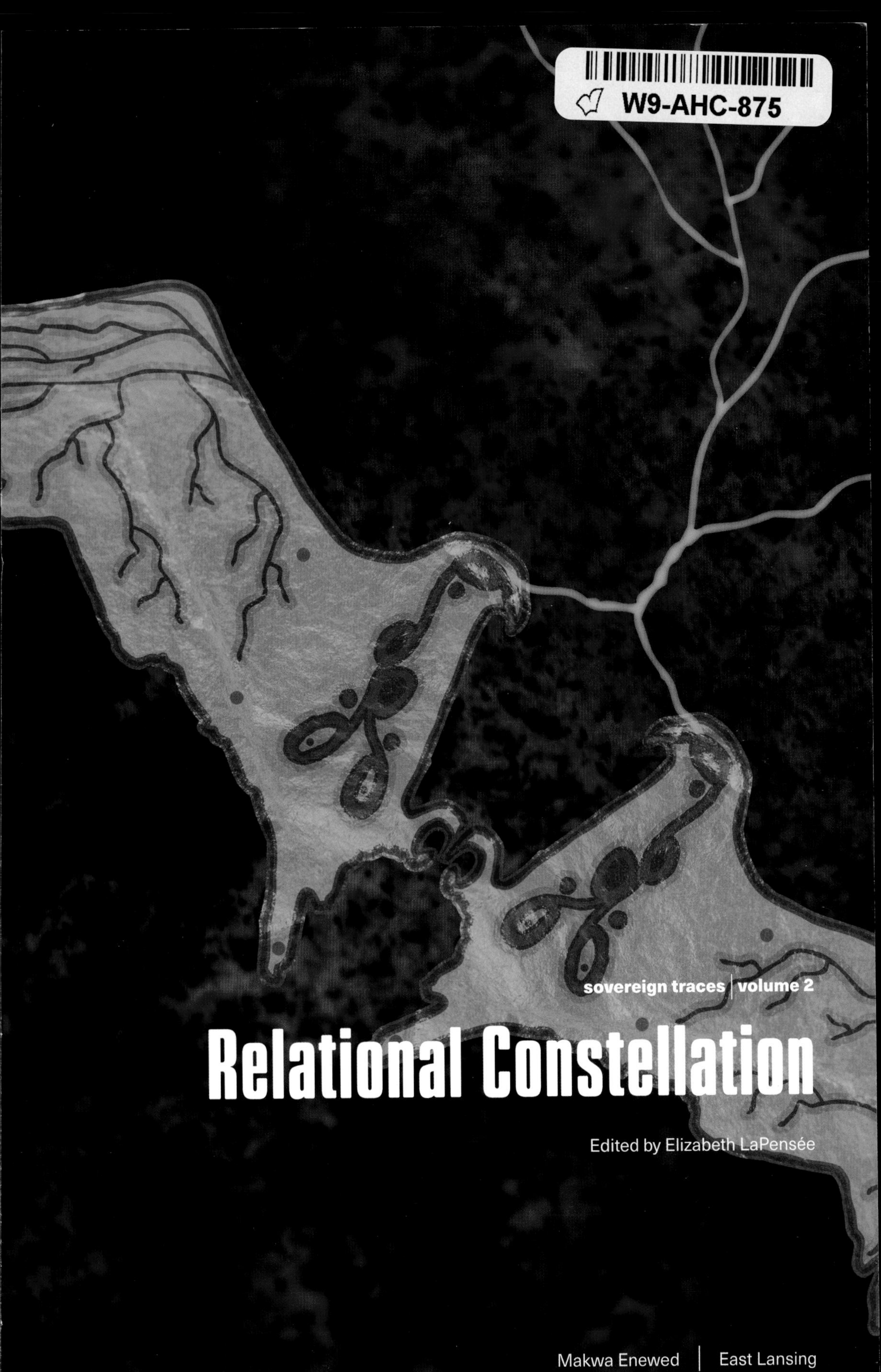

sovereign traces | volume 2

Relational Constellation

Edited by Elizabeth LaPensée

Makwa Enewed | East Lansing

♾ The paper used in this publication meets the minimum requirements of ANSI/NISO
Z39.48-1992 (R 1997) (Permanence of Paper).

SOVEREIGN
TRACES

Gordon Henry Jr. and Elizabeth LaPensée, *Series Editors*

Sovereign Traces, Volume 2: Relational Constellation | ISBN 978-1-938065-11-8
Edited by Elizabeth LaPensée

 Michigan State University Press
East Lansing, Michigan 48823-5245

 Makwa Enewed is an imprint of Michigan State University Press
East Lansing, Michigan 48823-5245

native
realities Published with the cooperation of Native Realities Press

Printed and bound in the United States of America.

28 27 26 25 24 23 22 21 20 19   1 2 3 4 5 6 7 8 9 10

Library of Congress Control Number: 2018952520 | ISBN: 978-1-938065-11-8 (pbk.)

Book and cover design by Charlie Sharp, Sharp Des!gns, East Lansing, Michigan.
Cover image is *Niimikodaadi'ing* ©2015 Elizabeth LaPensée and is used with permission
of the artist. All rights reserved. www.elizabethlapensee.com.

green
press Michigan State University Press is a member of the Green Press Initiative
INITIATIVE and is committed to developing and encouraging ecologically responsible
publishing practices. For more information about the Green Press Initiative and the use of
recycled paper in book publishing, please visit *www.greenpressinitiative.org*.

Visit Michigan State University Press at *www.msupress.org*

contents

foreword

Karyn Recollet

Of dust and stars
Born from destruction and chaos
Formed into the most beautiful
Alluring
Things
　　　　　　—Ishki Ricard, "Space"

Movement and migration—the radical reorientational capacities of water, the celestial, the "otherwise" relationalities—*constellations* claw their way out of that glitch space where rupture is love, because stars are exploding all of time in space. This I learned from Buffy St. Marie, as she recalled the fierce practices of love requirements for the postapocalyptic, post–residential school, post-millennial scoop time. These are times that call on us to love our rupturus selves . . . fiercely.

Water is that which moves between the maps fluidly, gently, forcefully, and fiercely: "we are the flood" (Niigaanwewidam James Sinclair). This space of futurisms honors those kin who have relationships with water that are fierce, fiery, rich, and loving. For those of us who occupy a displacement, exiles and 60s millennial scoops, water's migratory relationality—akin with the Milky Way—illuminates spatial freedoms in ways that produce "home" as ephemeral yet also quite rooted to the below and above. Our grounding becomes rhizomatically rooted upwards . . . as a kinstillatory connection—a radical reorientation toward all of lands' overflow. Illuminated by Gabriela Aveiro-Ojeda, intimacies in the slipstream are color coded in light's curves. So you see, our grounding may be celestial, and kinship for us . . . may be of stars. Kinstillations allow us to refuse the maps that have been determined by settler-coloniality and anti-Blackness. Kinstillations remind us that we can move, as in Renee Nejo's re-creation story ("You left . . . that's all you need to do today"), migratory patterns offer escape into otherwise spaces (Ashon Crawley) where toxic masculinities have no hold.

The writers in this gorgeous collection realign us to our future ancestors and illuminate our patterns of flight in how to be good kin. They are activating and recoding our many fractals of Indigeneity through a variety of technologies and mediums. Water is how we move through maps; waters are text too because they imprint. This collection brings to mind that the canoe is both a vessel of migration and space-time travel. It is akin to the offering of the time-travelling plant, tobacco (Lee Maracle), as a gesture of futurity building. Radical reorientations are love's overflow where sexuality and creative intimacies become, to borrow Kim Tallbear's terminology, "modes of being in good relation."

It is possible to mimic celestial bodies in the ways that we build and share creative intimacies. We learn how to pay attention to the sonic sovereignty of the sounds of celestial beings being in good relation. If this collection had a soundtrack, I don't doubt that I would hear Jeremy Dutcher, because that's what stars sound like.

This collection re-creates intimacies that imagine "otherwise" (Ashon Crawley), each offering a call and response, mimicking dark matters' gravitational pull, bringing us closer toward each other in cosmos. You see, we are kin in the making. We gather groundedness from the fall—fractals of light sent through sky. The cosmos are glyphed on our bodies, the shadow spaces holding intentions and spaces of care—this is the gathering you are about to witness.

introduction

Elizabeth LaPensée

Love is a constellation of our relations, our kinships, and our revelations. The ways in which we communicate shape the connections between us, much like the plasma running between stars. Pathways of reciprocity activate how we relate.

The intention of this collection is to create space for a myriad of Indigenous voices on the meaning of love. From the endearing to the funny to the sassy to the raunchy, whether merging or diverging, the works joined together here are a remembrance. We remember who we are and how we love, with hope for openness and shared understanding.

With gratitude to all of the contributors for expressing their ways of knowing and to all who look through these pages, considering and contemplating the meaning of love for themselves.

Miigwech.

sovereign traces

volume 2

Love Is for Everyone

Illustrated by Liv Barney

"Love Is for Everyone" is a black and white illustration I did in October 2016 as a part of an annual art challenge called "InkTober." The piece was also published in *Red Rising Magazine*'s issue 5: "Love." I see "Love Is for Everyone" as an important piece among my collection of work because it touches on the topic of love while also leaving the narrative open to interpretation by the viewer. The artwork shows two Natives leaning on one another while watching the sun. The individuals could be from different tribes, the same tribe, mixed, or not. Their gender, romantic, and sexual orientations and identities are not specified either. The piece is meant to be as open and inclusive as can be while still having a connection to my Indigenous identity.

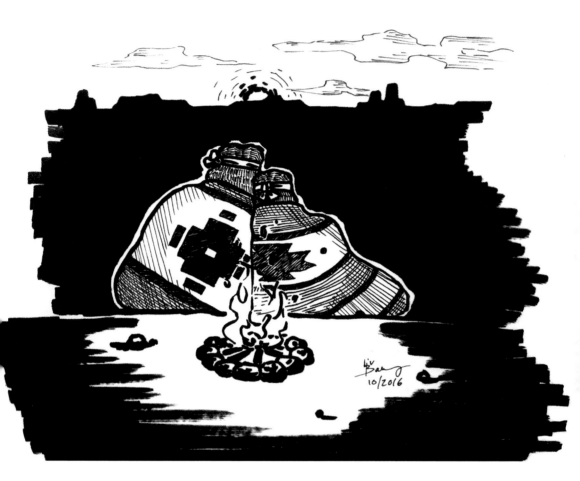

People Were Created to Be Loved

**Written by Margaret Noodin and Henrietta Black,
Illustrated by Bernard Perley**

"People Were Created to Be Loved" was written after a
student asked how a Tibetan idea expressed in English
would be translated into an Algonquian language.
Some parts of the idea moved easily into another
language; other parts were entirely transformed. A
direct translation of the quote serves as an epigraph
to the poem and is a much less direct response to
the idea of love. After Margaret wrote the poem in
Anishinaabemowin, Henrietta moved the ideas into
Maliseet, and her son Bernard brought them to life
visually.

Pəmawhsowinowok kisiyapənik weci kseləmot.

People were created to be loved.

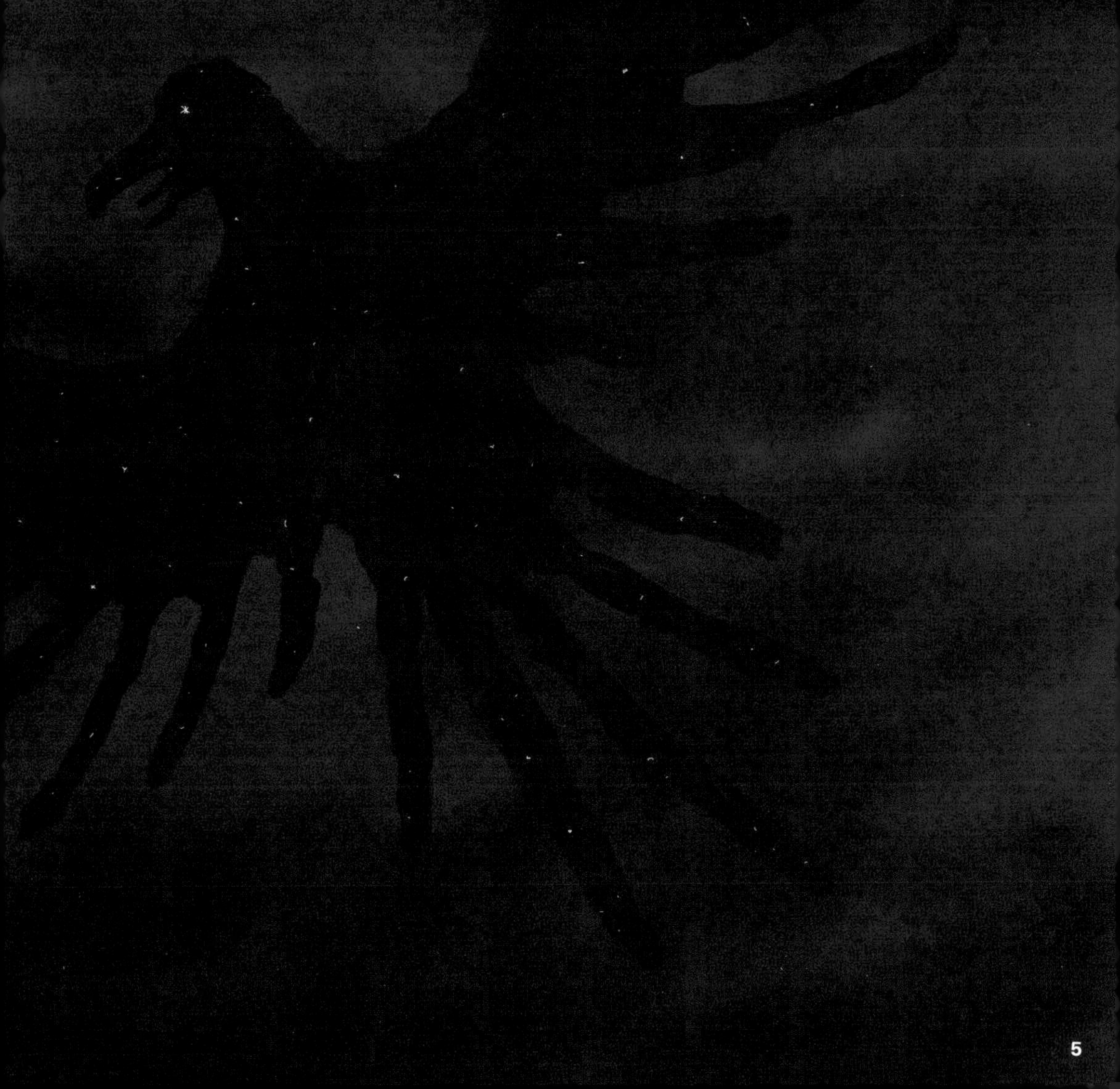

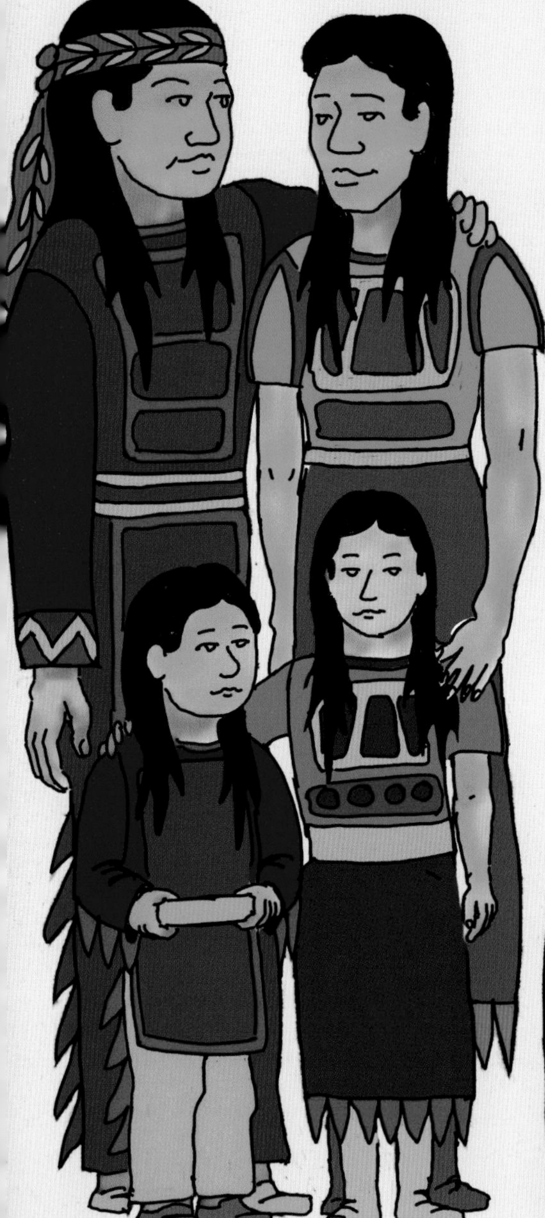

Gegoon gaa giizhenindaagwadoon ji-aabajichigaadeg.

Psiwte kekw piləway kisihtasopən weci wehkasik.

Things were created to be used.

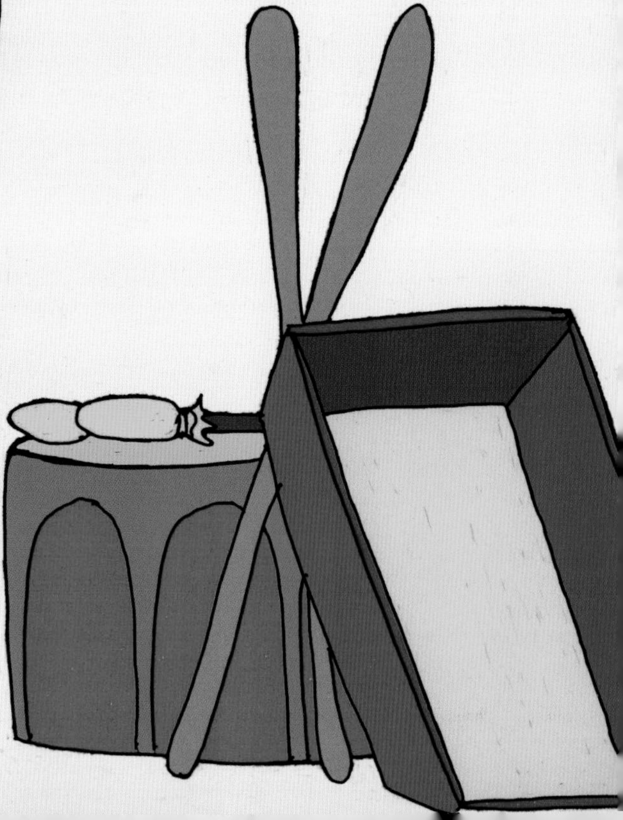

Noongom gegoon onzaam
zaagitoowaad gaye bimaadizijig
aabji'idiwaad...

Təkec psiwte kekw ksitahataso
naka pəmawhsowinowok
wehkahak...

Today things are loved and people
are used...

. . . wenji majizhe\vebag.

. . . nit nit weci psiwte kekw
waplehsik.

. . . this is the reason for bad
happenings.

-Lhamo Dondrub, The 14th Dalai

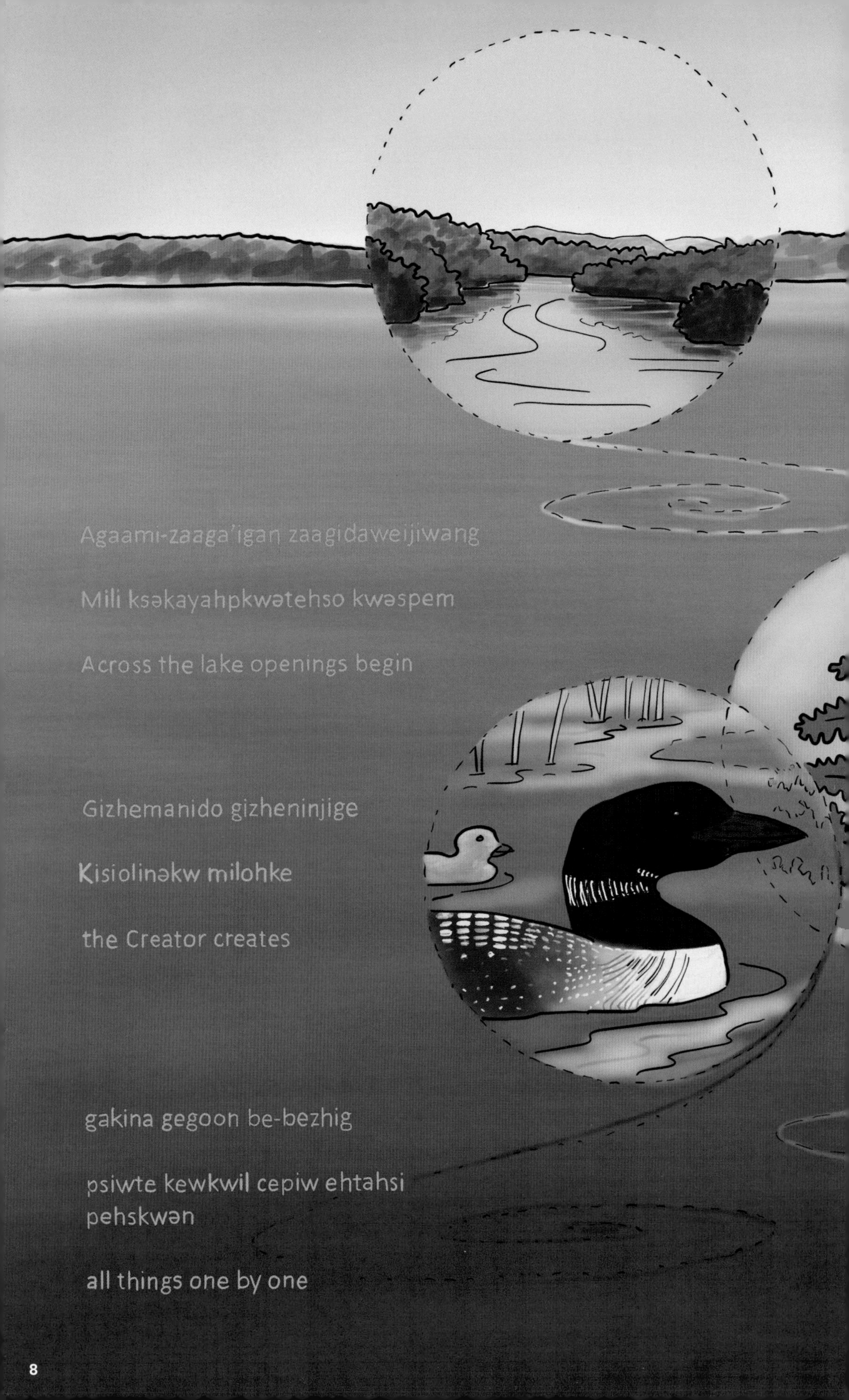

Agaami-zaaga’igan zaagidaweijiwang

Mili ksəkayahpkwətehso kwəspem

Across the lake openings begin

Gizhemanido gizheninjige

Kisiolinəkw milohke

the Creator creates

gakina gegoon be-bezhig

psiwte kewkwil cepiw ehtahsi pehskwən

all things one by one

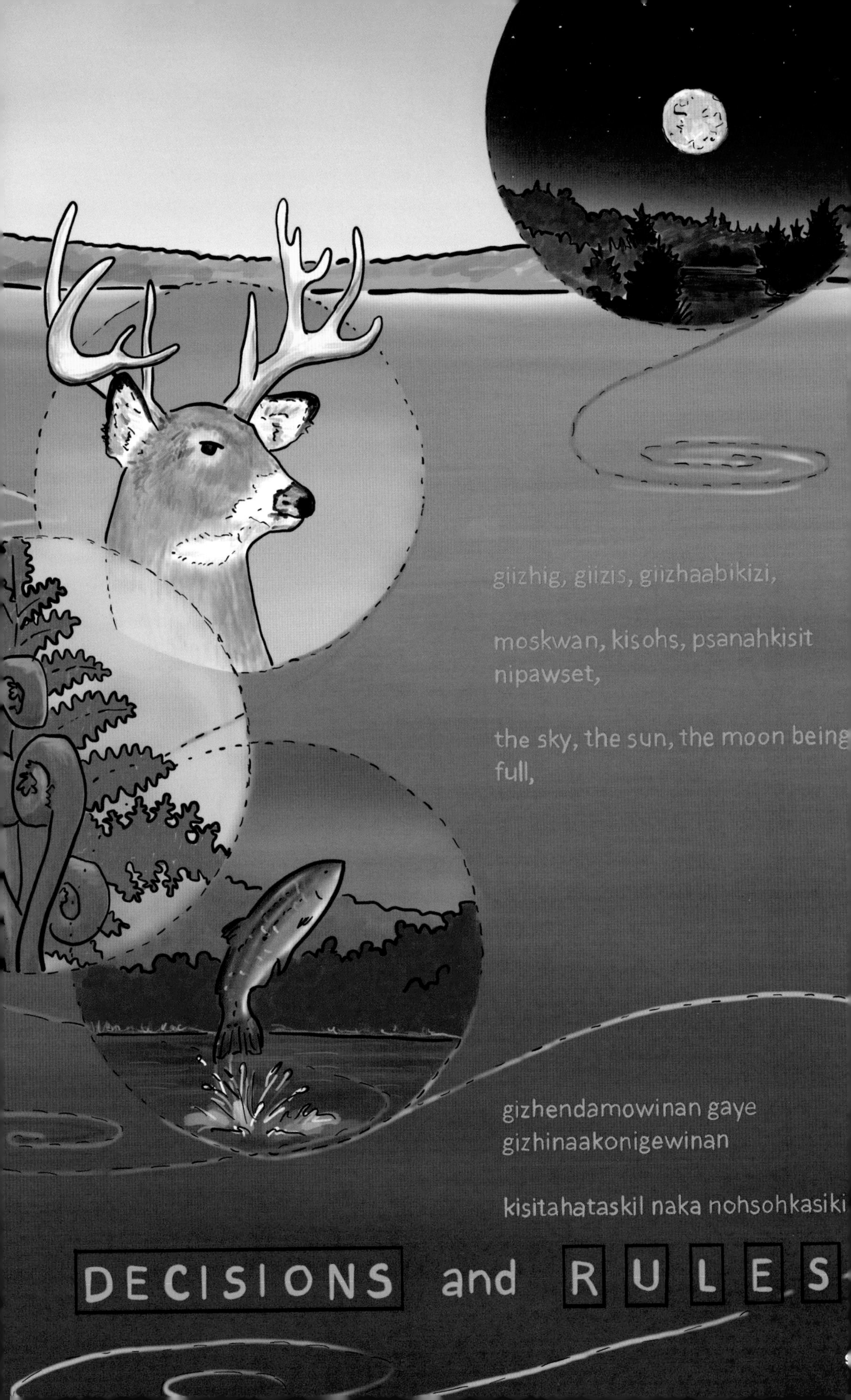

giizhig, giizis, giizhaabikizi,

moskwan, kisohs, psanahkisit nipawset,

the sky, the sun, the moon being full,

gizhendamowinan gaye gizhinaakonigewinan

kisitahataskil naka nohsohkasiki

DECISIONS and RULES

mii dash epiichii giiwitaashkaamagag

nita psiwte nəlwiw eli amniyak

then amidst the turning cycles

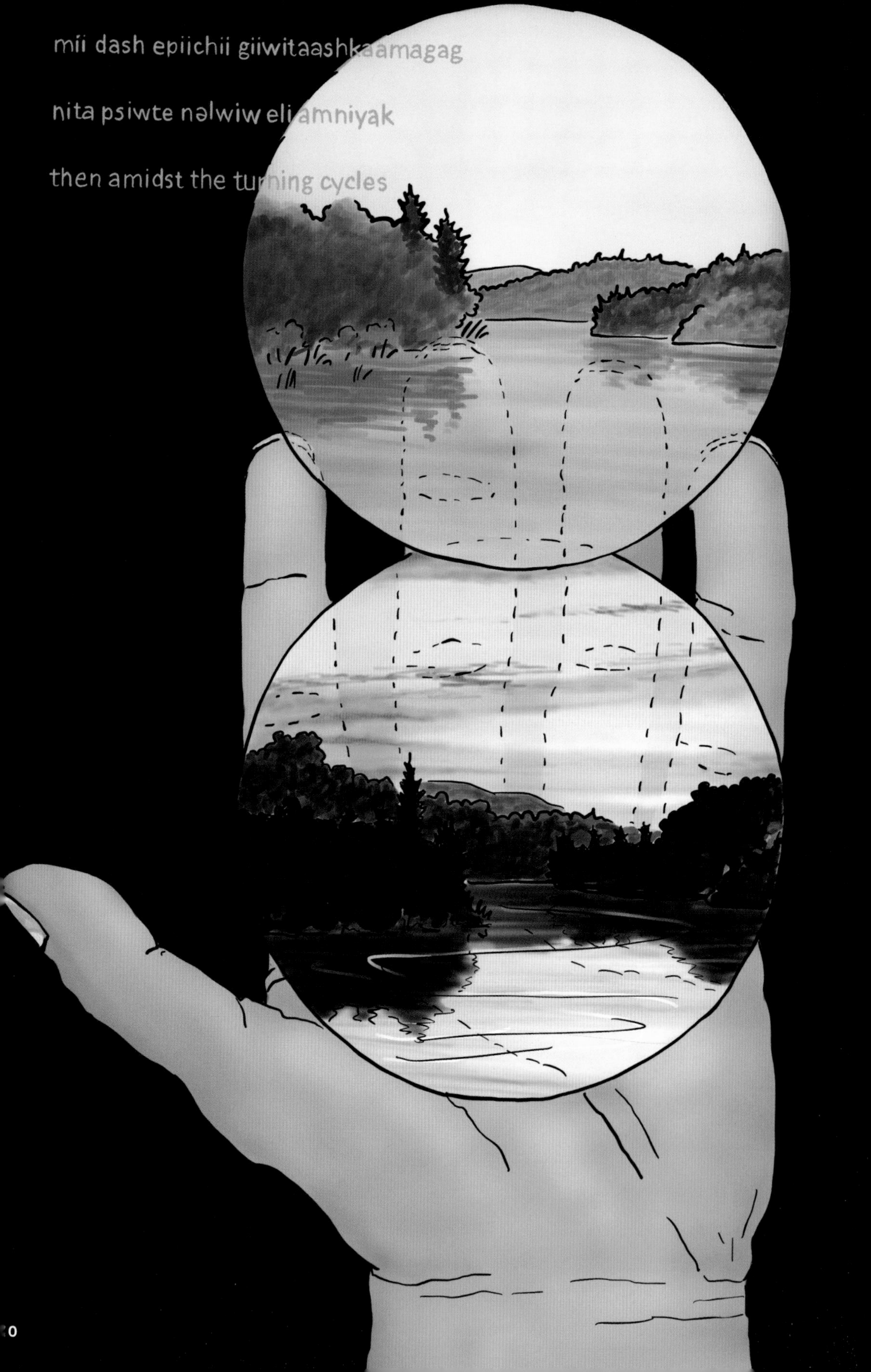

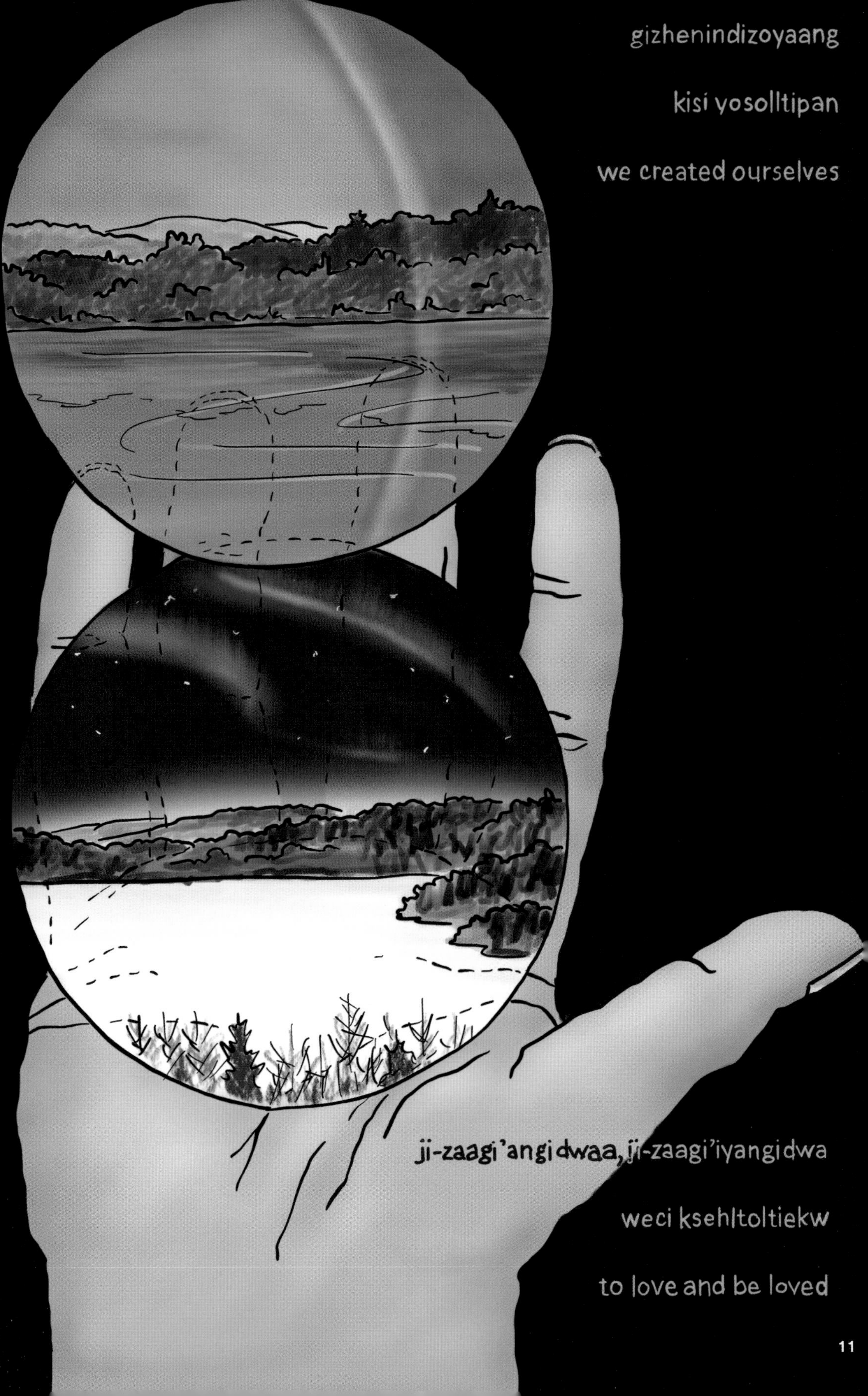

gizhenindizoyaang

kisi yosolltipan

we created ourselves

ji-zaagi'angidwaa, ji-zaagi'iyangidwa

weci ksehltoltiekw

to love and be loved

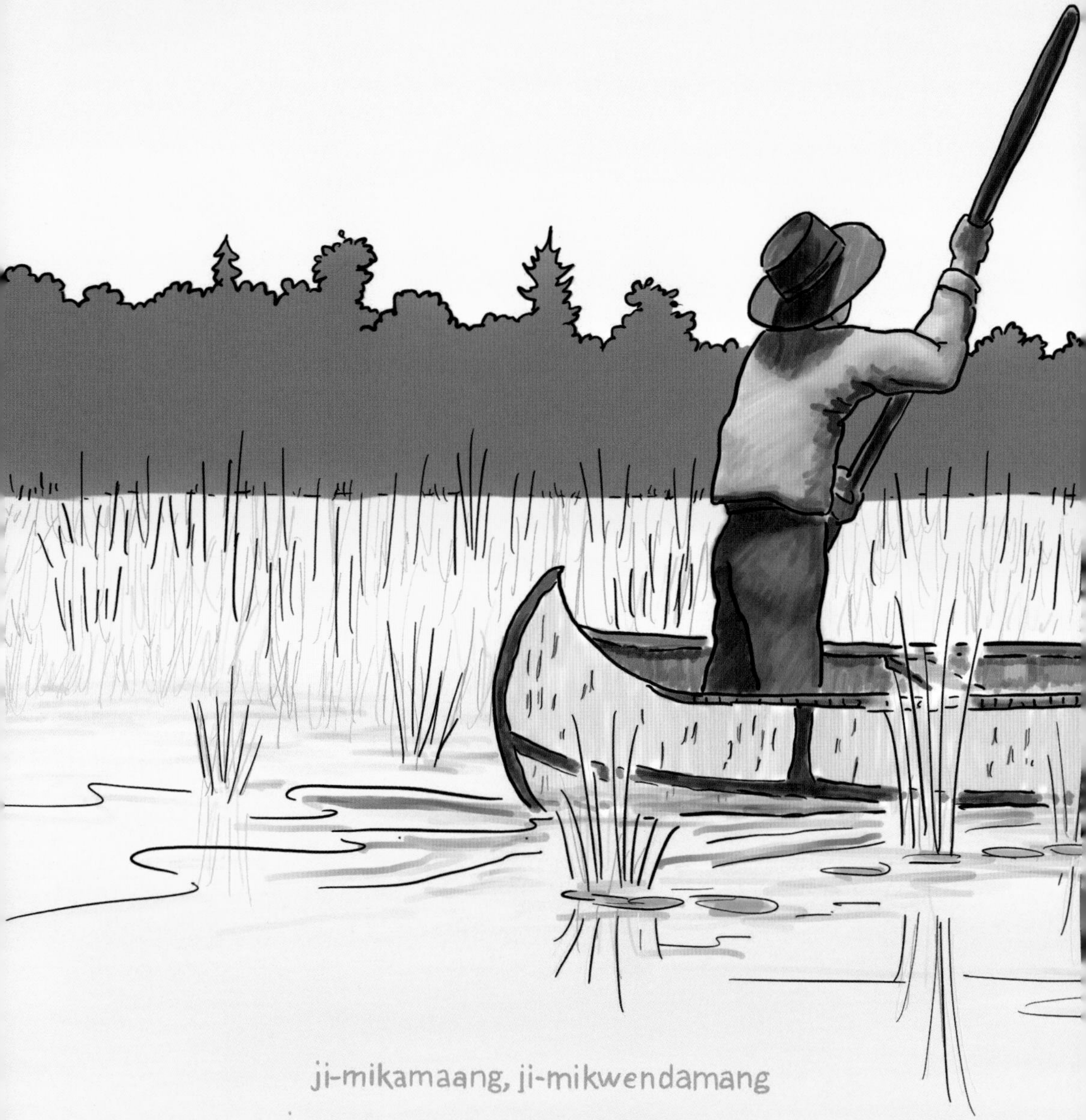

ji-mikamaang, ji-mikwendamang

weci pskəmahsolltiekw naka mikwitahasolltiekw

to find and to remember

gakina gegoon ezhi-aabajichigaadeg

psiwte kekw ellwehkasik

the use for everything

ji-mikawangidwaa, ji-mikwenimangidwaa

weci pskəmąhsoḷltiekw naka mikwitahasoḷltiekw

to find and remember

be-bezhig bimaadizijig ezhi-zhaawenimangidwaa

psiwte cepiw eli wolitahamkwəhsoḷtiekw

the singular blessing of every being

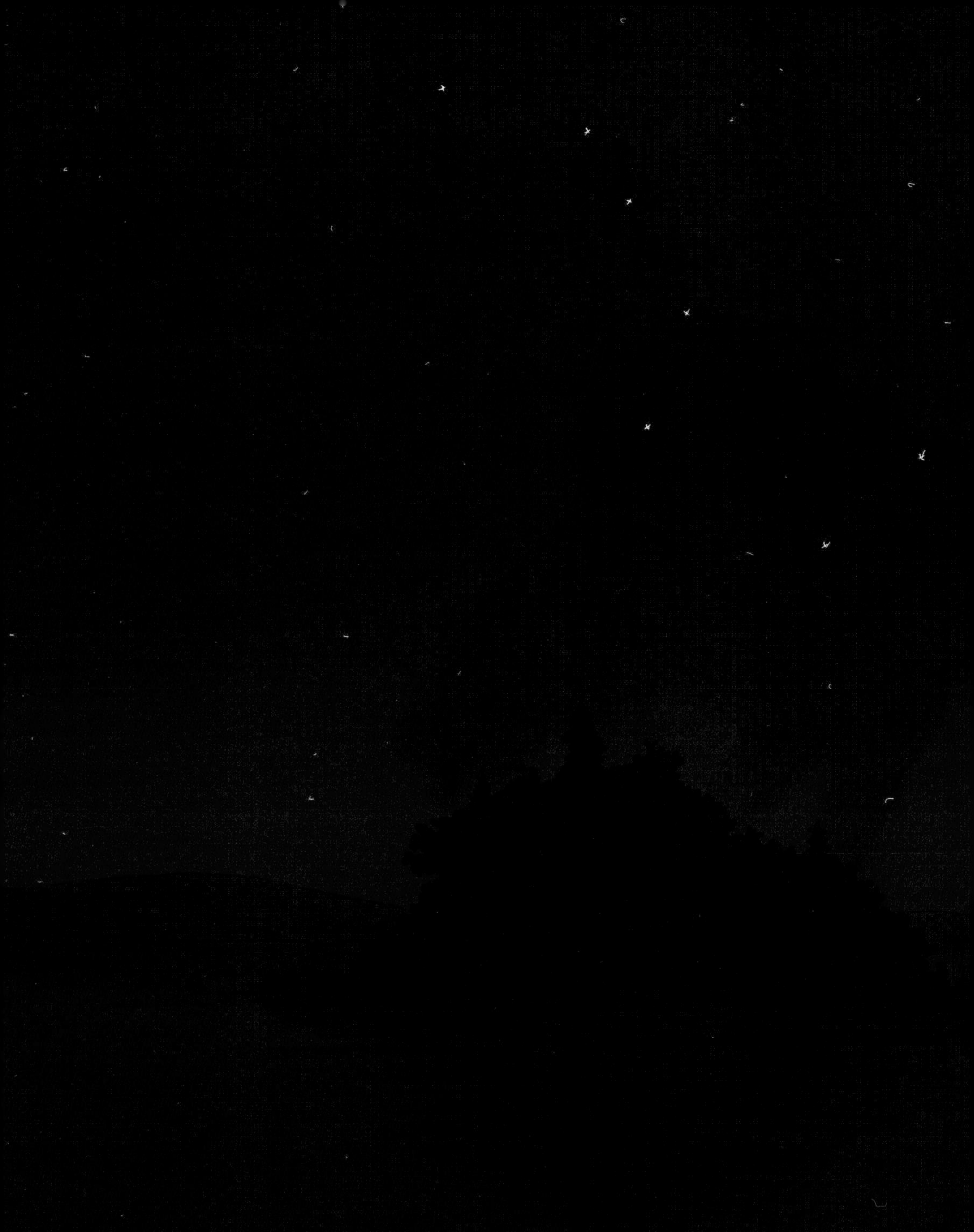

minisan giishkijigwenaag gichigaming

tahalo əte psiwte manikwəl tehkəhskwənkoniya sopekw

---

the way every island is embraced by the sea

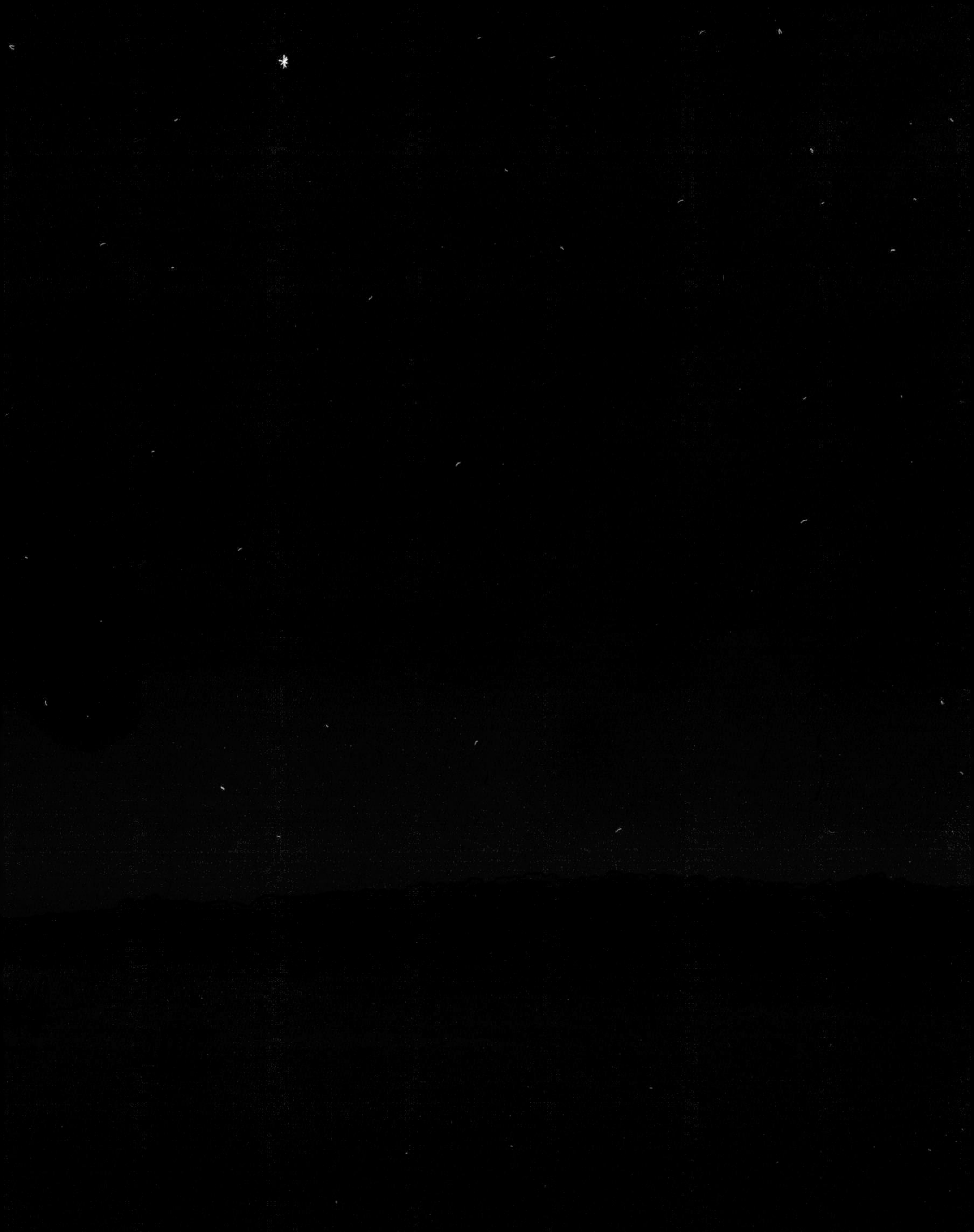

Maang Anongan zagaakwaa'igenid giizhigong.

tahalo tehpLahtəkwehsnowi Pəhsesem petkwənkon moskwan.

the way the North Star is held by the sky.

Changing Woman

Written and Illustrated by Shaun Beyale

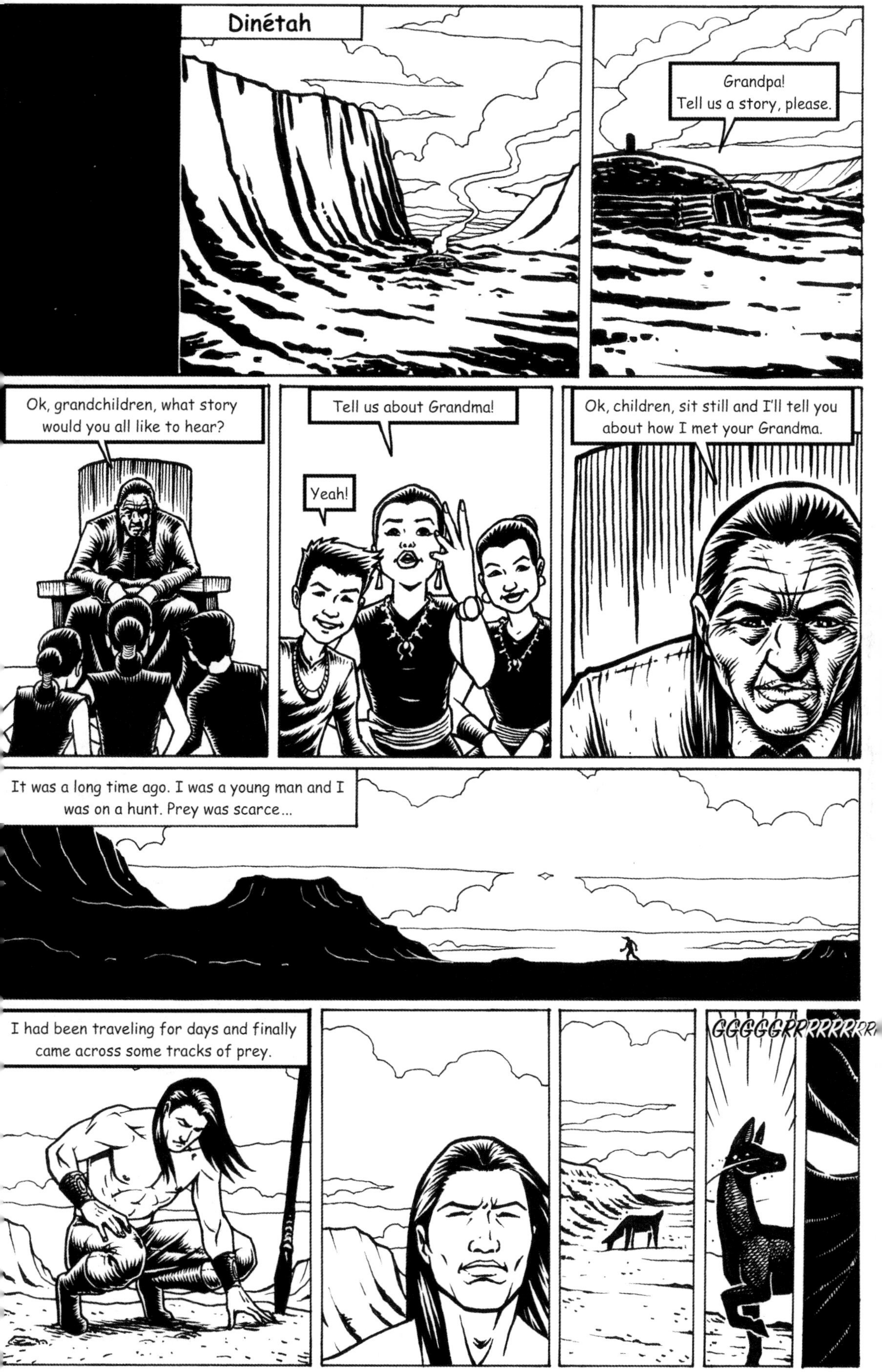
Dinétah
Grandpa! Tell us a story, please.
Ok, grandchildren, what story would you all like to hear?
Tell us about Grandma!
Yeah!
Ok, children, sit still and I'll tell you about how I met your Grandma.
It was a long time ago. I was a young man and I was on a hunt. Prey was scarce...
I had been traveling for days and finally came across some tracks of prey.
GGGGGRRRRRRR

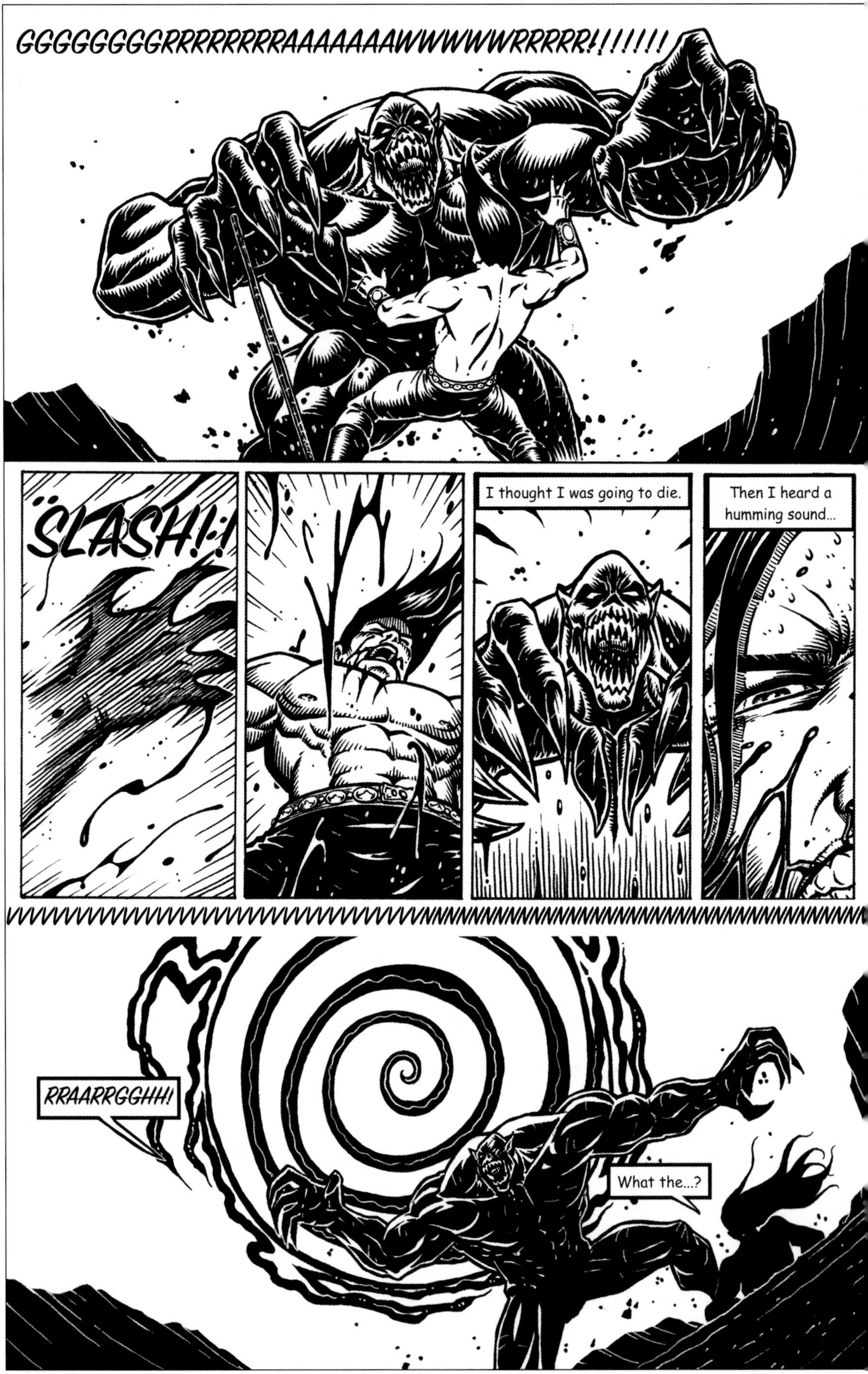
GGGGGGGRRRRRRRAAAAAAAWWWWRRRRRR!!!!!!!
SLASH!!
I thought I was going to die.
Then I heard a humming sound...
RRAARRGGHH!
What the...?

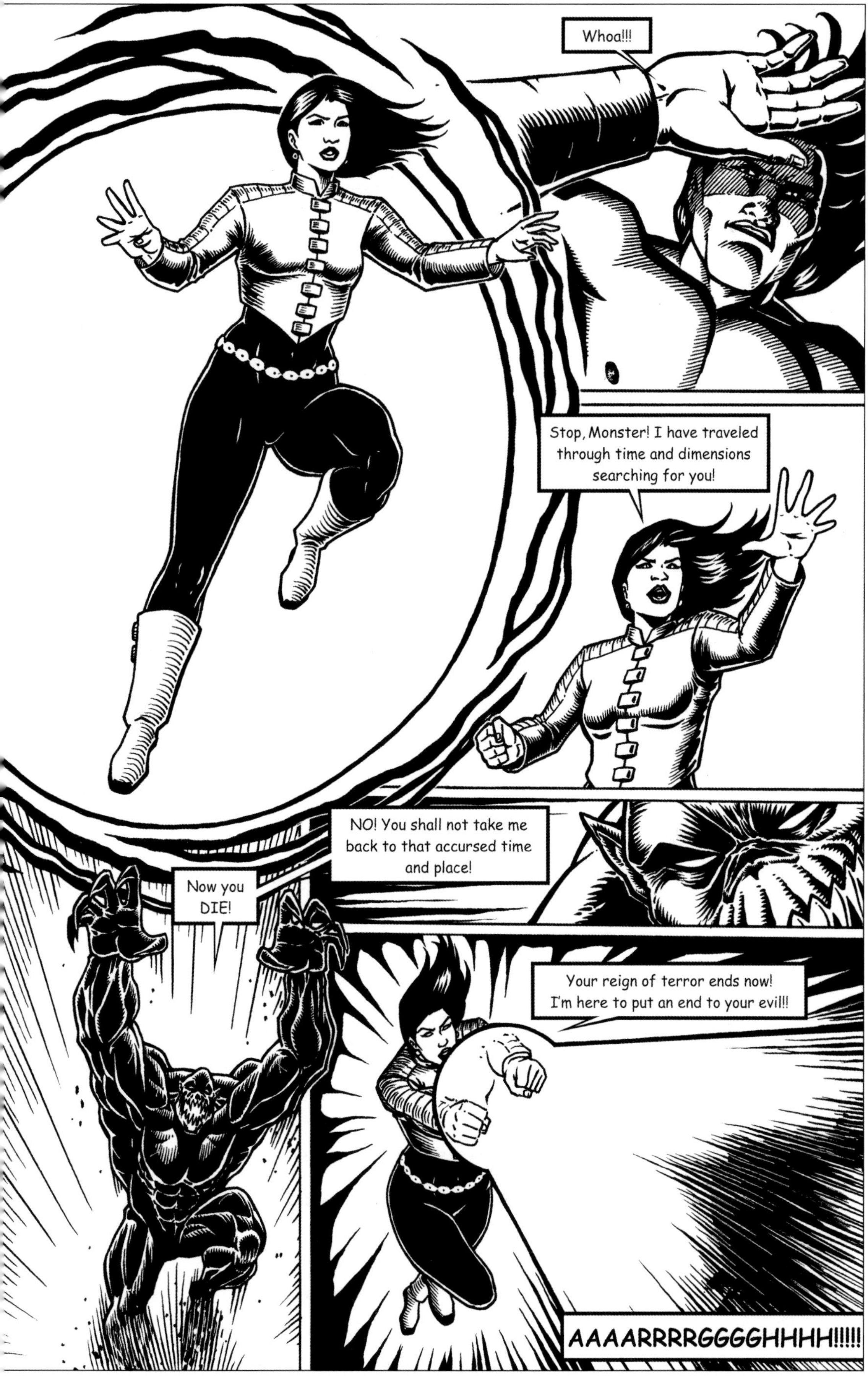
Whoa!!!
Stop, Monster! I have traveled through time and dimensions searching for you!
NO! You shall not take me back to that accursed time and place!
Now you DIE!
Your reign of terror ends now! I'm here to put an end to your evil!!
AAAARRRRGGGGHHHH!!!!!!

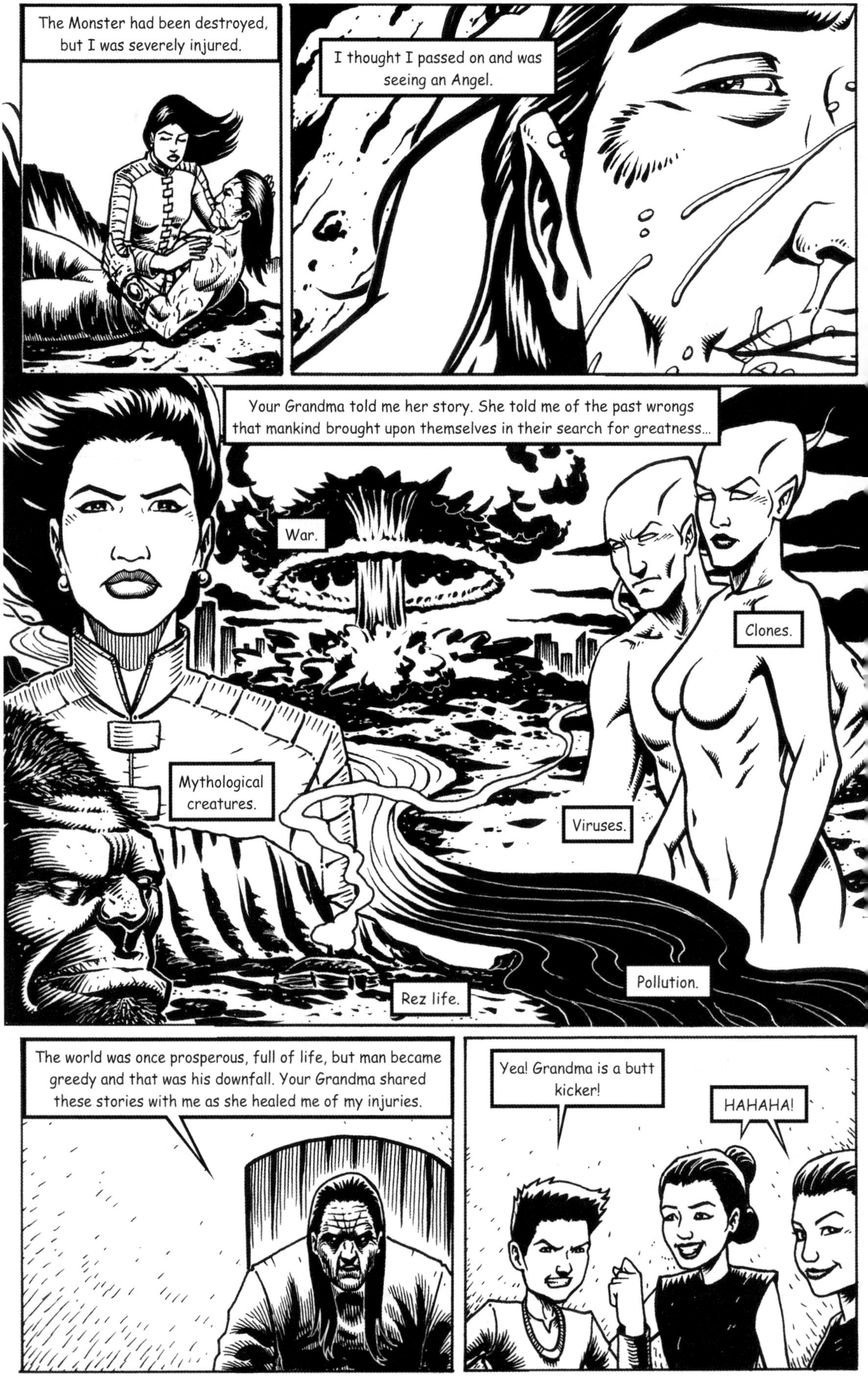
The Monster had been destroyed, but I was severely injured.
I thought I passed on and was seeing an Angel.
Your Grandma told me her story. She told me of the past wrongs that mankind brought upon themselves in their search for greatness...
War.
Clones.
Mythological creatures.
Viruses.
Rez life.
Pollution.
The world was once prosperous, full of life, but man became greedy and that was his downfall. Your Grandma shared these stories with me as she healed me of my injuries.
Yea! Grandma is a butt kicker!
HAHAHA!

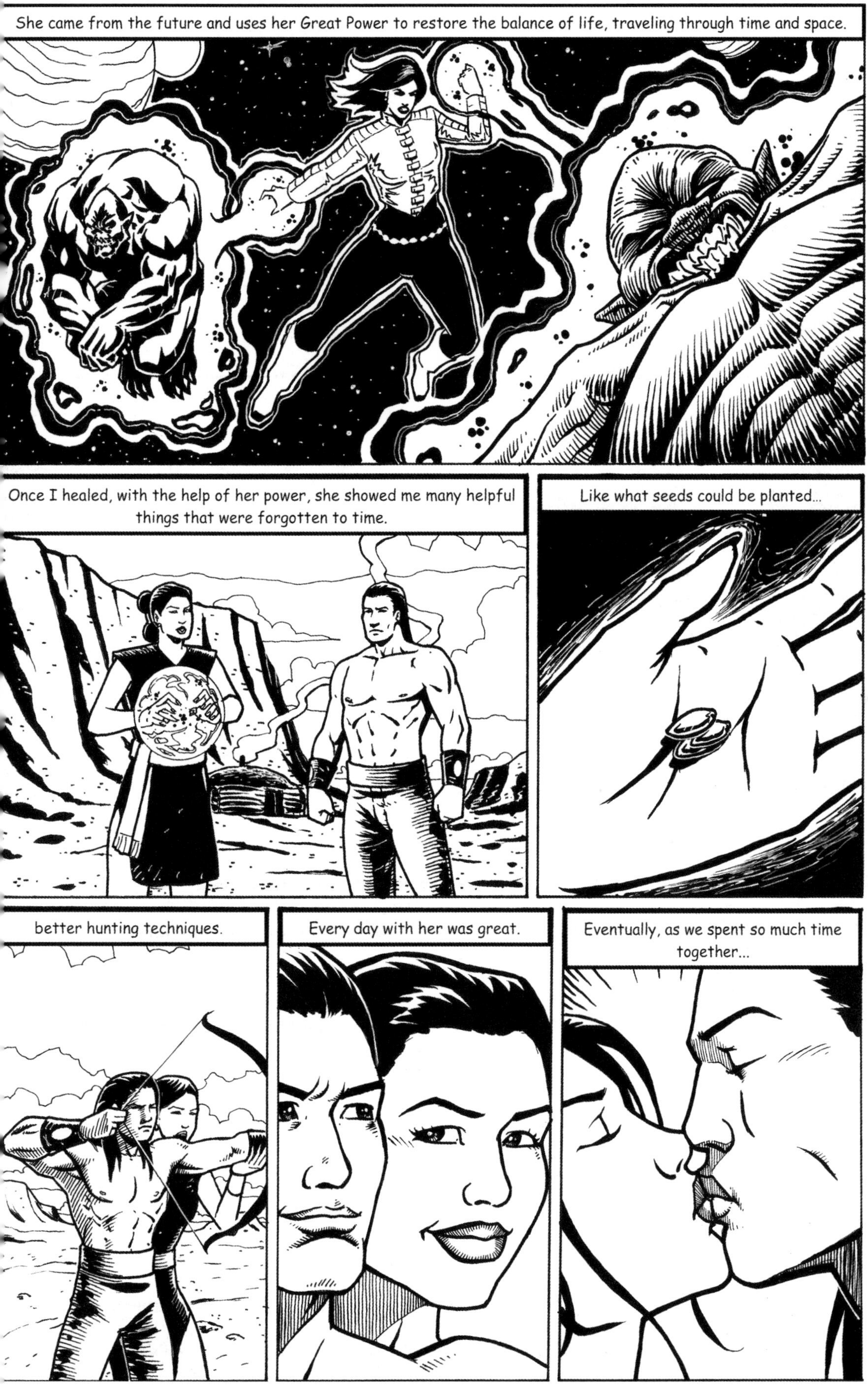
She came from the future and uses her Great Power to restore the balance of life, traveling through time and space.
Once I healed, with the help of her power, she showed me many helpful things that were forgotten to time.
Like what seeds could be planted...
better hunting techniques.
Every day with her was great.
Eventually, as we spent so much time together...

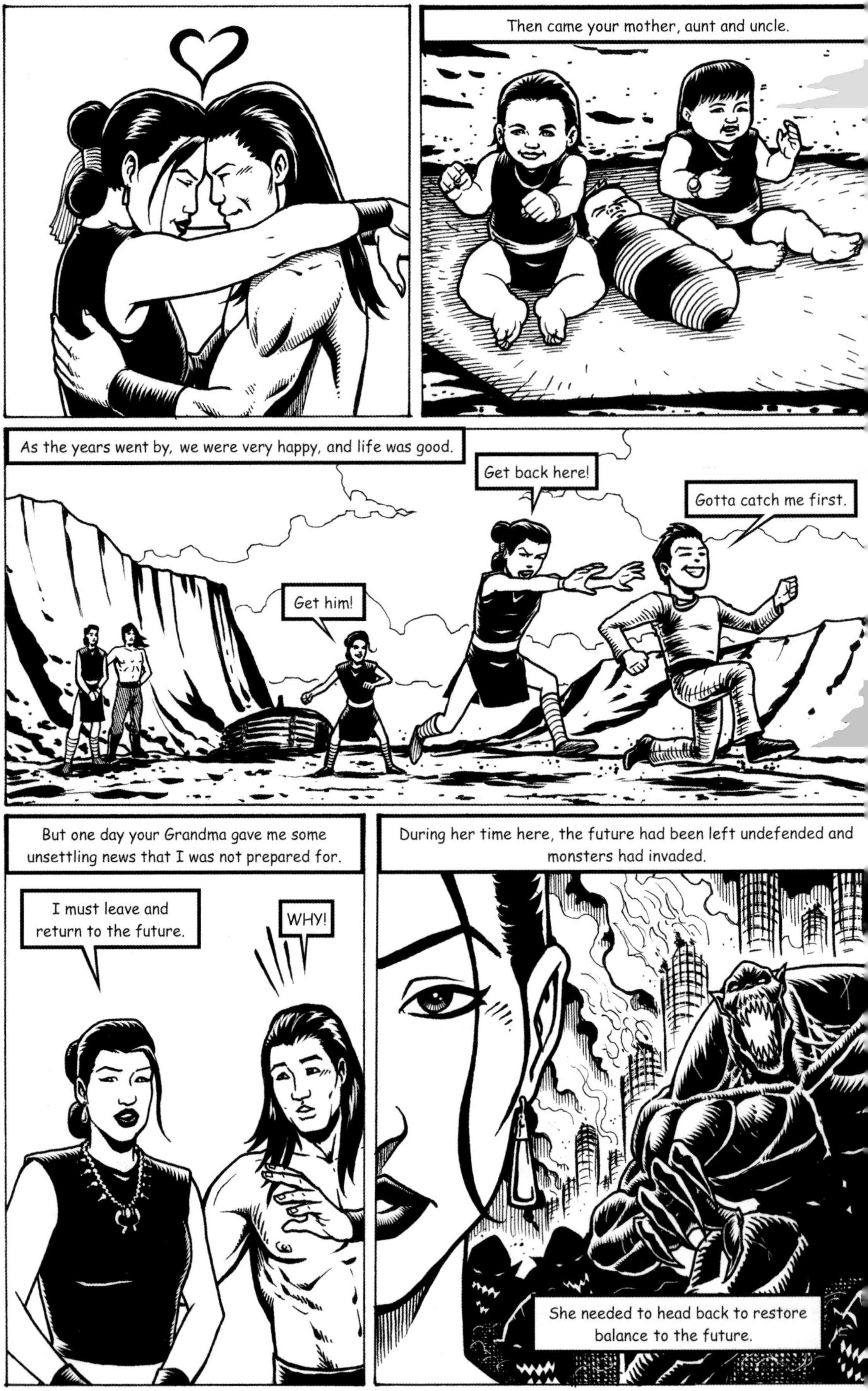
Then came your mother, aunt and uncle.
As the years went by, we were very happy, and life was good.
Get back here!
Gotta catch me first.
Get him!
But one day your Grandma gave me some unsettling news that I was not prepared for.
I must leave and return to the future.
WHY!
During her time here, the future had been left undefended and monsters had invaded.
She needed to head back to restore balance to the future.

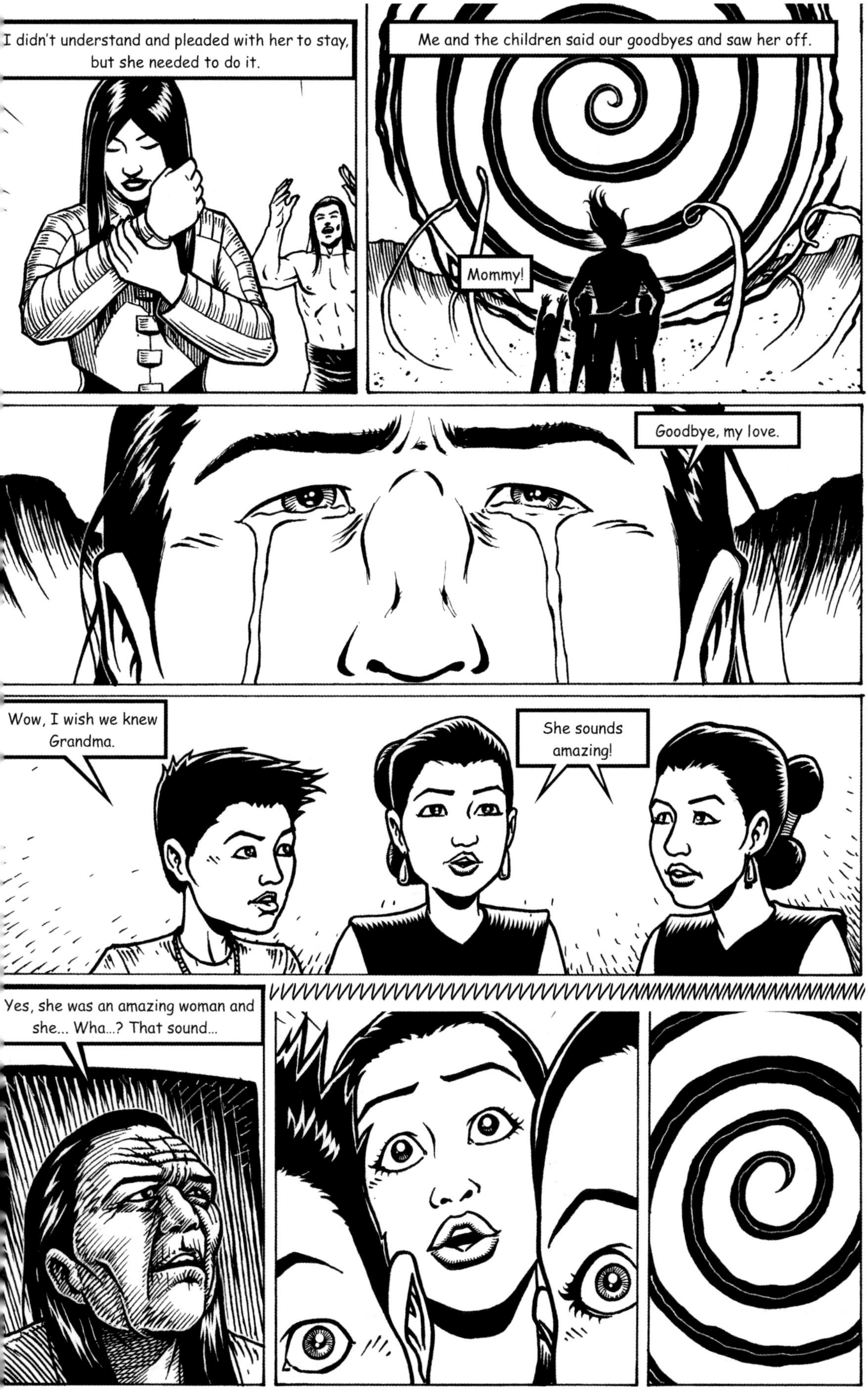
I didn't understand and pleaded with her to stay, but she needed to do it.
Me and the children said our goodbyes and saw her off.
Mommy!
Goodbye, my love.
Wow, I wish we knew Grandma.
She sounds amazing!
Yes, she was an amazing woman and she... Wha...? That sound...
VVVVVVVVVVVVVVVVVVVVVVVVVVVVNNNNNNNNNNNNNNNNNNNNN

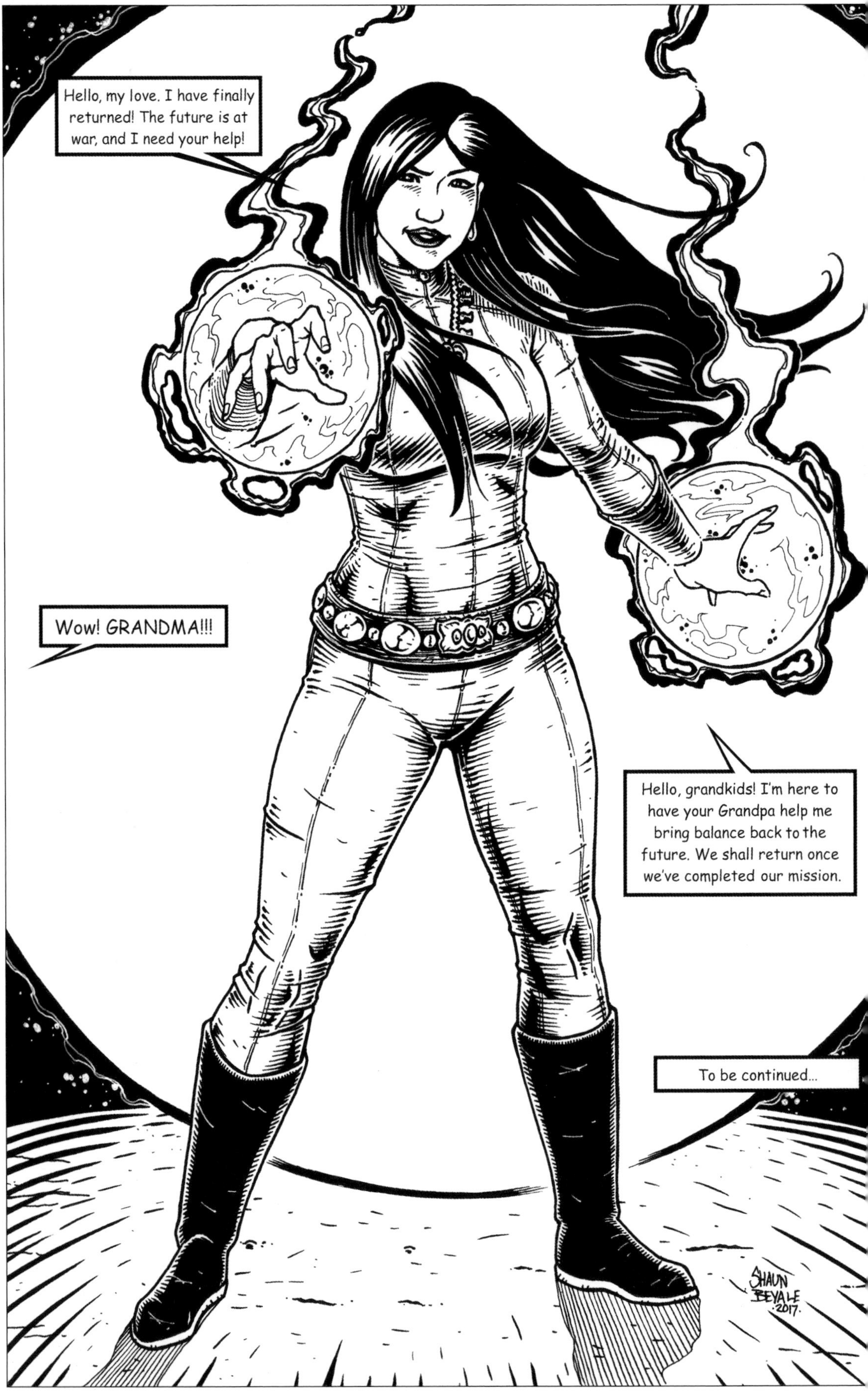
Hello, my love. I have finally returned! The future is at war, and I need your help!
Wow! GRANDMA!!!
Hello, grandkids! I'm here to have your Grandpa help me bring balance back to the future. We shall return once we've completed our mission.
To be continued...
SHAUN BEYALE 2017.

denim regalia

Molly Billows

I use the blanket stitch my auntie taught me
attach patches to denim,
create my queer dance party regalia.

Attach a screenprint of the word "killjoy,"
a white moth cut from an old T-shirt.
Add my first beadwork— a blue flower and little green leaves
in the style a Gwich'in friend taught me,
a barret I no longer need since I cut my hair too short to use it.
Across my shoulders I draw the mountains and rivers of my territory.
Below, the words "qʷagə hošt čičɬem: Come on, let's go dancing!"

I know, for us, the dance floor is a sacred space.
I know our bodies moving together are ceremony and protest.
I know, like any form of resistance, it can be enough to get us killed.

There is a sadness in watching us dance here together.
The flash of strobe lights gives me glimpses
of our queer, trans, indigenous, black and brown bodies.
I am so tired of seeing us in missing posters and in memoriams,
in racist media coverage and mugshots.

Here we move, we laugh, we love
        unapologetically.
I long for us to feel this kind of freedom in the streets,
in our workplaces, our schools, our childhood homes.

Here, the flash of strobe lights gives me glimpses of release and escape.
We take these moments to witness each other's beauty illuminated.
I know ours is a radical love. And being here
our sovereign bodies dancing
is a radical act.

In Aunties We Trust

Illustrated by Kimberly Robertson

Some people measure their wealth in fast cars or fat wallets, in fancy dinners and fine jewelry. Where I come from, we measure our wealth in aunties. I like to think of the process of auntification as a Native feminist practice of radical kinship—an intentional and deliberate practice of making relations beyond the limitations of Western concepts of family, time, space, and place. Under settler colonialism and heteropatriarchy, auntie alliances are particularly critical. These carefully curated crews of knowledge-wielding warriors love our communities into our best selves. They possess, share with one another, and transmit to future generations knowledge of the stories, languages, ceremonies, and medicines that form the very foundation of our survivance.

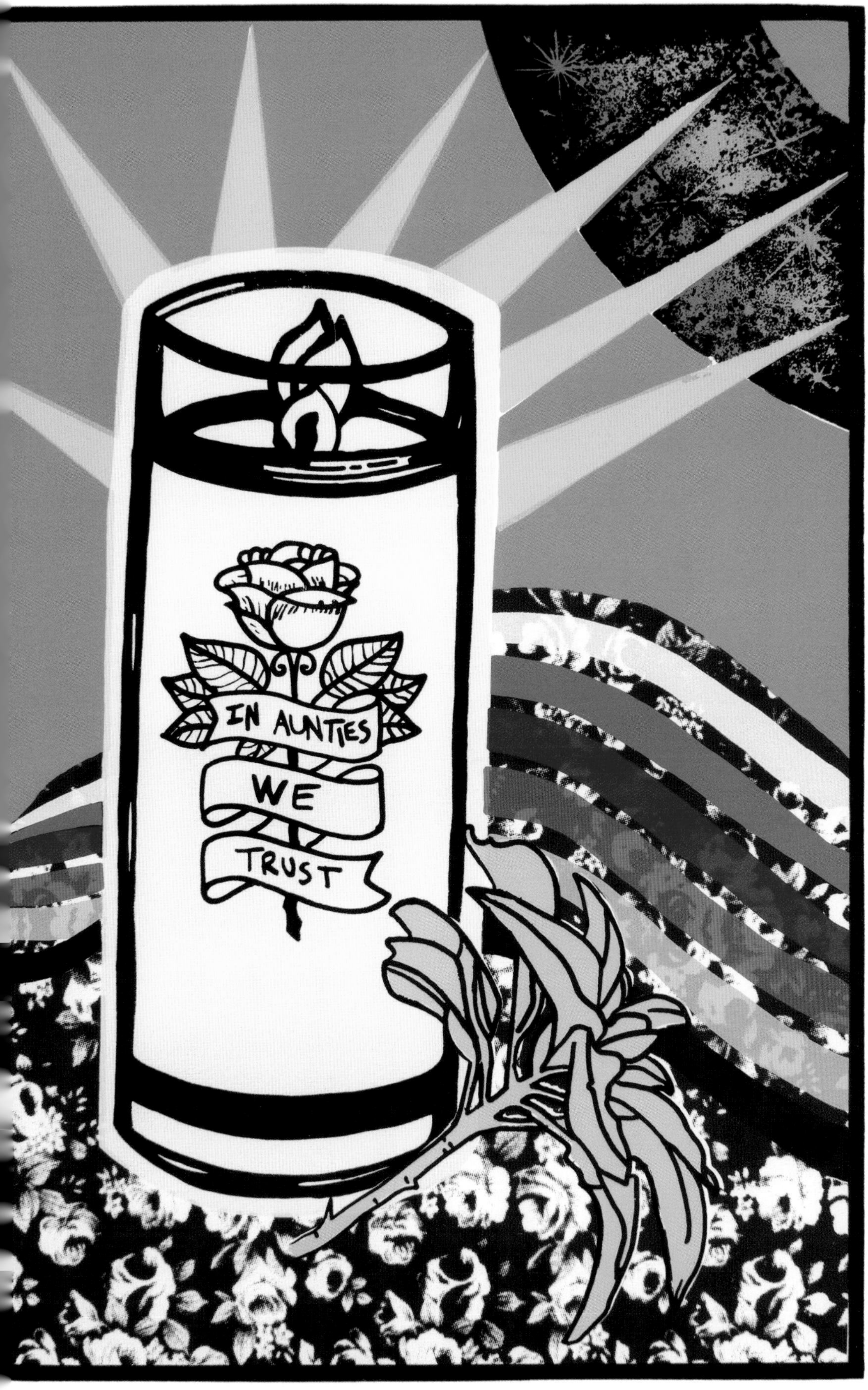
IN AUNTIES
WE
TRUST

Atoruk: Auntie Cameo

Written by Lucas Rowley,
Illustrated by Dale Ray Deforest

Atoruk is a detective comic series featuring an Alaska Native hero in *First Alaskans Magazine*, which is made by and for Alaska Natives. This one-page excerpt reflects on the role of aunties in love.

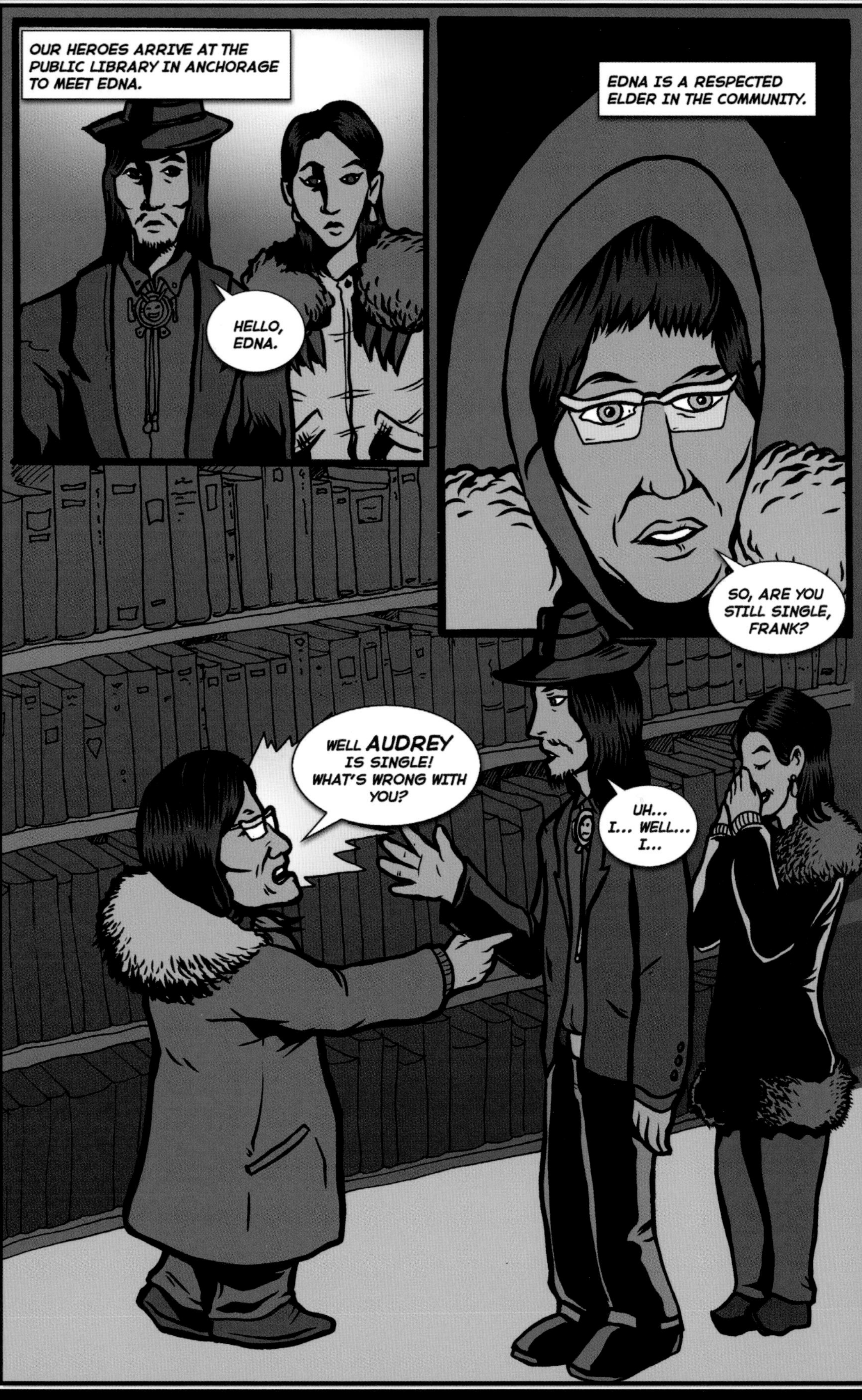
OUR HEROES ARRIVE AT THE PUBLIC LIBRARY IN ANCHORAGE TO MEET EDNA.
HELLO, EDNA.
EDNA IS A RESPECTED ELDER IN THE COMMUNITY.
SO, ARE YOU STILL SINGLE, FRANK?
WELL AUDREY IS SINGLE! WHAT'S WRONG WITH YOU?
UH... I... WELL... I...

Big Mama Pearl

Written and Illustrated by Renee Nejo

For me, love is about the mountains of care shown to me by my family, my grandmother in particular. She was always so steadfast and unwavering. When I thought of her, I thought of her strength, and it was always placed safely in that love. It's inspiring to me. She's why I'm the way I am. I get my strength and steady balance from her and her example. "Big Mama Pearl" was inspired by many real events in my family's history—fiction inspired by reality.

MY GRANDMOTHER WAS A HARD WOMAN,

HARDENED BY HER LIFE. HARD TO UNDERSTAND.

TO ME,

SHE SPOKE IN RIDDLES.

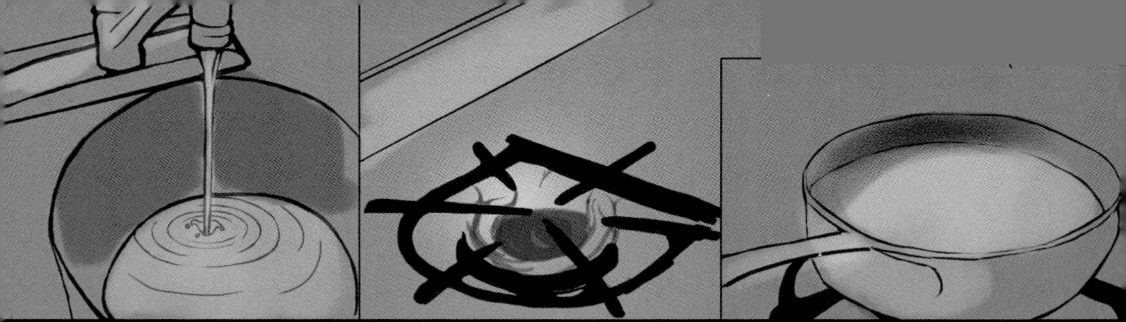

NO COFFEEPOT IN HER HOUSE, BUT EVERY DAY THERE WAS COFFEE IN THE MORNING. THAT INSTANT STUFF.

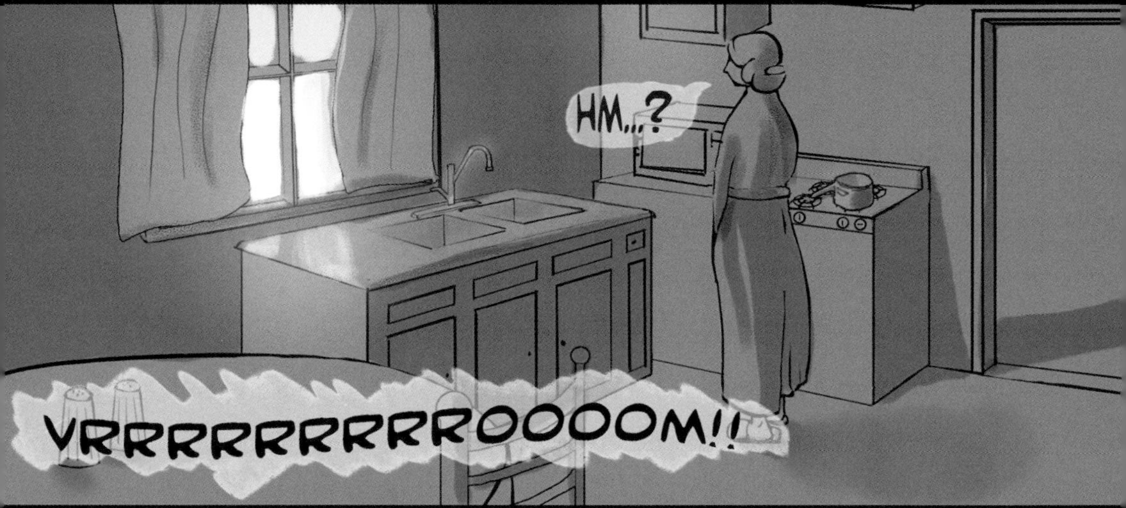
HM...?
VRRRRRRRRROOOOM!!

THE DAY MY MOM LEFT MY DAD WAS NO DIFFERENT. WE DROVE TO GRANDMA'S.

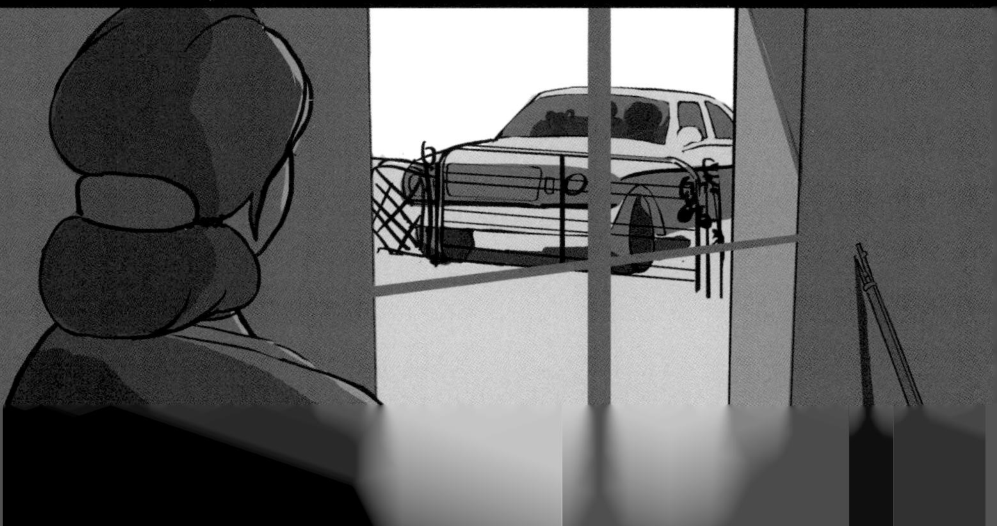

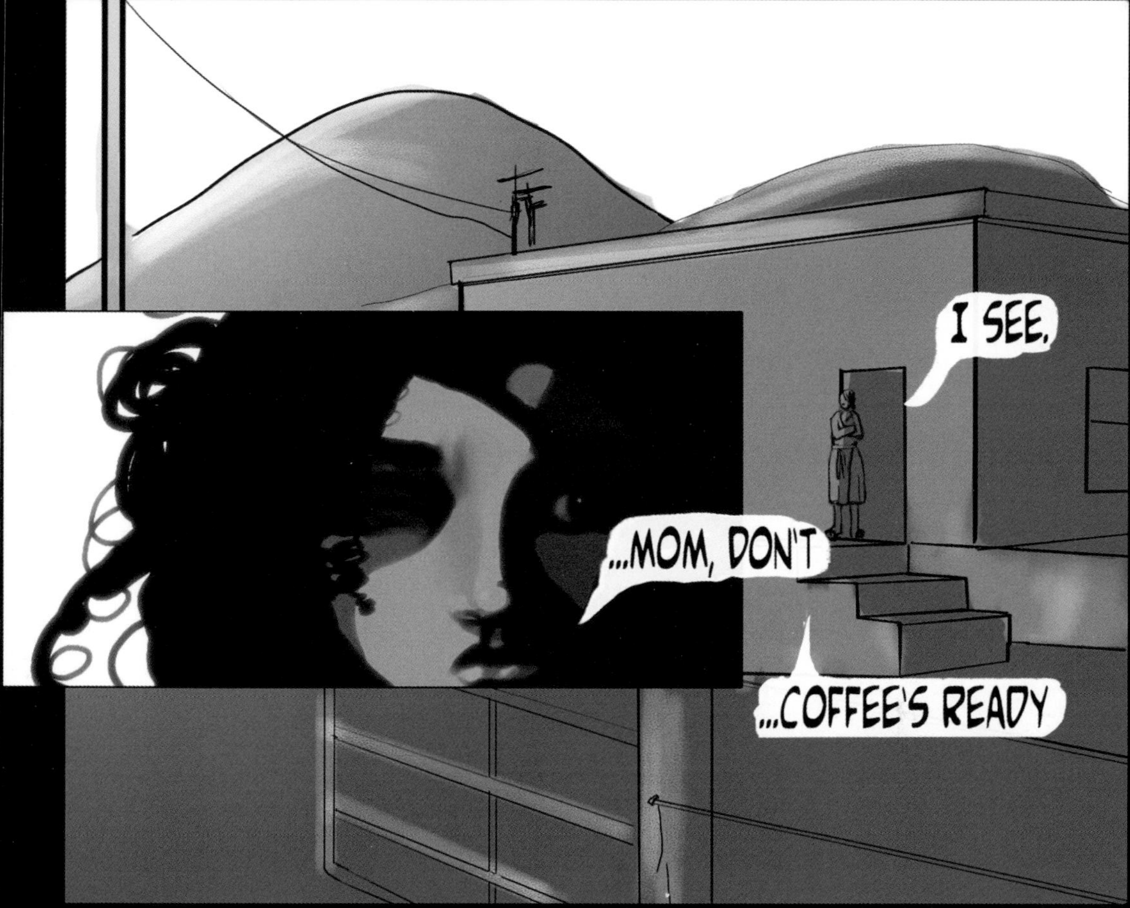
I SEE.
...MOM, DON'T
...COFFEE'S READY

WE DIDN'T KNOW WHY WE WERE THERE, BUT WE BROUGHT OUR SUITCASE. WE LOVED PLAYING ON THE GATE TO PASS THE TIME... AND THAT BUSTED ANTIQUE STOVE IN THE FRONT YARD.

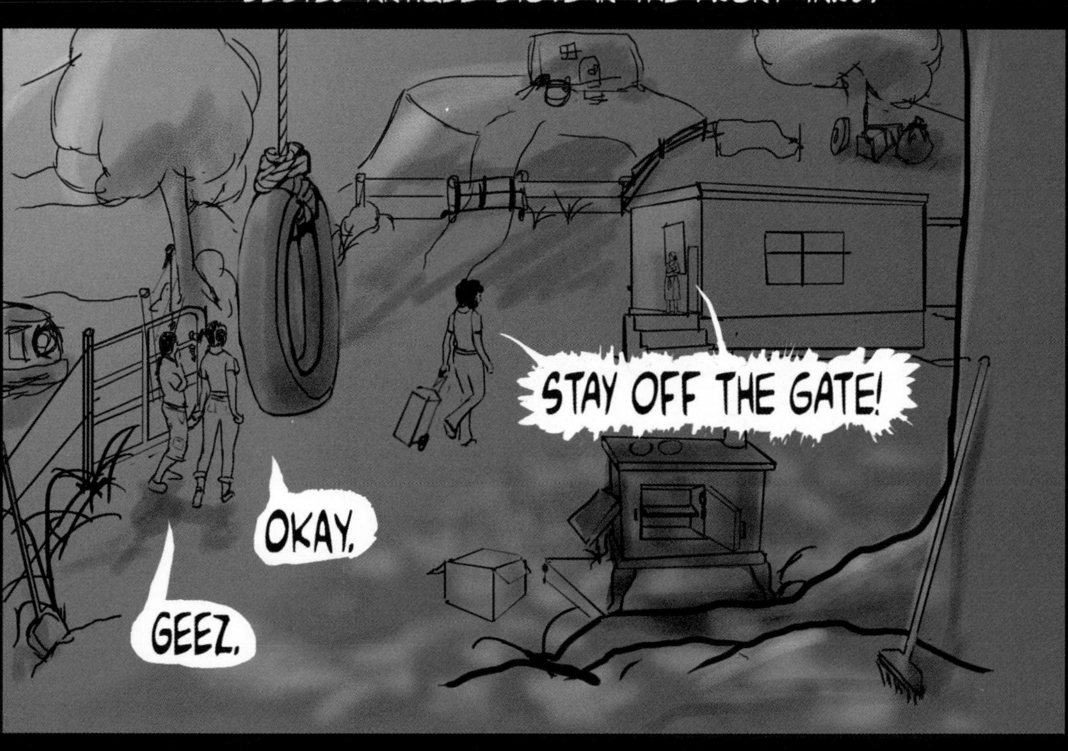
STAY OFF THE GATE!
OKAY.
GEEZ.

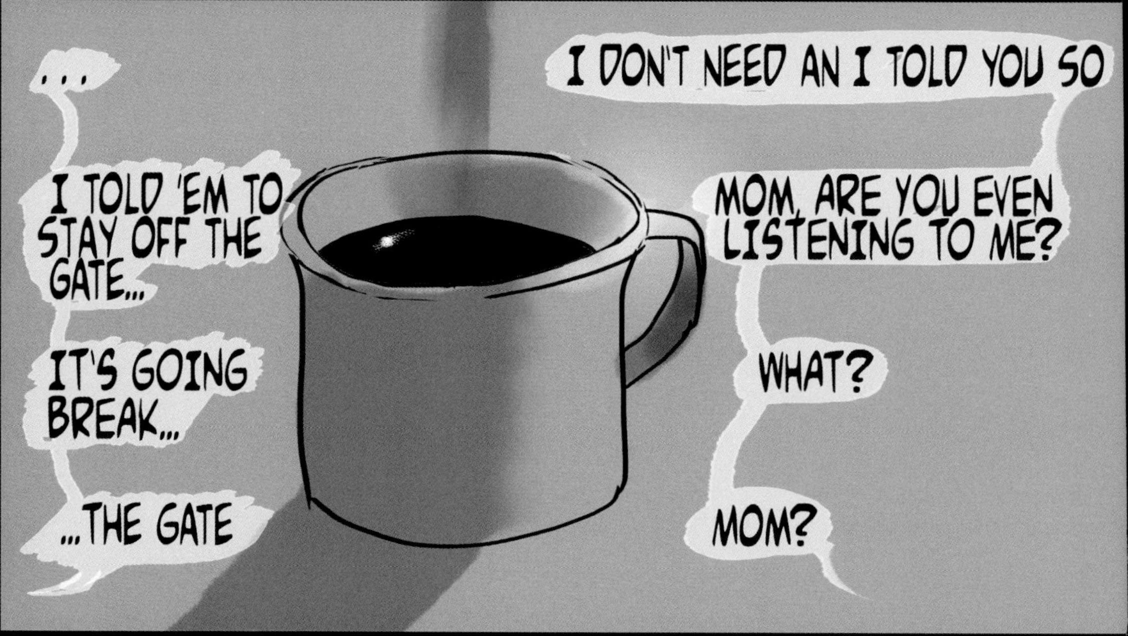
. . .
I TOLD 'EM TO STAY OFF THE GATE...
IT'S GOING BREAK...
...THE GATE
I DON'T NEED AN I TOLD YOU SO
MOM, ARE YOU EVEN LISTENING TO ME?
WHAT?
MOM?

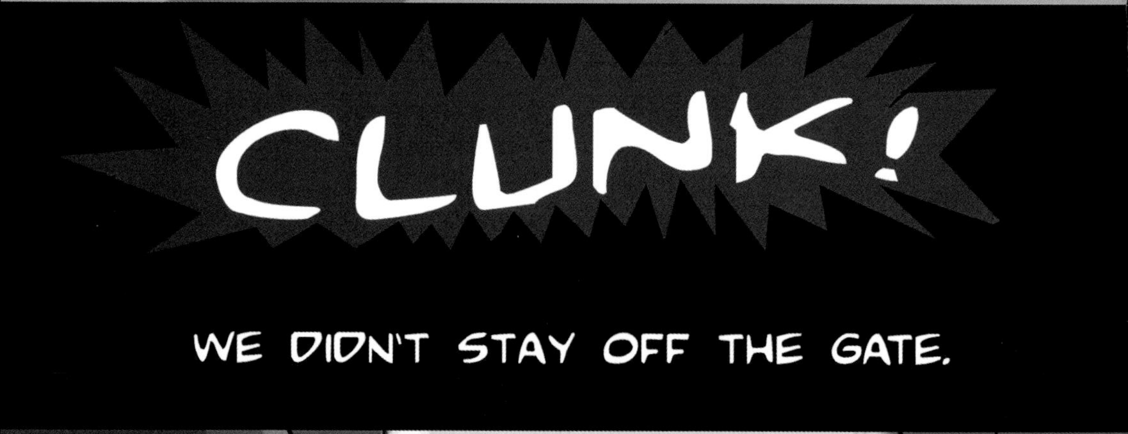
CLUNK!
WE DIDN'T STAY OFF THE GATE.

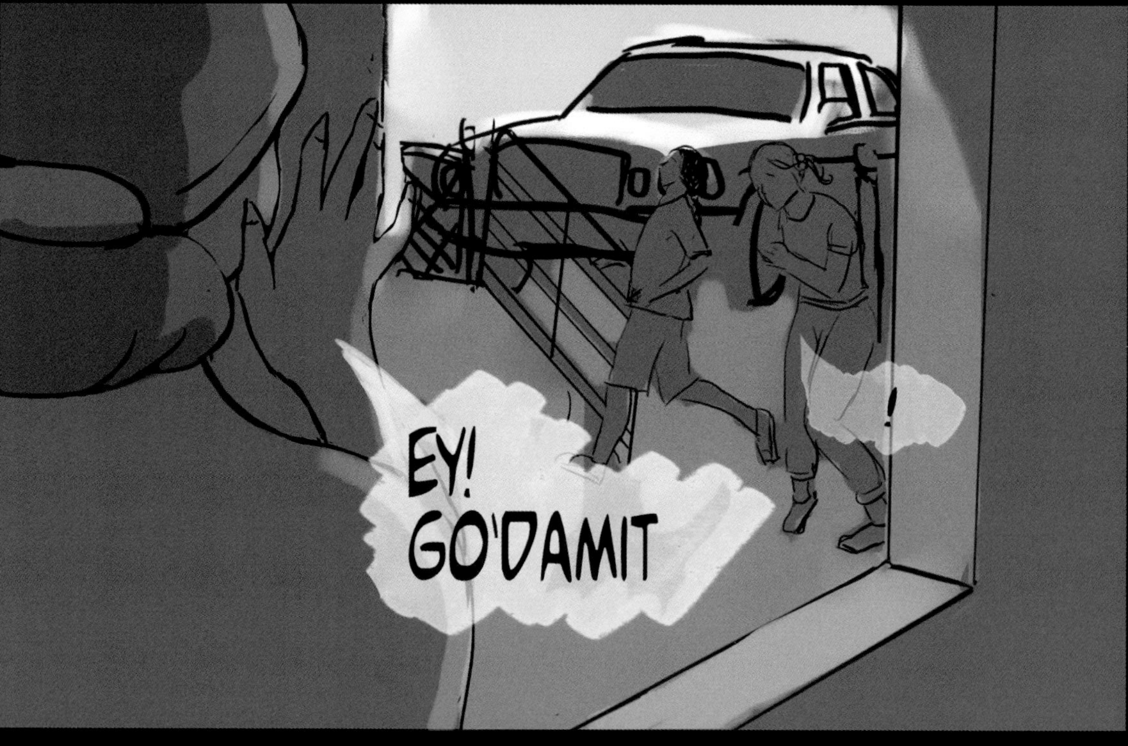
EY!
GO'DAMIT

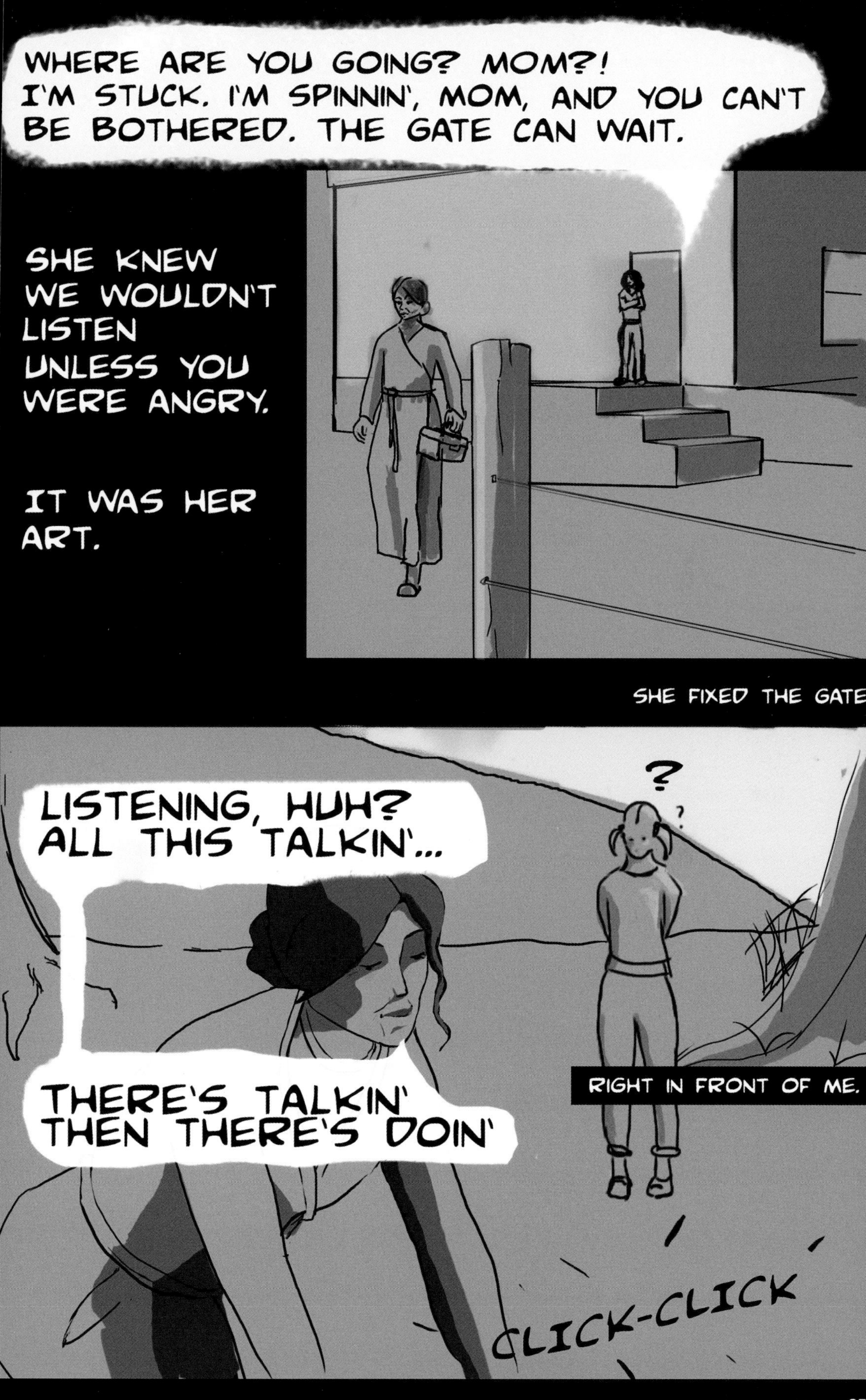
WHERE ARE YOU GOING? MOM?! I'M STUCK. I'M SPINNIN', MOM, AND YOU CAN'T BE BOTHERED. THE GATE CAN WAIT.
SHE KNEW WE WOULDN'T LISTEN UNLESS YOU WERE ANGRY.
IT WAS HER ART.
SHE FIXED THE GATE
LISTENING, HUH? ALL THIS TALKIN'...
THERE'S TALKIN' THEN THERE'S DOIN'
?
?
RIGHT IN FRONT OF ME.
CLICK-CLICK

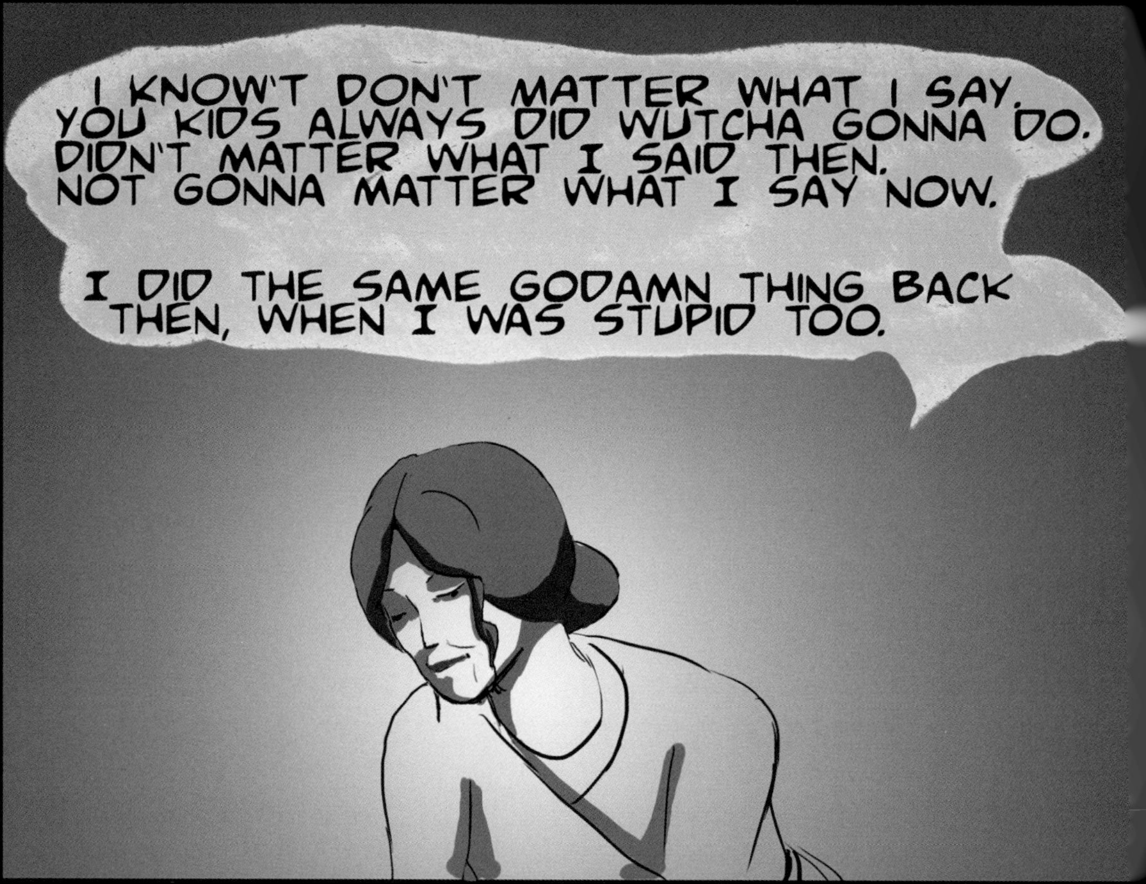
I KNOW'T DON'T MATTER WHAT I SAY. YOU KIDS ALWAYS DID WUTCHA GONNA DO. DIDN'T MATTER WHAT I SAID THEN. NOT GONNA MATTER WHAT I SAY NOW.
I DID THE SAME GODAMN THING BACK THEN, WHEN I WAS STUPID TOO.

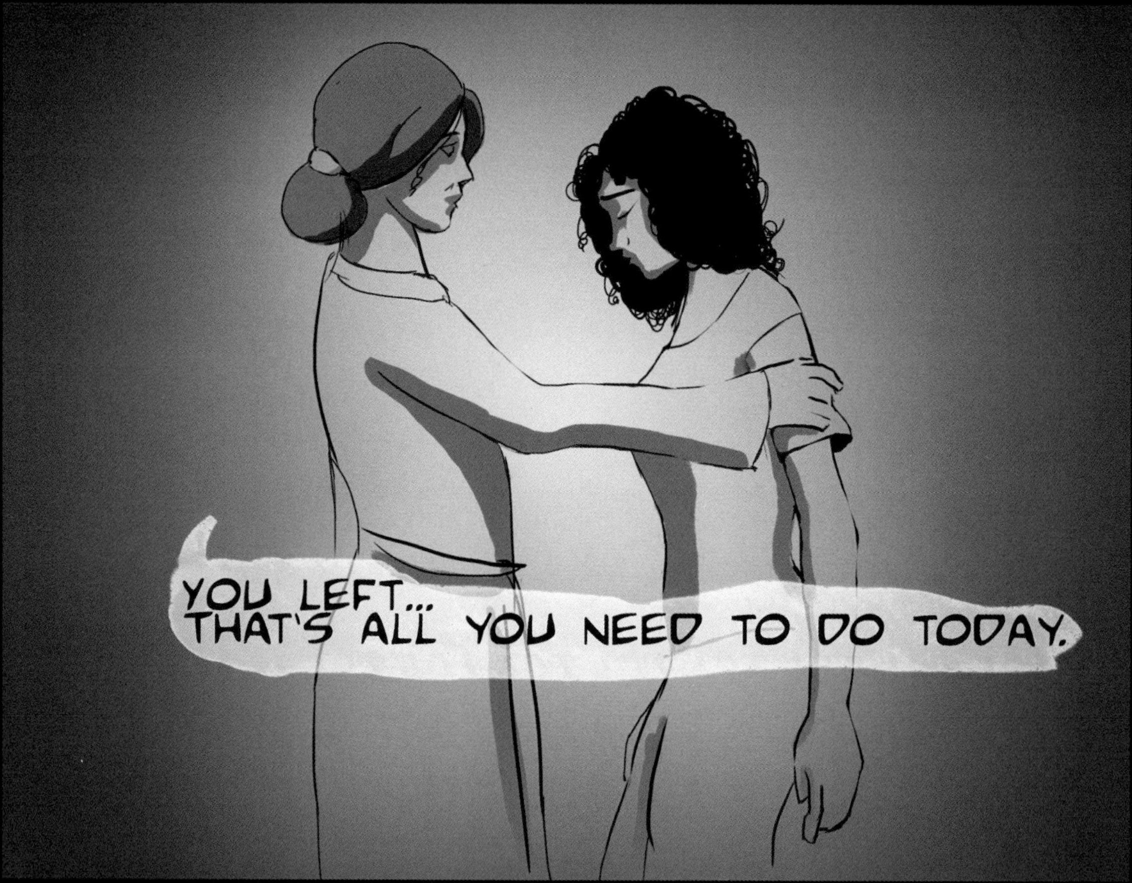
YOU LEFT... THAT'S ALL YOU NEED TO DO TODAY.

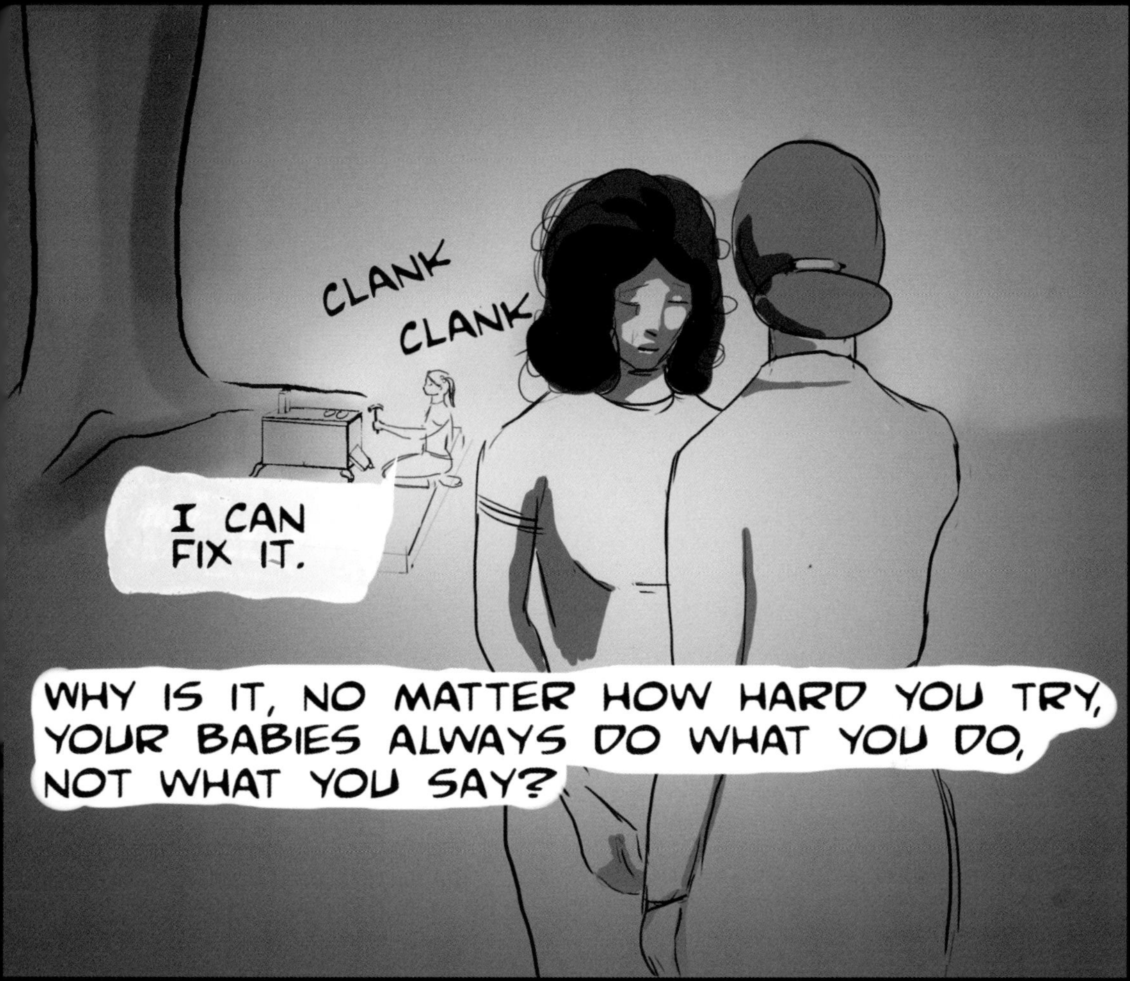
CLANK
CLANK
I CAN FIX IT.
WHY IS IT, NO MATTER HOW HARD YOU TRY, YOUR BABIES ALWAYS DO WHAT YOU DO, NOT WHAT YOU SAY?

THAT DAY I LEARNED YOU FIX WHAT YOU WANT TO LAST. YOU TAKE CARE OF WHAT YOU LOVE.

I FIXED THE BROKEN STOVE.

I WILL TEACH MY DAUGHTER TO FIX HER STOVE.

AND I WILL NOT TELL HER TO LOVE HERSELF.

I WILL SHOW HER.

THE END

Pathetic

Written and Illustrated
by Dale Ray Deforest

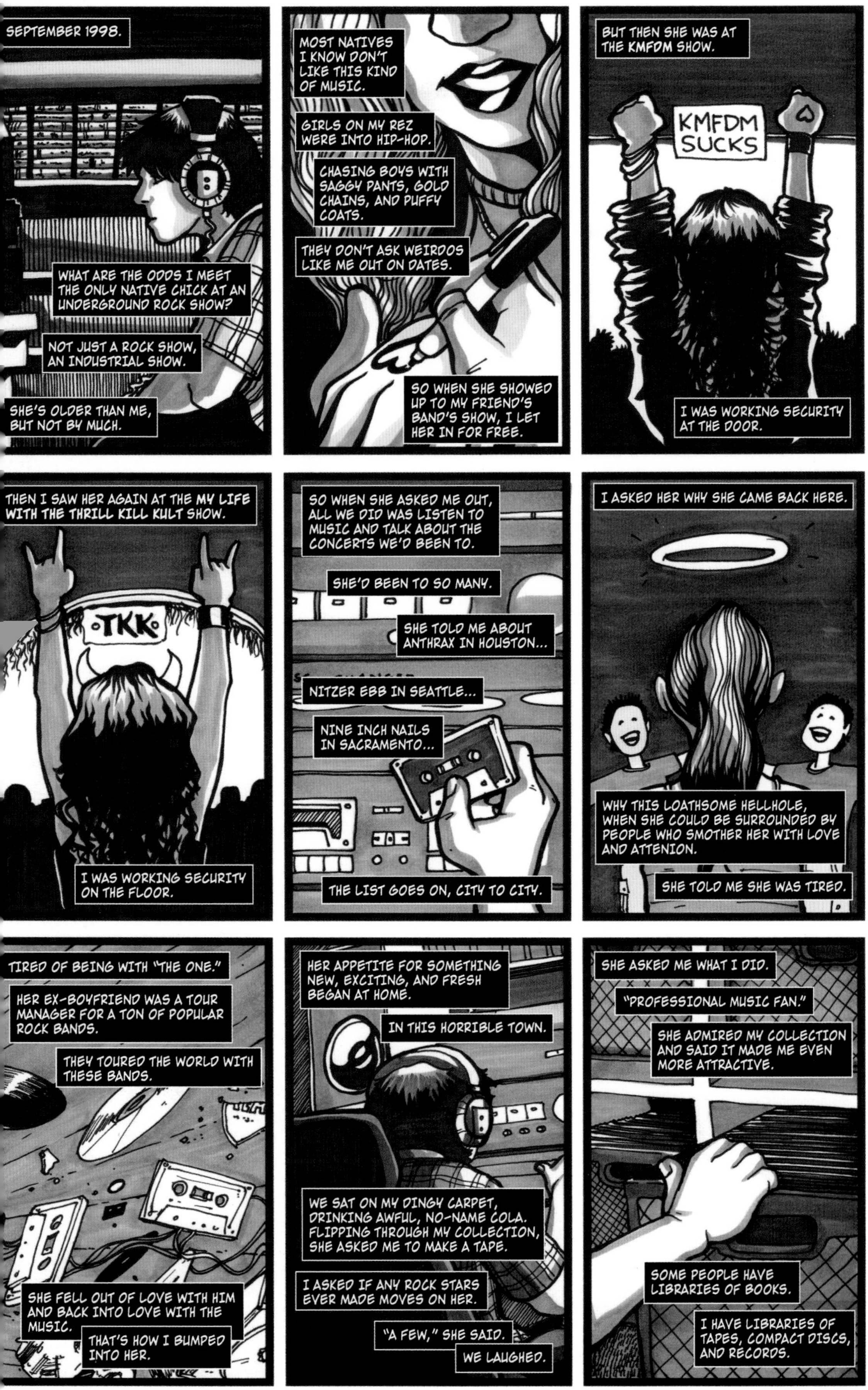
SEPTEMBER 1998.
WHAT ARE THE ODDS I MEET THE ONLY NATIVE CHICK AT AN UNDERGROUND ROCK SHOW?
NOT JUST A ROCK SHOW, AN INDUSTRIAL SHOW.
SHE'S OLDER THAN ME, BUT NOT BY MUCH.
MOST NATIVES I KNOW DON'T LIKE THIS KIND OF MUSIC.
GIRLS ON MY REZ WERE INTO HIP-HOP.
CHASING BOYS WITH SAGGY PANTS, GOLD CHAINS, AND PUFFY COATS.
THEY DON'T ASK WEIRDOS LIKE ME OUT ON DATES.
SO WHEN SHE SHOWED UP TO MY FRIEND'S BAND'S SHOW, I LET HER IN FOR FREE.
BUT THEN SHE WAS AT THE KMFDM SHOW.
KMFDM SUCKS
I WAS WORKING SECURITY AT THE DOOR.
THEN I SAW HER AGAIN AT THE MY LIFE WITH THE THRILL KILL KULT SHOW.
TKK
I WAS WORKING SECURITY ON THE FLOOR.
SO WHEN SHE ASKED ME OUT, ALL WE DID WAS LISTEN TO MUSIC AND TALK ABOUT THE CONCERTS WE'D BEEN TO.
SHE'D BEEN TO SO MANY.
SHE TOLD ME ABOUT ANTHRAX IN HOUSTON...
NITZER EBB IN SEATTLE...
NINE INCH NAILS IN SACRAMENTO...
THE LIST GOES ON, CITY TO CITY.
I ASKED HER WHY SHE CAME BACK HERE.
WHY THIS LOATHSOME HELLHOLE, WHEN SHE COULD BE SURROUNDED BY PEOPLE WHO SMOTHER HER WITH LOVE AND ATTENTION.
SHE TOLD ME SHE WAS TIRED.
TIRED OF BEING WITH "THE ONE."
HER EX-BOYFRIEND WAS A TOUR MANAGER FOR A TON OF POPULAR ROCK BANDS.
THEY TOURED THE WORLD WITH THESE BANDS.
SHE FELL OUT OF LOVE WITH HIM AND BACK INTO LOVE WITH THE MUSIC.
THAT'S HOW I BUMPED INTO HER.
HER APPETITE FOR SOMETHING NEW, EXCITING, AND FRESH BEGAN AT HOME.
IN THIS HORRIBLE TOWN.
WE SAT ON MY DINGY CARPET, DRINKING AWFUL, NO-NAME COLA. FLIPPING THROUGH MY COLLECTION, SHE ASKED ME TO MAKE A TAPE.
I ASKED IF ANY ROCK STARS EVER MADE MOVES ON HER.
"A FEW," SHE SAID.
WE LAUGHED.
SHE ASKED ME WHAT I DID.
"PROFESSIONAL MUSIC FAN."
SHE ADMIRED MY COLLECTION AND SAID IT MADE ME EVEN MORE ATTRACTIVE.
SOME PEOPLE HAVE LIBRARIES OF BOOKS.
I HAVE LIBRARIES OF TAPES, COMPACT DISCS, AND RECORDS.

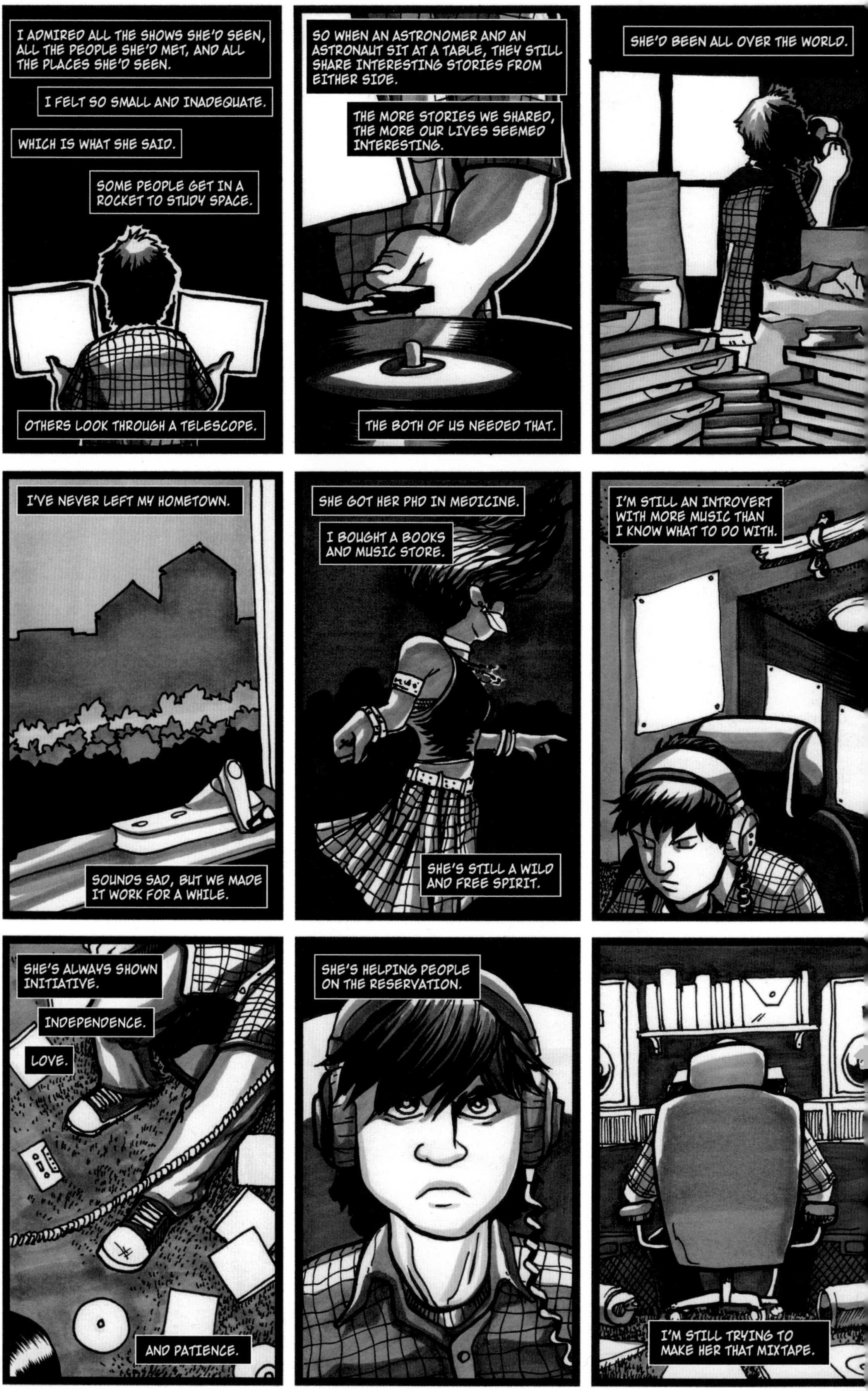
I ADMIRED ALL THE SHOWS SHE'D SEEN, ALL THE PEOPLE SHE'D MET, AND ALL THE PLACES SHE'D SEEN.
I FELT SO SMALL AND INADEQUATE.
WHICH IS WHAT SHE SAID.
SOME PEOPLE GET IN A ROCKET TO STUDY SPACE.
OTHERS LOOK THROUGH A TELESCOPE.
SO WHEN AN ASTRONOMER AND AN ASTRONAUT SIT AT A TABLE, THEY STILL SHARE INTERESTING STORIES FROM EITHER SIDE.
THE MORE STORIES WE SHARED, THE MORE OUR LIVES SEEMED INTERESTING.
THE BOTH OF US NEEDED THAT.
SHE'D BEEN ALL OVER THE WORLD.
I'VE NEVER LEFT MY HOMETOWN.
SOUNDS SAD, BUT WE MADE IT WORK FOR A WHILE.
SHE GOT HER PHD IN MEDICINE.
I BOUGHT A BOOKS AND MUSIC STORE.
SHE'S STILL A WILD AND FREE SPIRIT.
I'M STILL AN INTROVERT WITH MORE MUSIC THAN I KNOW WHAT TO DO WITH.
SHE'S ALWAYS SHOWN INITIATIVE.
INDEPENDENCE.
LOVE.
AND PATIENCE.
SHE'S HELPING PEOPLE ON THE RESERVATION.
I'M STILL TRYING TO MAKE HER THAT MIXTAPE.

END

Memories of the Future

Illustrated by Elizabeth LaPensée

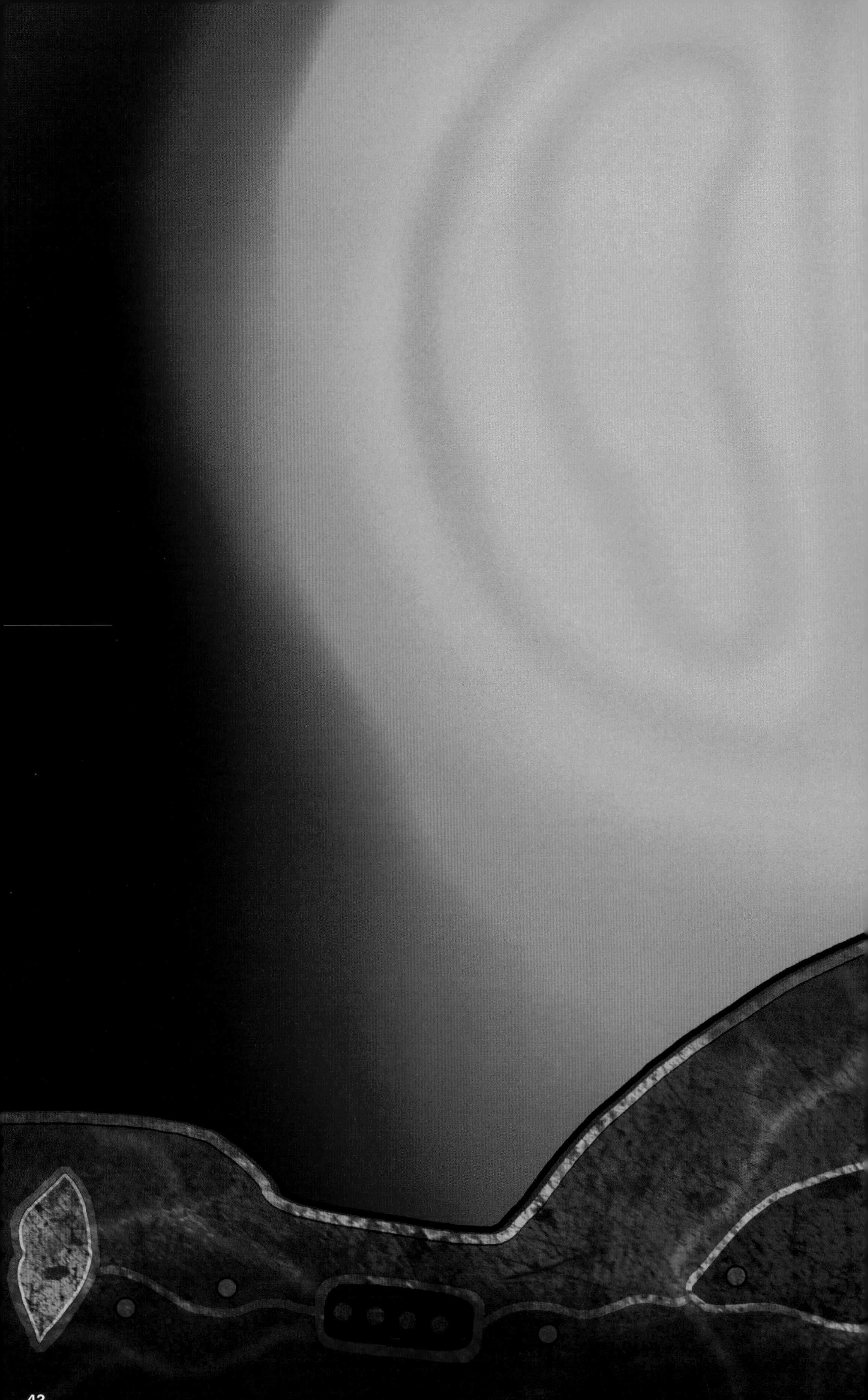

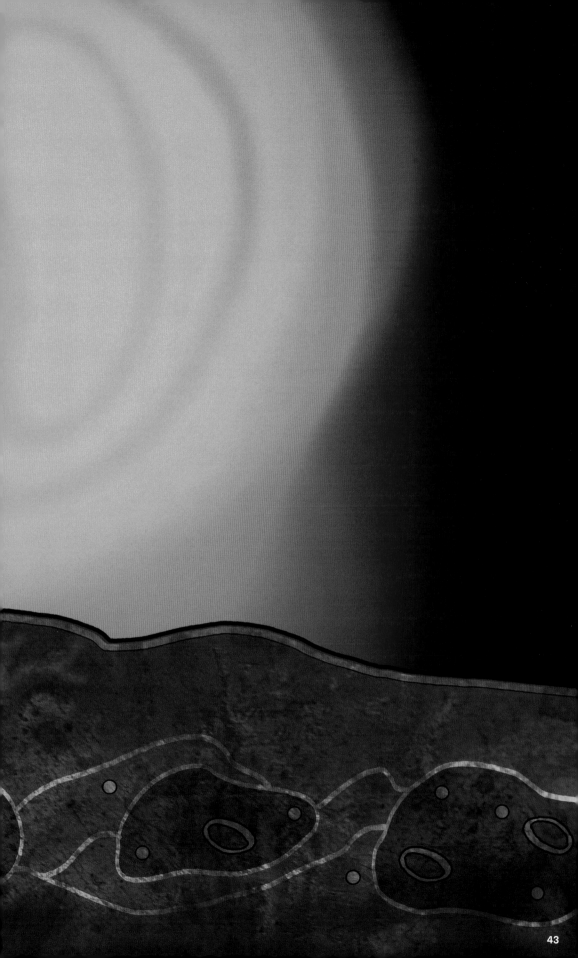

Oceanographer

Written and Illustrated by Darcie Little Badger

Shinch'oonii ashííìì Shila.

"Oceanographer" explores my love for the ocean, which is tightly linked to my love of self and others. It is also a contemplation of endurance. Yes, things are tough. Our land—and, as a consequence, our bodies—are being poisoned. The climate is changing. The sea is rising. Species are dying. We are trapped in an apocalypse that started before the industrial revolution, and the odds of survival seem slim. In times like these, it is crucial to find strength within family, self, and *hope*.

It may be a challenge to continue resisting. The weight of all the apathy, greed, and cruelty in the world is great. Sometimes even I feel like giving up, but then I remember Badger, the first Badger. I'm named after her. Her persistence and determination brought life to the world. I may not be able to save every endemic bird, prevent every pipeline, or stop the coral reefs from dying, but I can make the world *better*, even just a little. It's so important.

We and our land are worth love and protection.

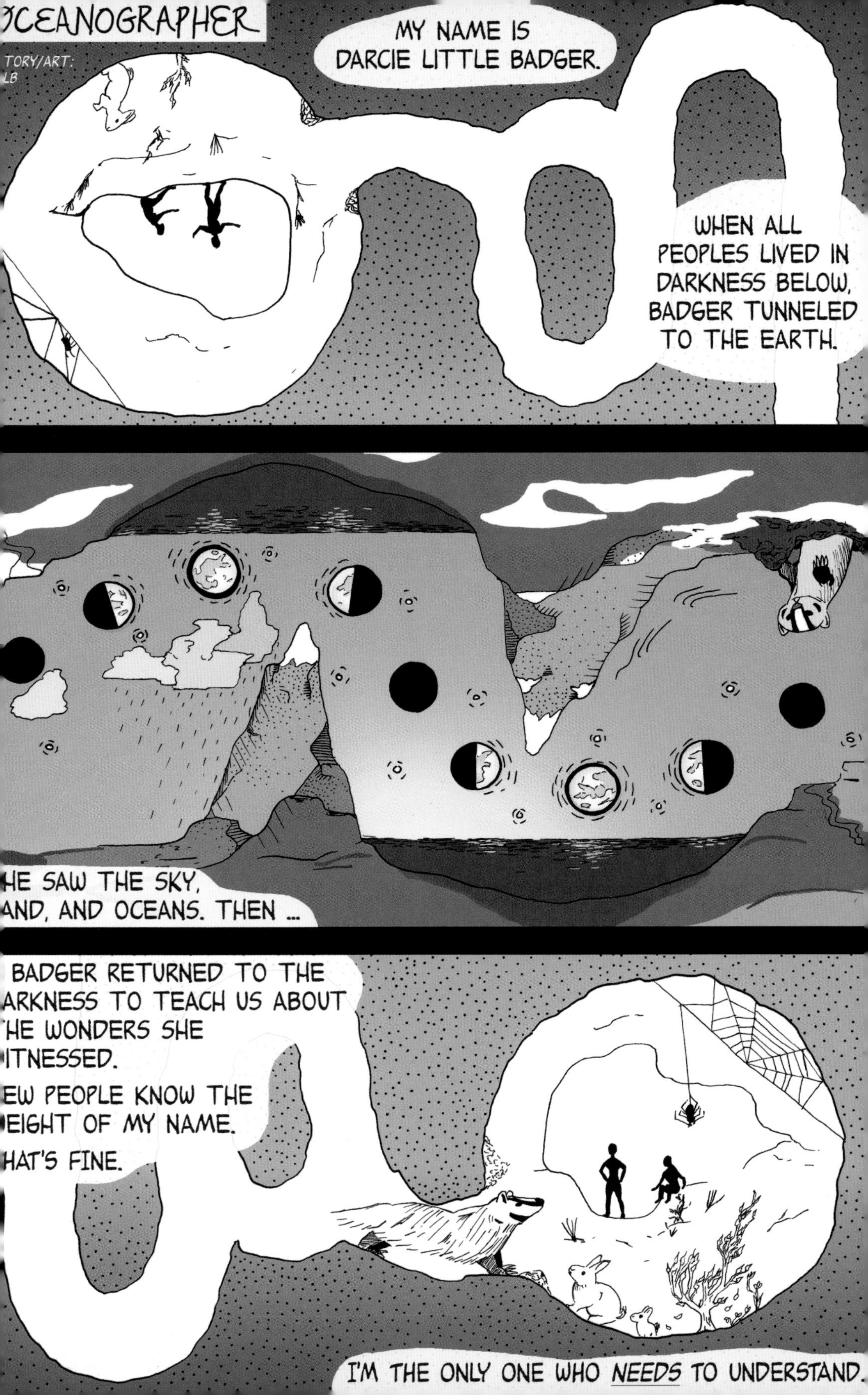

OCEANOGRAPHER
TORY/ART:
LB
MY NAME IS DARCIE LITTLE BADGER.
WHEN ALL PEOPLES LIVED IN DARKNESS BELOW, BADGER TUNNELED TO THE EARTH.
HE SAW THE SKY,
AND, AND OCEANS. THEN ...
BADGER RETURNED TO THE ARKNESS TO TEACH US ABOUT HE WONDERS SHE ITNESSED.
EW PEOPLE KNOW THE EIGHT OF MY NAME.
HAT'S FINE.
I'M THE ONLY ONE WHO NEEDS TO UNDERSTAND.

I FOUND THE WORLD BY STUDYING GEOSCIENCE AND OCEANOGRAPHY.

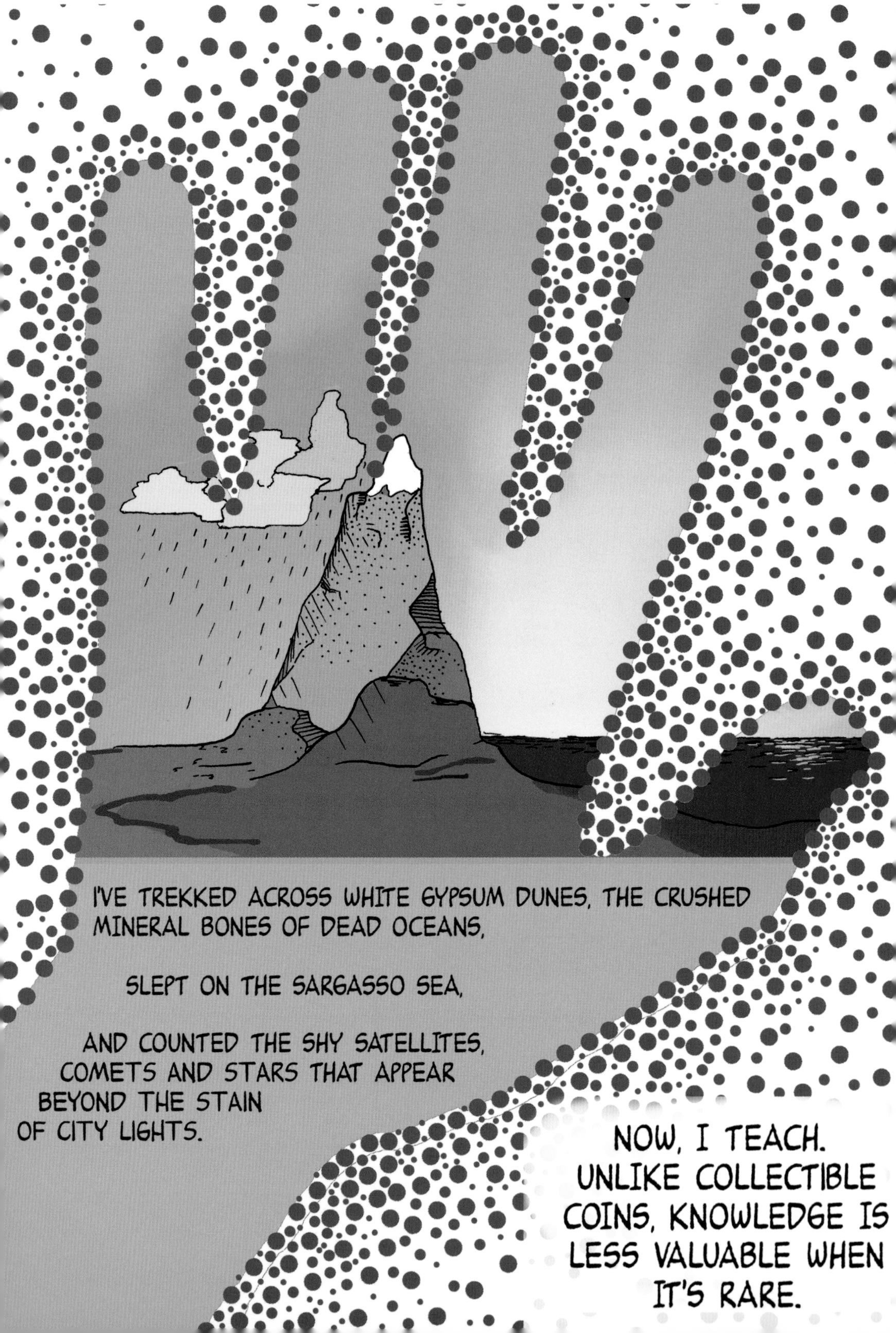
I'VE TREKKED ACROSS WHITE GYPSUM DUNES, THE CRUSHED MINERAL BONES OF DEAD OCEANS,
SLEPT ON THE SARGASSO SEA,
AND COUNTED THE SHY SATELLITES, COMETS AND STARS THAT APPEAR BEYOND THE STAIN OF CITY LIGHTS.
NOW, I TEACH. UNLIKE COLLECTIBLE COINS, KNOWLEDGE IS LESS VALUABLE WHEN IT'S RARE.

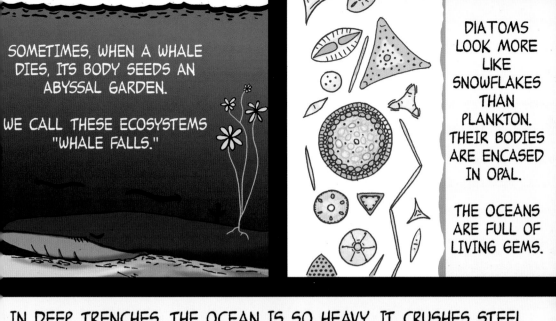

SOMETIMES, WHEN A WHALE DIES, ITS BODY SEEDS AN ABYSSAL GARDEN.

WE CALL THESE ECOSYSTEMS "WHALE FALLS."

DIATOMS LOOK MORE LIKE SNOWFLAKES THAN PLANKTON. THEIR BODIES ARE ENCASED IN OPAL.

THE OCEANS ARE FULL OF LIVING GEMS.

IN DEEP TRENCHES, THE OCEAN IS SO HEAVY, IT CRUSHES STEEL. HOLOTHURIANS, AMPHIPODS, AND OTHER WONDERS THRIVE UNDER PRESSURE. WITHOUT THE WEIGHT OF THE OCEAN ON THEIR BACKS, TRENCH ANIMALS DIE.

EVERY YEAR, THE ATLANTIC OCEAN WIDENS BY AN INCH. MY HAIR GROWS MORE QUICKLY THAN THAT.

IF MY HAIR BECAME AN OCEAN, IT WOULD SWALLOW THE WORLD.

ODDLY ENOUGH... ON BAD DAYS, I FEEL LIKE THE WORLD IS DROWNING _ME_.

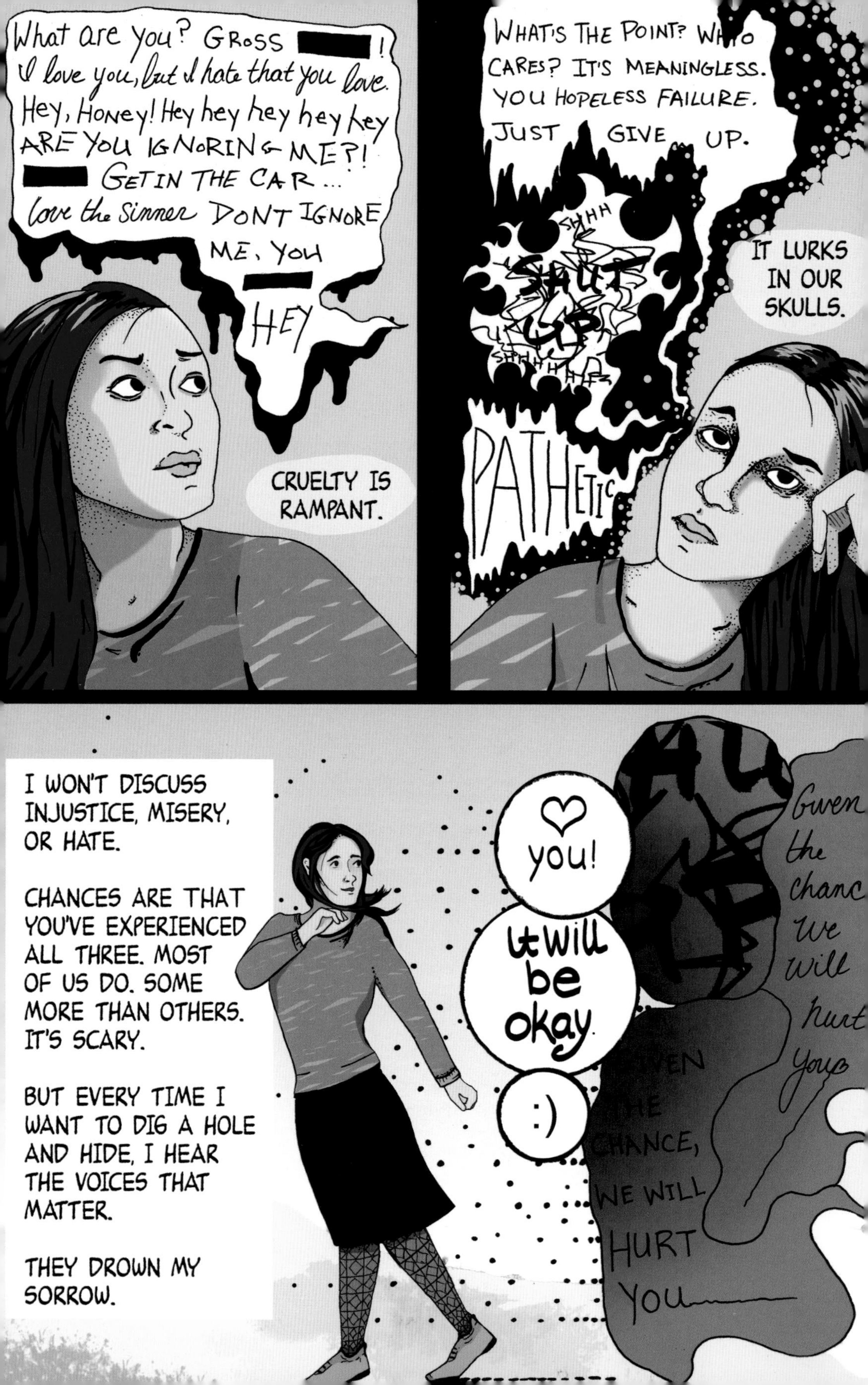
What are you? GROSS [redacted]!
I love you, but I hate that you love.
Hey, Honey! Hey hey hey hey hey
ARE YOU IGNORING ME?!
[redacted] GET IN THE CAR...
love the sinner DONT IGNORE
ME, YOU [redacted]
HEY
CRUELTY IS RAMPANT.
WHAT'S THE POINT? WHO CARES? IT'S MEANINGLESS.
YOU HOPELESS FAILURE.
JUST GIVE UP.
PATHETIC
IT LURKS IN OUR SKULLS.
I WON'T DISCUSS INJUSTICE, MISERY, OR HATE.
CHANCES ARE THAT YOU'VE EXPERIENCED ALL THREE. MOST OF US DO. SOME MORE THAN OTHERS. IT'S SCARY.
BUT EVERY TIME I WANT TO DIG A HOLE AND HIDE, I HEAR THE VOICES THAT MATTER.
THEY DROWN MY SORROW.
♡ you!
it will be okay.
:)
Given the chanc We will hurt you
CHANCE, WE WILL HURT YOU

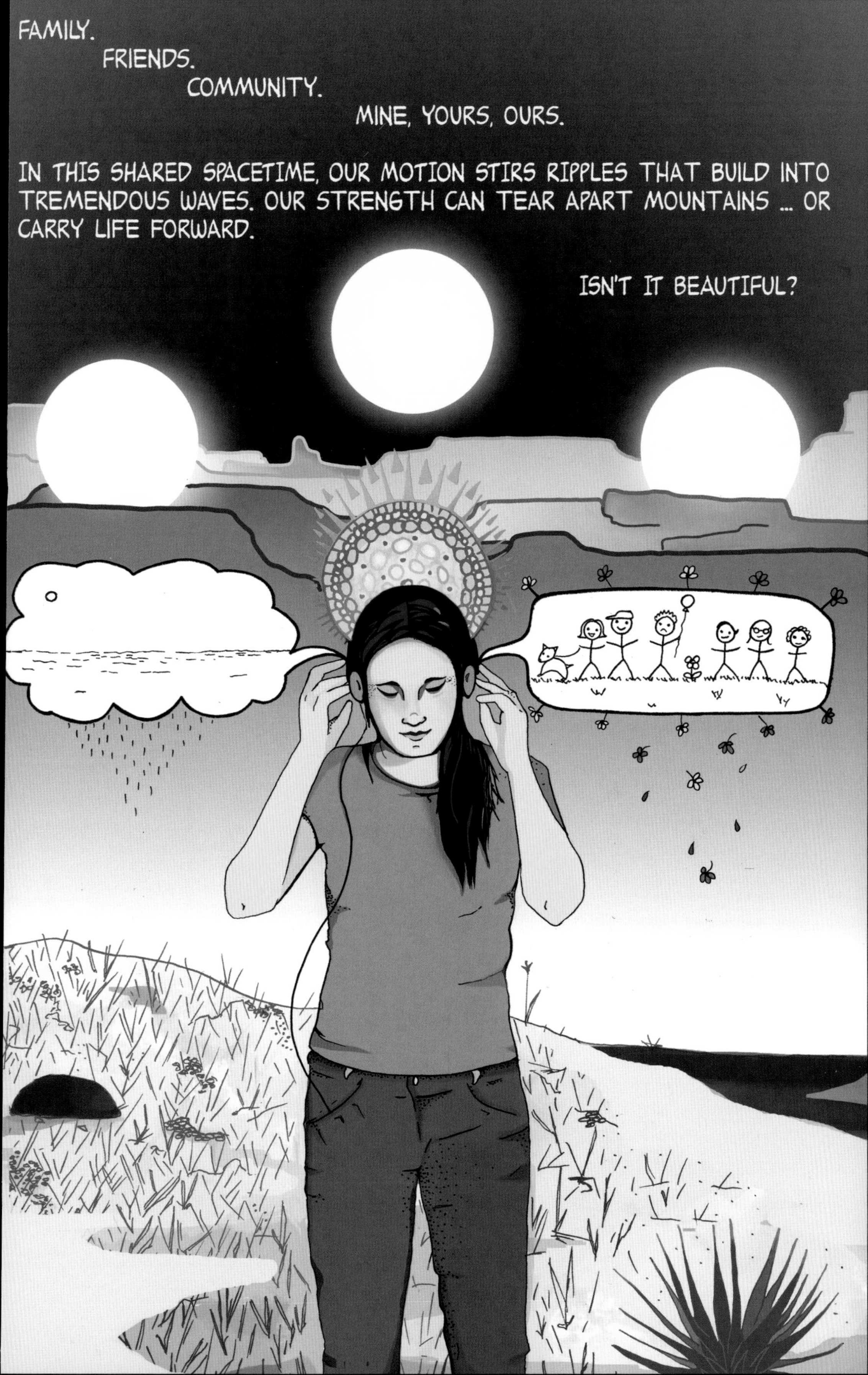
FAMILY.
FRIENDS.
COMMUNITY.
MINE, YOURS, OURS.
IN THIS SHARED SPACETIME, OUR MOTION STIRS RIPPLES THAT BUILD INTO TREMENDOUS WAVES. OUR STRENGTH CAN TEAR APART MOUNTAINS ... OR CARRY LIFE FORWARD.
ISN'T IT BEAUTIFUL?

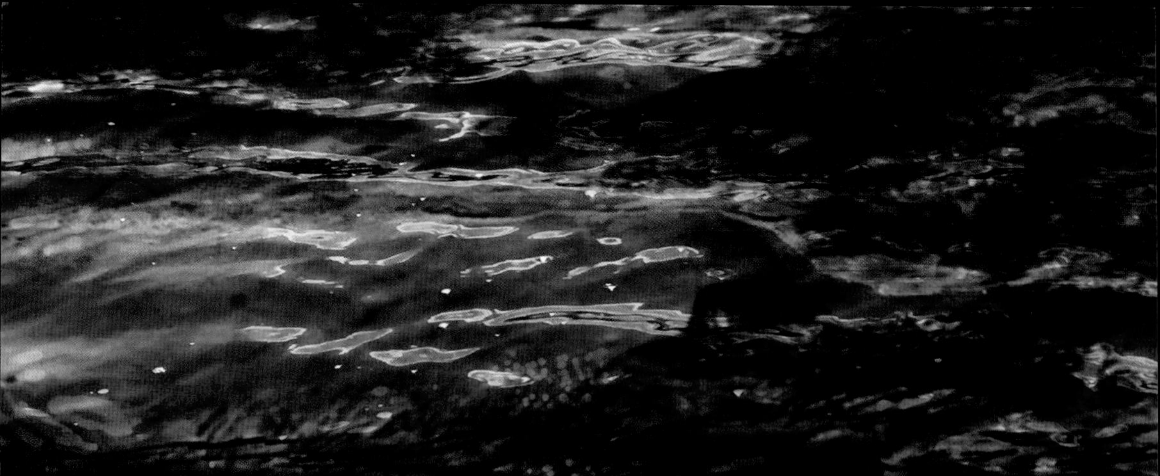

Space

Written by Ishki Ricard

"Space" is about seeing below the surface and into the depths, making a soul connection, and finding a feeling like home with someone special. Whether that's a friend, a family member, an acquaintance, or a romantic partner is up to interpretation, and I feel can be found with any of those. It's about seeing something more, something different where others dismiss, and finding beauty in all of creation. It's being fascinated by the simultaneous simplicity and complexity of existence itself.

You are
So many hidden colors, things
Hidden warmth and brilliance
So much more than what could ever be seen
Depth
And pervasive support

Space is thought as empty
But it is so full

You are so full

All of life and creation is made of you
And you, all of life and creation

Of dust and stars
Born from destruction and chaos
Formed into the most beautiful
Alluring
Things

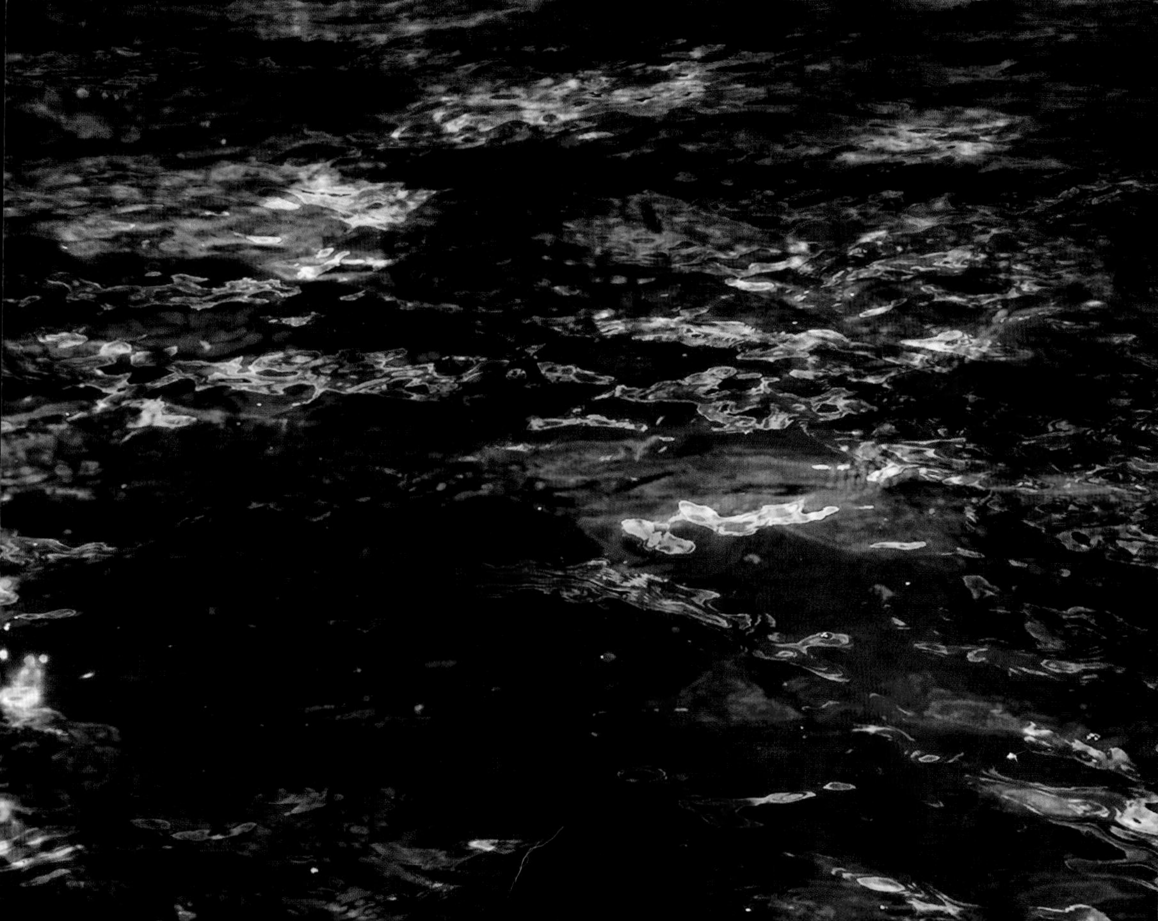

Breathtaking in depth and measure
Expansive and awesome and
Illuminating

You are not the empty darkness that is assumed
That is shown
You are all matter
All of the universe in such beauty
And grace
And fluidity

You are what keeps people up at night with
Existential ponderings
Of suns and earths and moons and love and life and *what-ifs* and *will-I-evers*

And *dreams*
Swirling, elusive dreams

You are a hazy comfortable sleep
filled to the brim with pleasantness
and ease
and the softest sweetest thoughts . . . of love

Liminal

**Written and Illustrated
by Michelle Lee Brown**

We are coastal people (the only province in Iparralde, that is; though I grew up nourished by the beaches and waters of traditional Wampanoag territory and I am currently supported by the 'āina of the Kānaka Maoli while I finish my PhD). Even now as I move into spaces and places, it's important for me to touch the waters there. To offer thanks. To know (a little bit) and connect. Moving in this piece doesn't mean not rooted, rather a sense of routedness, of multilayered cycles and flows, as other amazing Indigenous feminists have noted.

But moving in between-spaces is both comforting and discomforting. There are frictions and other sticky energies that took me years to learn to respect and work with. I'm still learning. Still messing up, adjusting, growing. My Nana made it look so fluid and easy. I know now it took her a lifetime or more to get to that level. Maybe there's still hope for me, though I imagine her shaking her head as I walk into doorframes now and then.

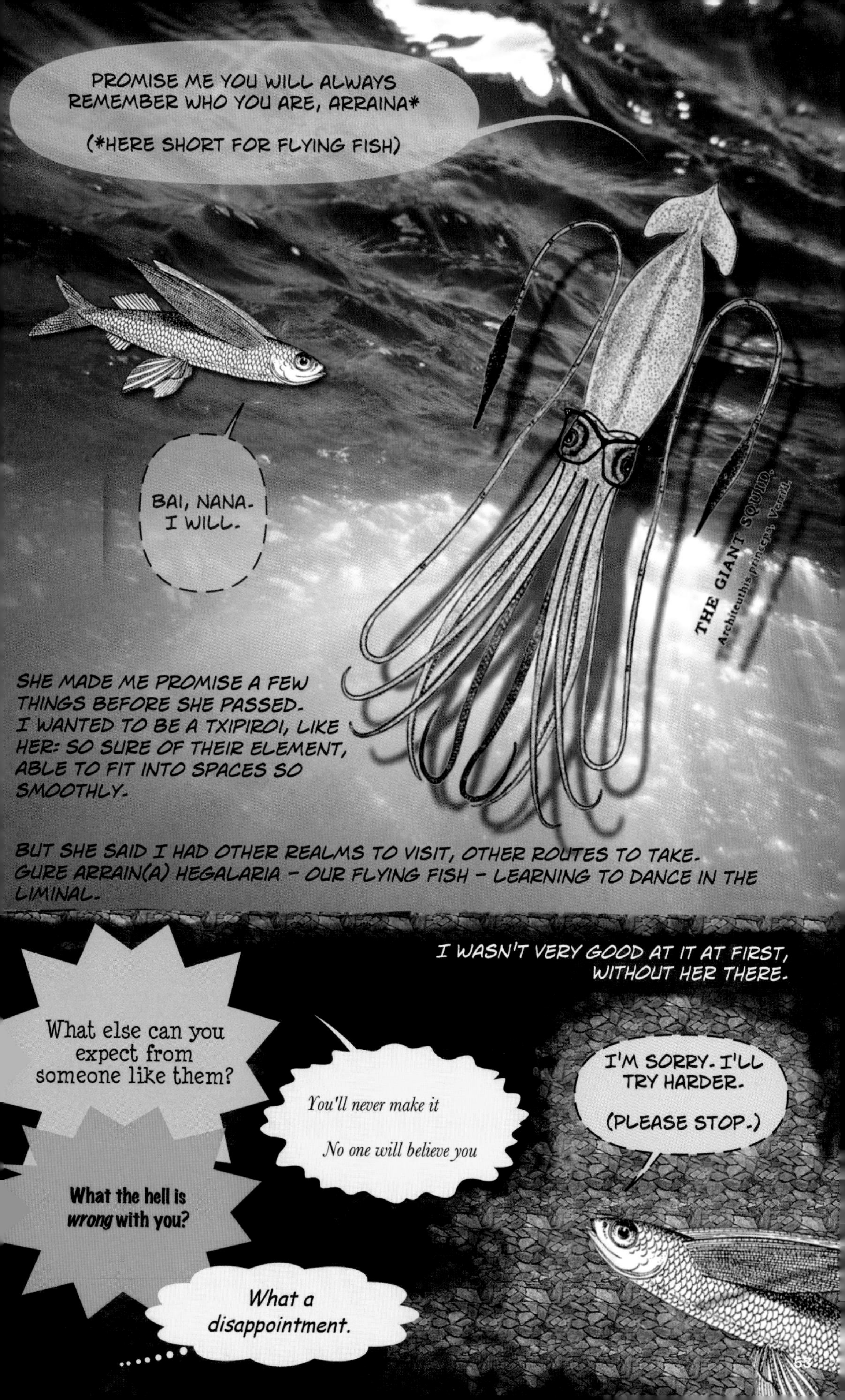
PROMISE ME YOU WILL ALWAYS REMEMBER WHO YOU ARE, ARRAINA*
(*HERE SHORT FOR FLYING FISH)
BAI, NANA. I WILL.
THE GIANT SQUID.
Architeuthis princeps, Verrill.
SHE MADE ME PROMISE A FEW THINGS BEFORE SHE PASSED. I WANTED TO BE A TXIPIROI, LIKE HER: SO SURE OF THEIR ELEMENT, ABLE TO FIT INTO SPACES SO SMOOTHLY.
BUT SHE SAID I HAD OTHER REALMS TO VISIT, OTHER ROUTES TO TAKE. GURE ARRAIN(A) HEGALARIA – OUR FLYING FISH – LEARNING TO DANCE IN THE LIMINAL.
I WASN'T VERY GOOD AT IT AT FIRST, WITHOUT HER THERE.
What else can you expect from someone like them?
You'll never make it
No one will believe you
I'M SORRY. I'LL TRY HARDER.
(PLEASE STOP.)
What the hell is *wrong* with you?
What a disappointment.

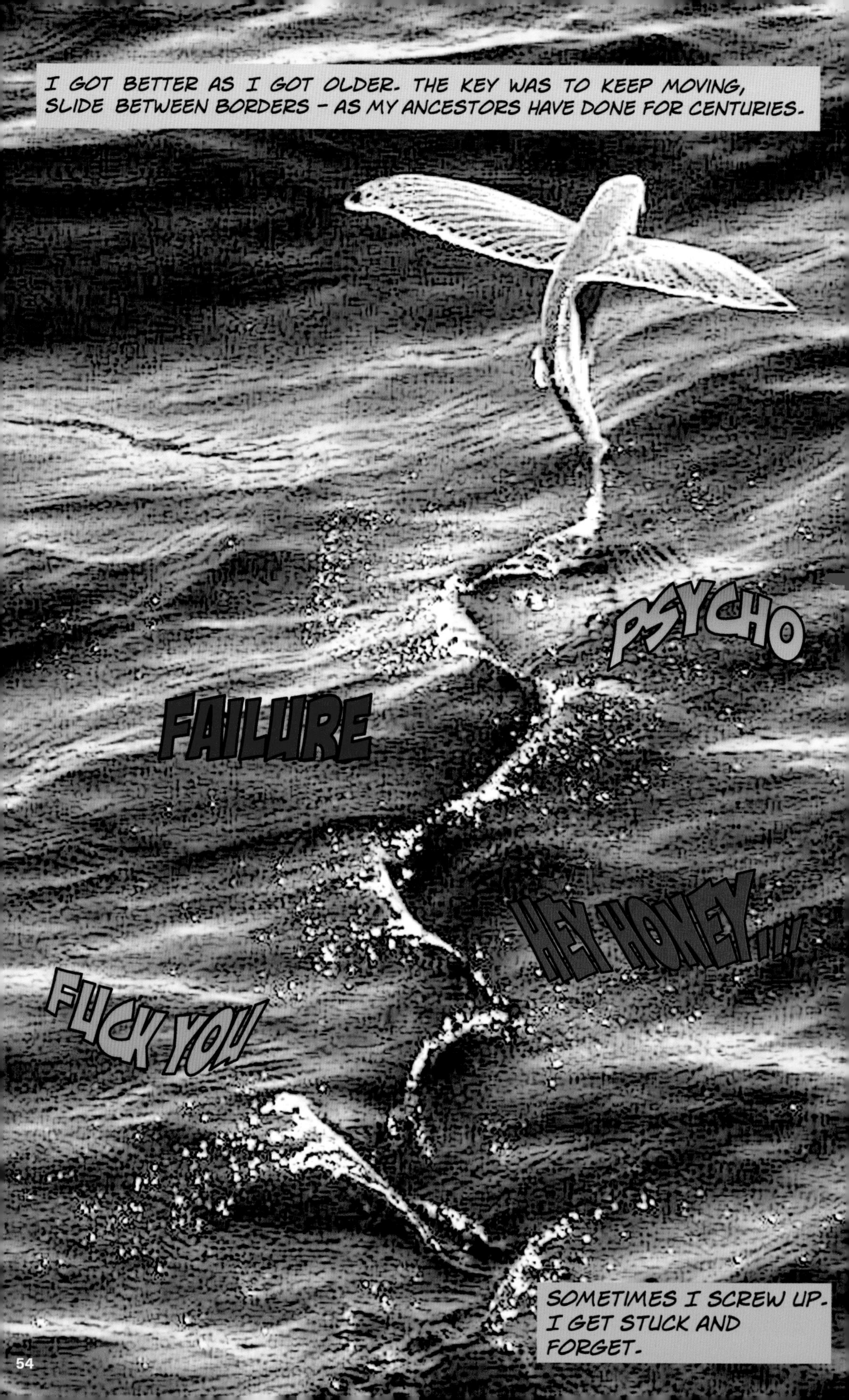
I GOT BETTER AS I GOT OLDER. THE KEY WAS TO KEEP MOVING, SLIDE BETWEEN BORDERS – AS MY ANCESTORS HAVE DONE FOR CENTURIES.
PSYCHO
FAILURE
HEY HONEY!!!!
FUCK YOU
SOMETIMES I SCREW UP. I GET STUCK AND FORGET.

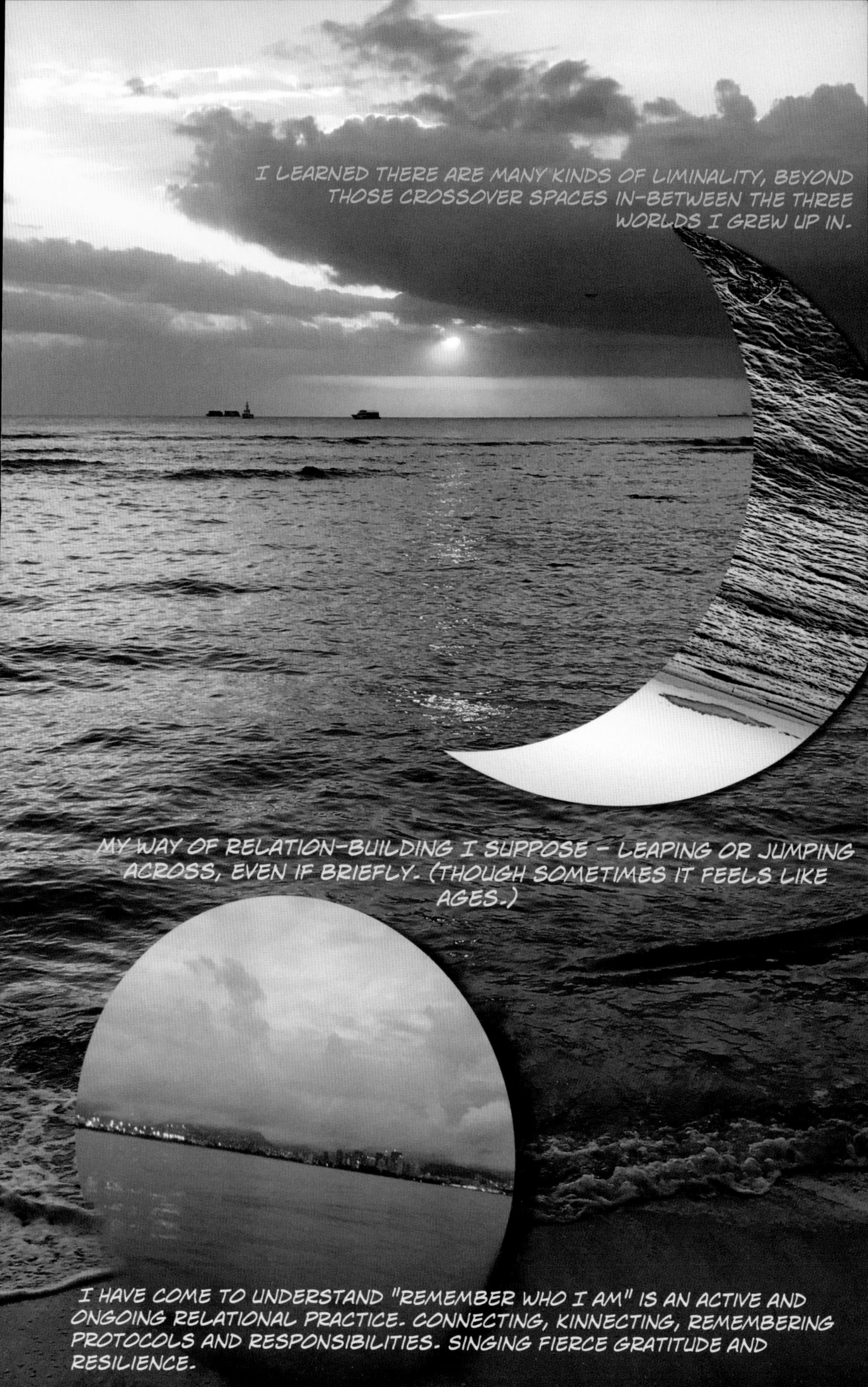
I LEARNED THERE ARE MANY KINDS OF LIMINALITY, BEYOND THOSE CROSSOVER SPACES IN-BETWEEN THE THREE WORLDS I GREW UP IN.
MY WAY OF RELATION-BUILDING I SUPPOSE - LEAPING OR JUMPING ACROSS, EVEN IF BRIEFLY. (THOUGH SOMETIMES IT FEELS LIKE AGES.)
I HAVE COME TO UNDERSTAND "REMEMBER WHO I AM" IS AN ACTIVE AND ONGOING RELATIONAL PRACTICE. CONNECTING, KINNECTING, REMEMBERING PROTOCOLS AND RESPONSIBILITIES. SINGING FIERCE GRATITUDE AND RESILIENCE.

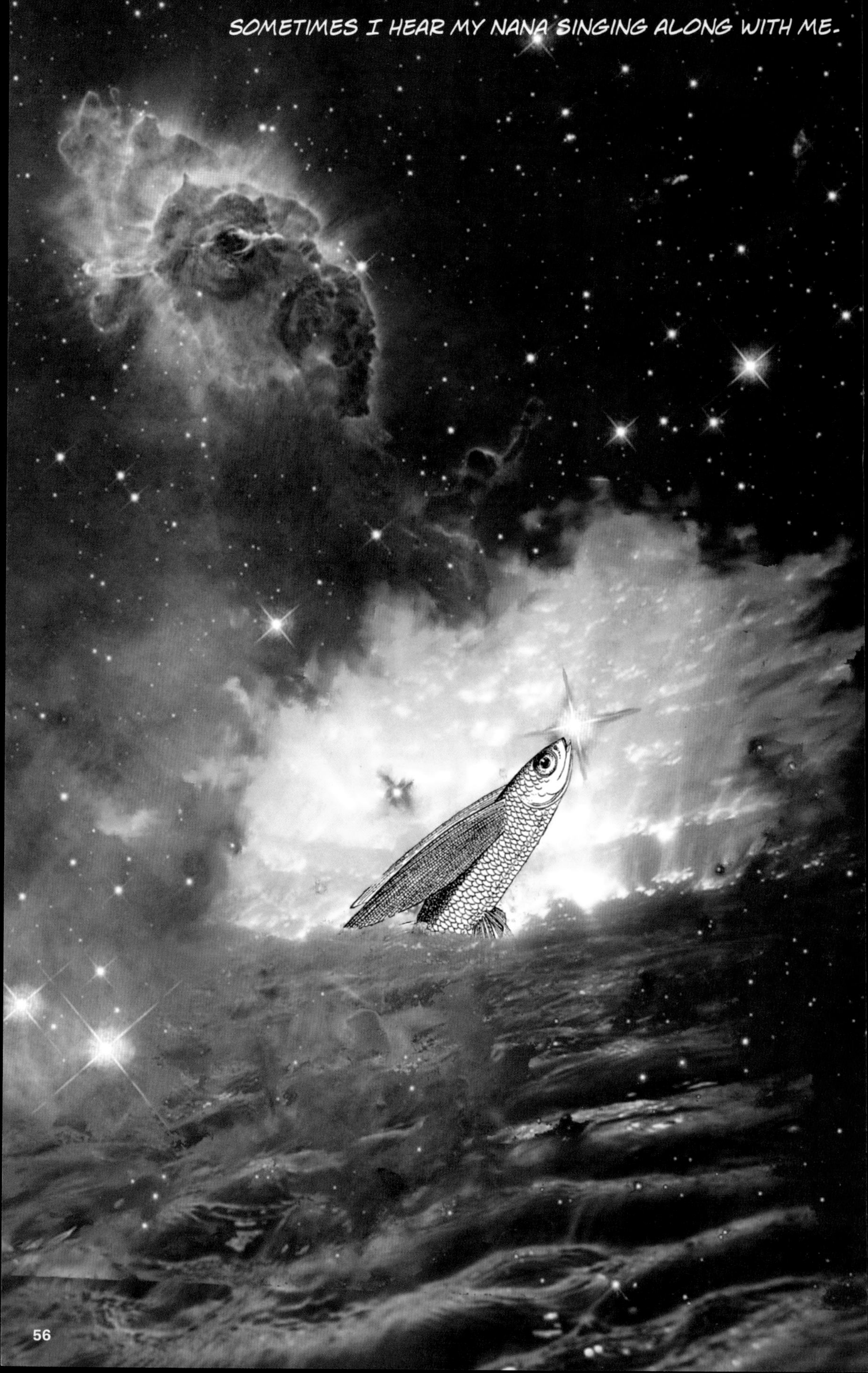
SOMETIMES I HEAR MY NANA SINGING ALONG WITH ME.

Unrequited

Written and Illustrated by Jason Sikoak

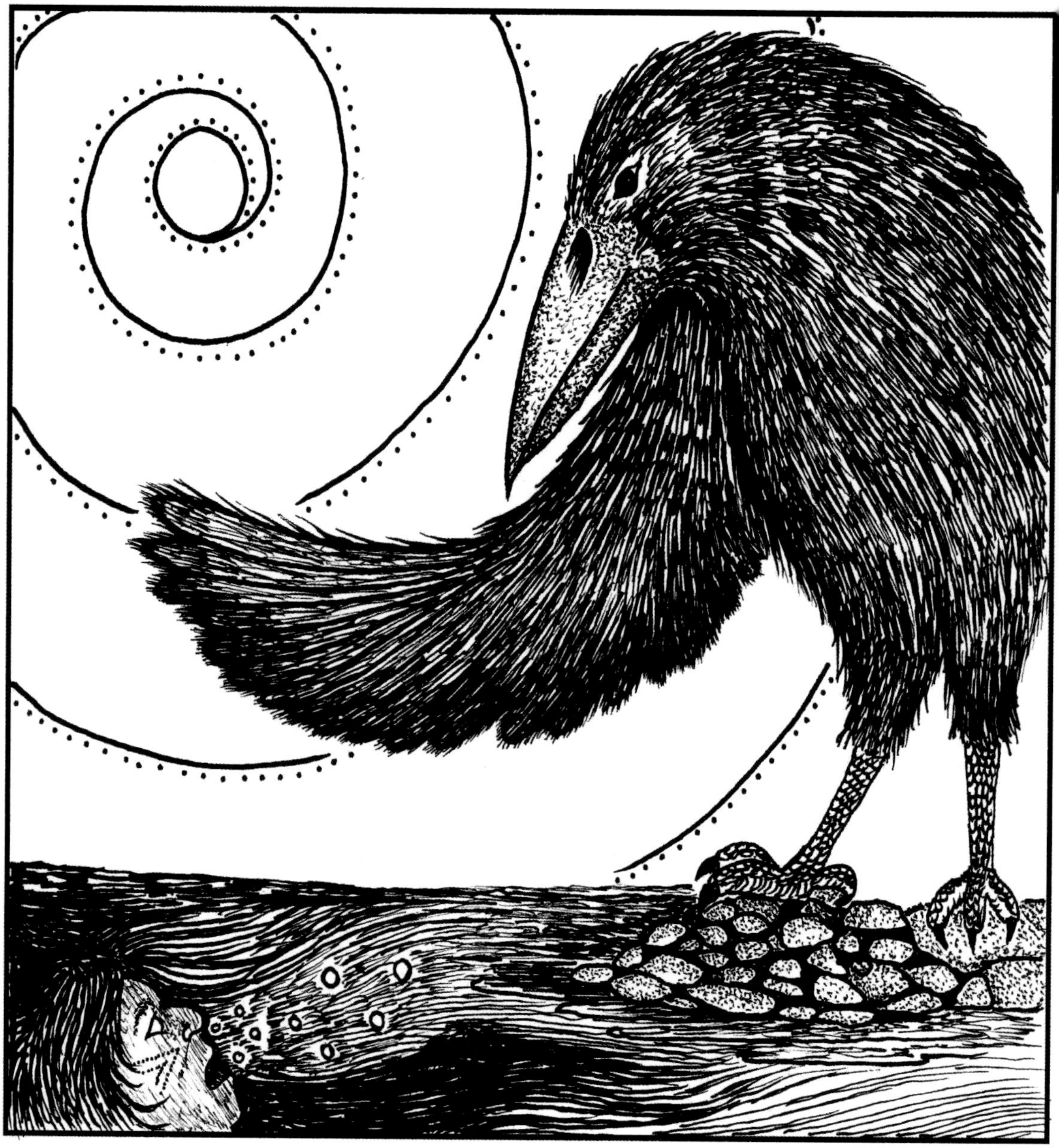

He loves her still...
Although she hated his true form, he loved her.
She was afraid!
She risked her family's lives to escape.
His rage caused her death,
But he loves her still.

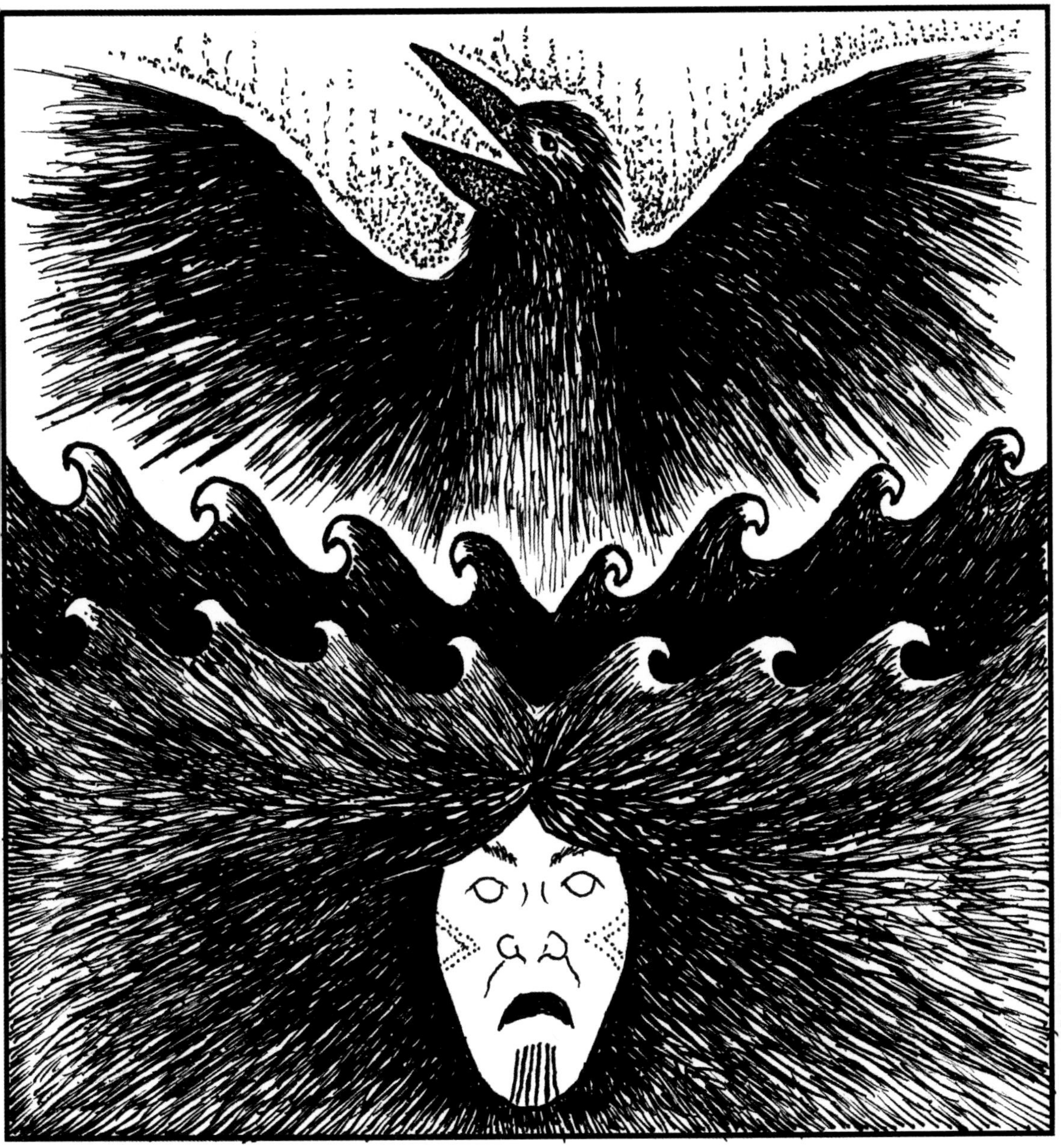

He rages now in mourning, causing the storms...
Causing her hair to become tangled and unkempt.
Trapping the food of her people,
They must sing the song, to comb and braid her hair, so they may eat of the sea again.

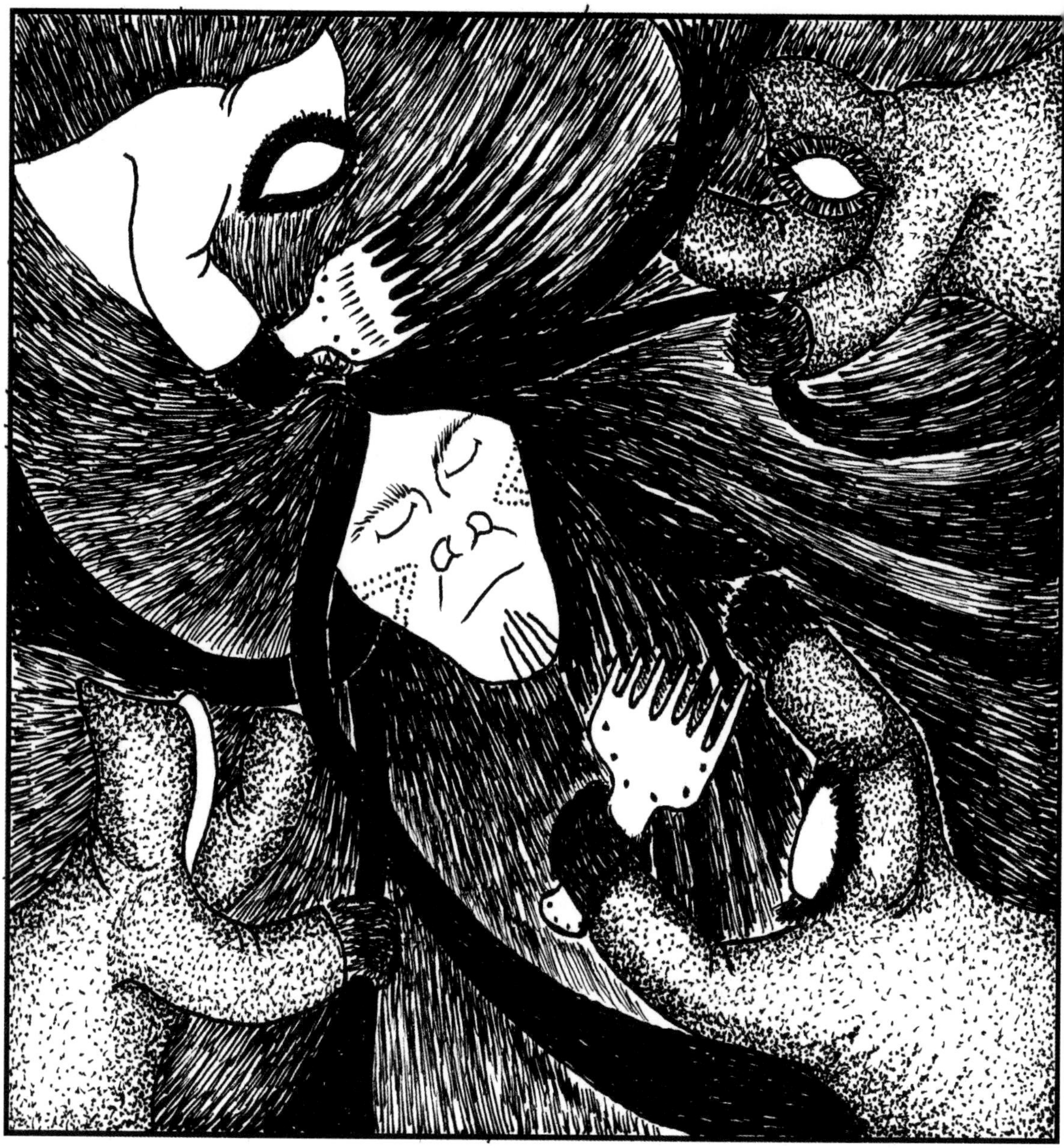

The children of her father, who cut off her fingers and hands
To save his own soul...
They reconcile with her, combing and braiding her hair, to free the mammals to feed them once again...

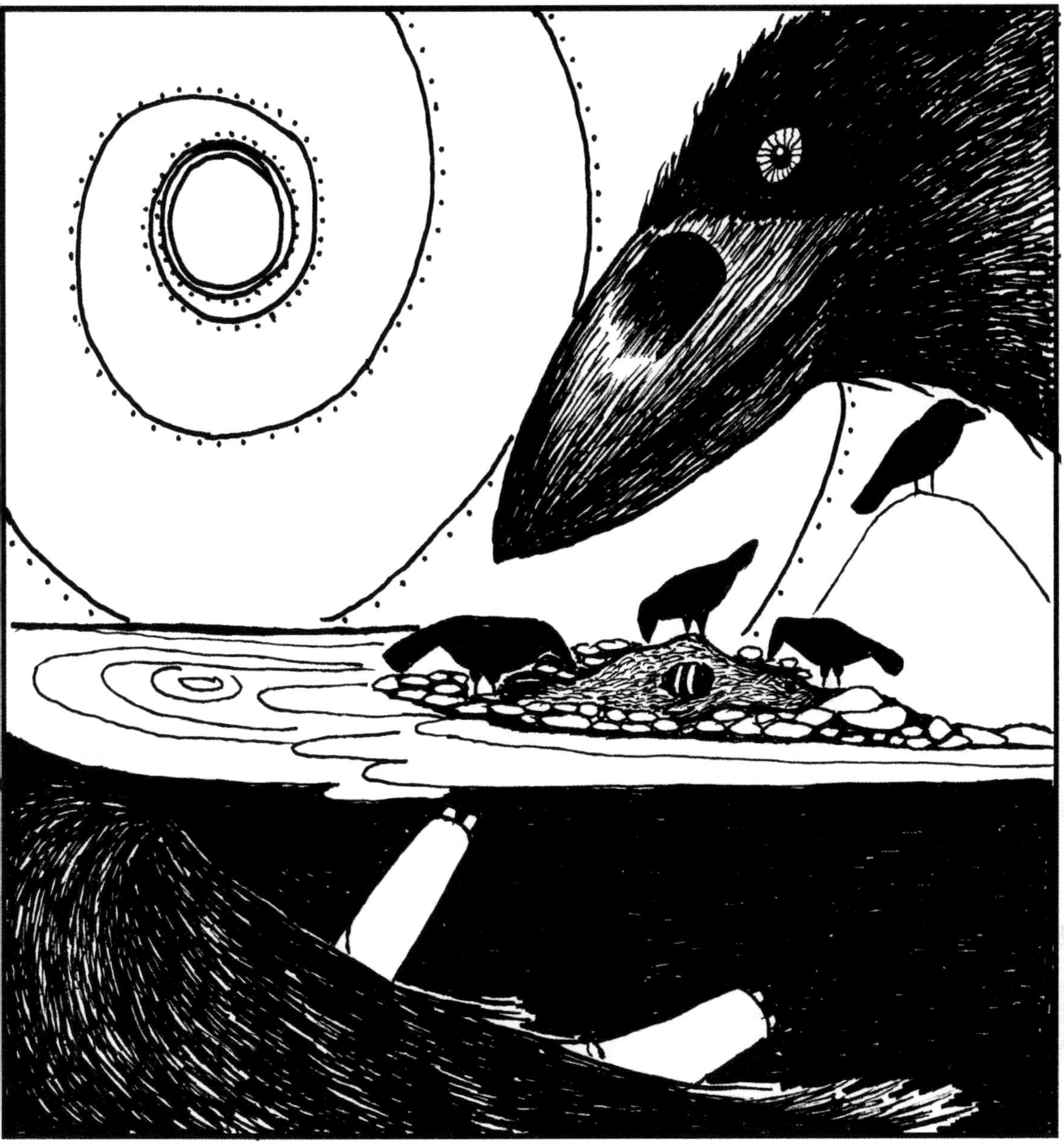

The sea is calm. The storm has passed. The song is sung.
Her hair is tidy and beautiful once more.
He wonders if she loves him still...
For sometimes she sends food to feed his children as well.

Moose Crossing

Written by Dawn Karima

Tracks lead straight to the heart of the matter,
Songs of the stars made flesh and bone.
Lamentation lost in the whirlwind,
An ache for wherever you are is home.
A lullaby spun from the Sun and Moon crying,
Sighing, scorching Earth as a soulful pyre,
Turning tides meant to inspire desire,
We make a map of the world in the flames of
Our fire.

All Things

Written by Dawn Karima

Sing medicine songs full of Southern low moaning,
Drum beats taut against the seams of our souls,
Trick Coyote with hand games and mirrors,
Bead broken hearts until they are whole.
The weight of the heart is a cruel transaction.
Trading in leather and feathers and glass,
Lasts beyond Earth and Wind and Water.
Passion peaks, surrenders to rag and bone,
As Eagle Whistles make our hearts our home.

Dandelion

Illustrated by beyon wren moor

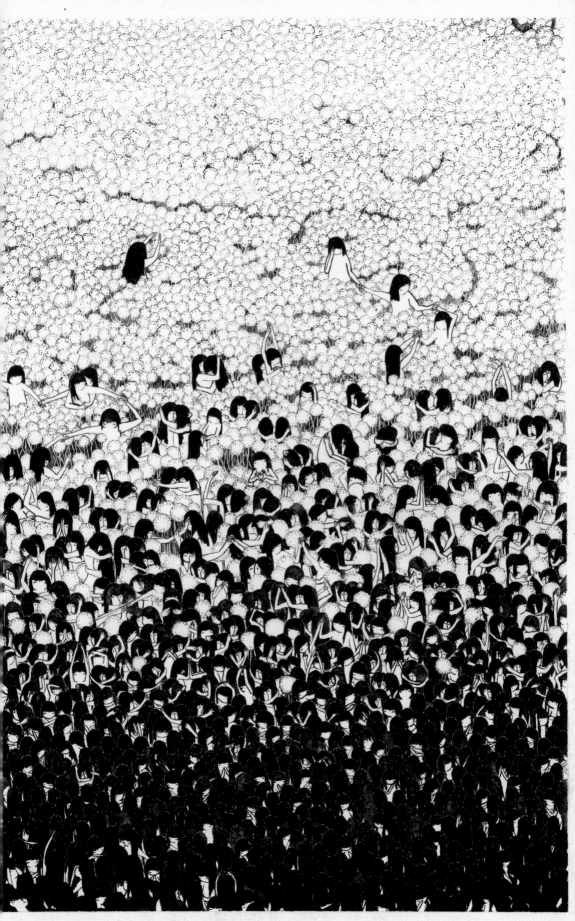

Two Spirit Step

Written and Illustrated by Dan Stinehart

Inspired by a story I've been working on for a while, I wanted to challenge myself on how a narrative would fare without any written dialogue or exposition. In my Ojibwe culture (among other Indigenous cultures), we pass on our stories and teachings orally, thus the interpretations and dialects come about as generations come and go. I wanted to give that same impression. The narrative can be interpreted, but the message remains the same. "Two Spirit Step" was my first attempt at a wordless comic.

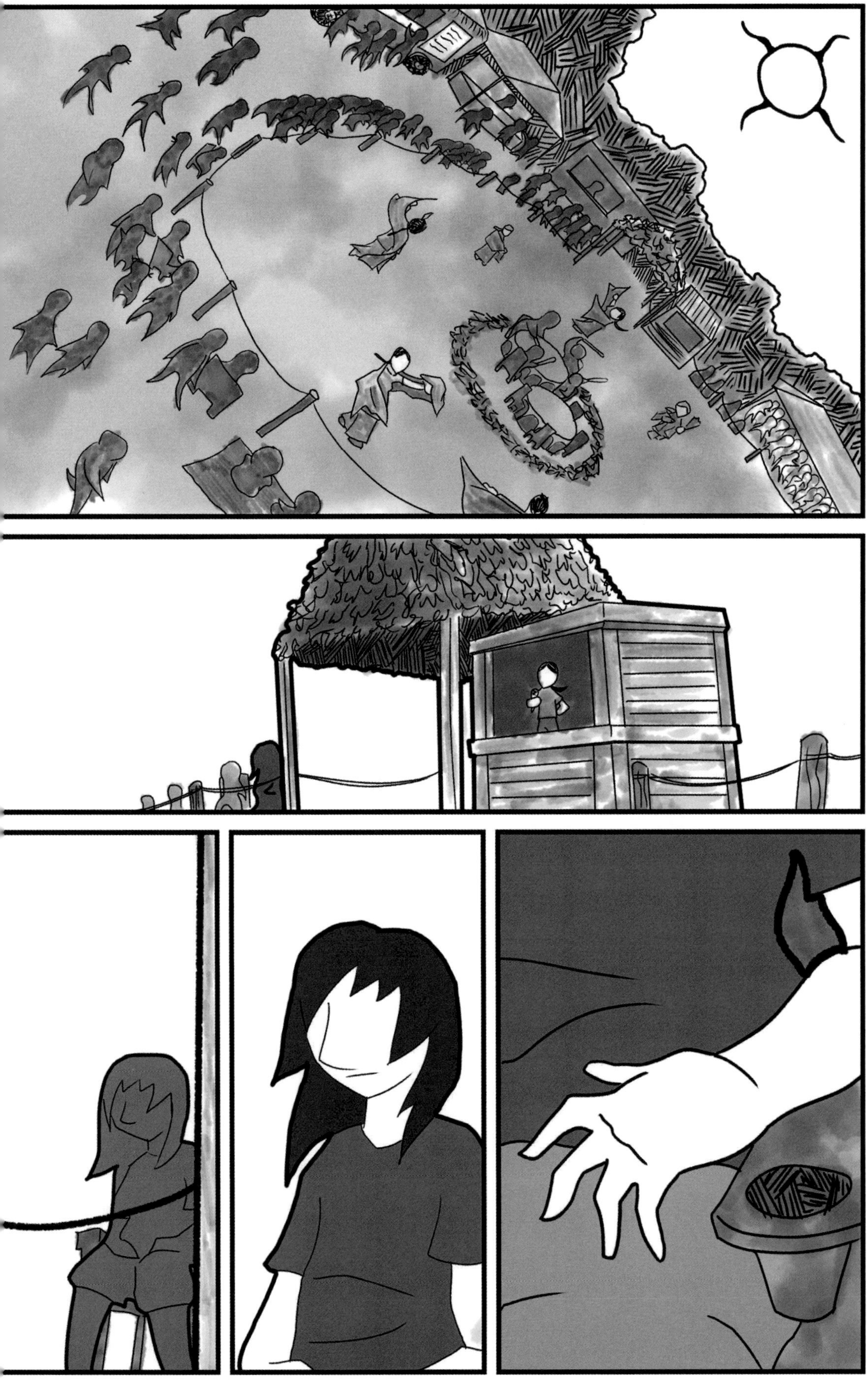

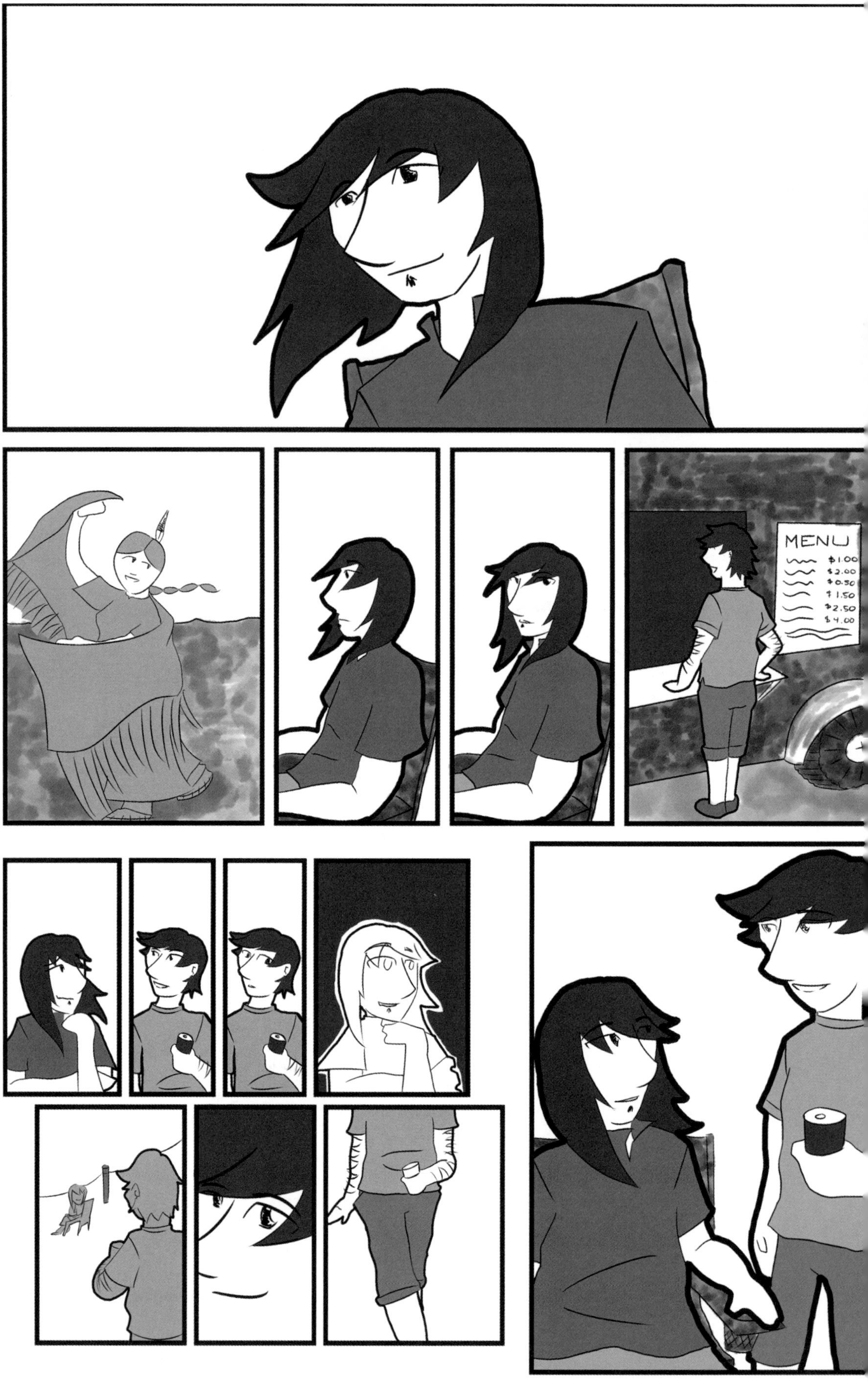
MENU
$1.00
$2.00
$0.50
$1.50
$2.50
$4.00

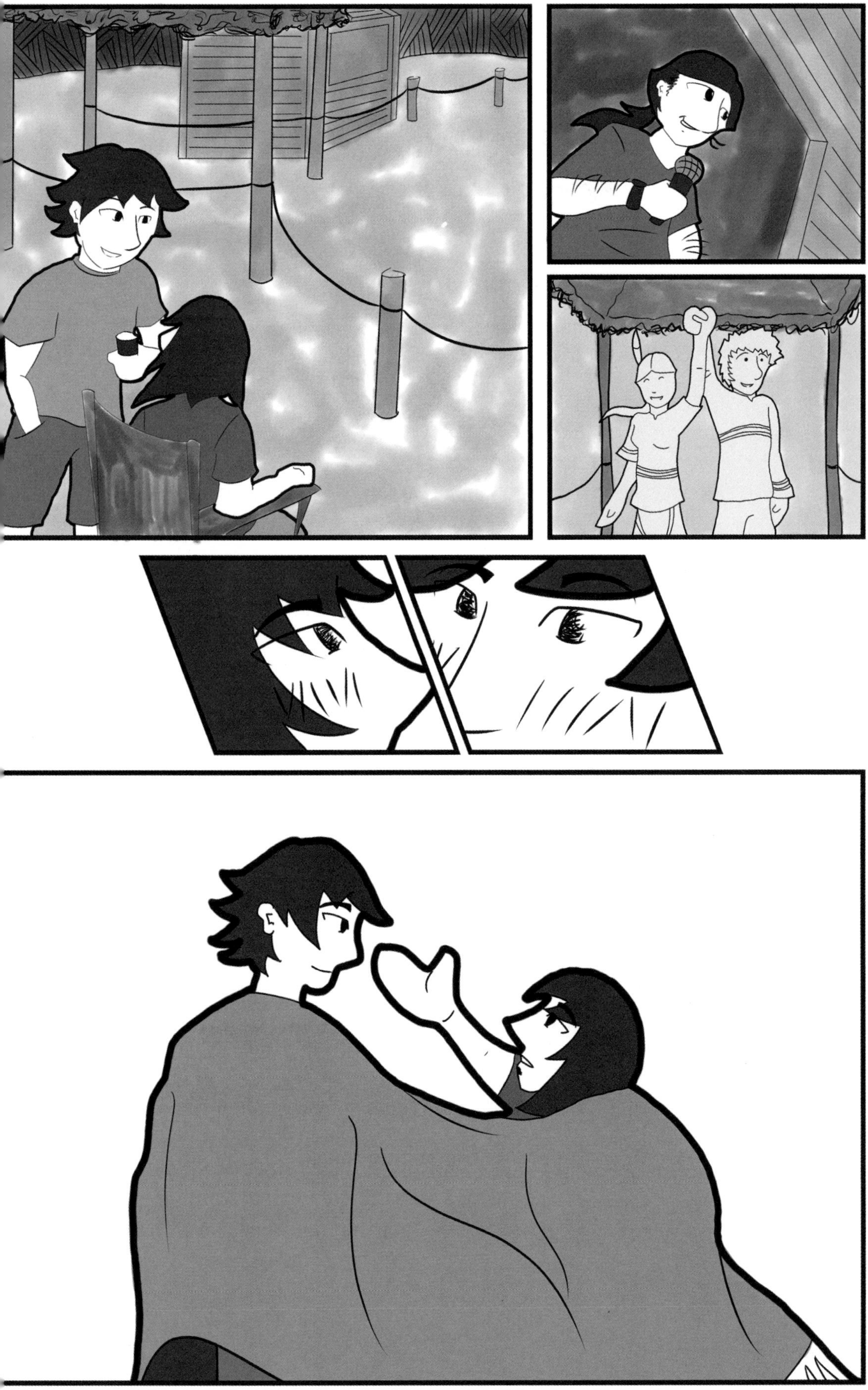

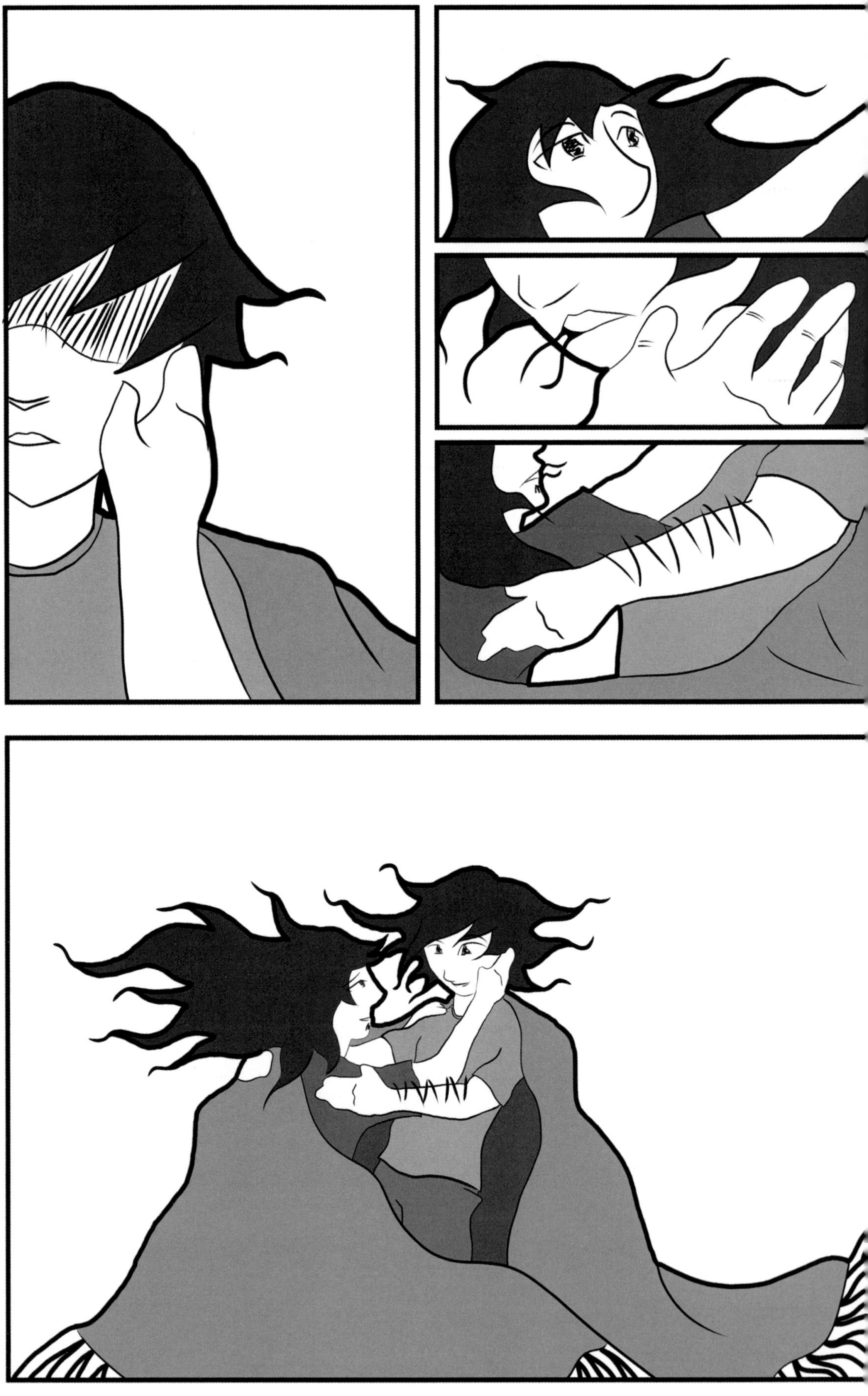

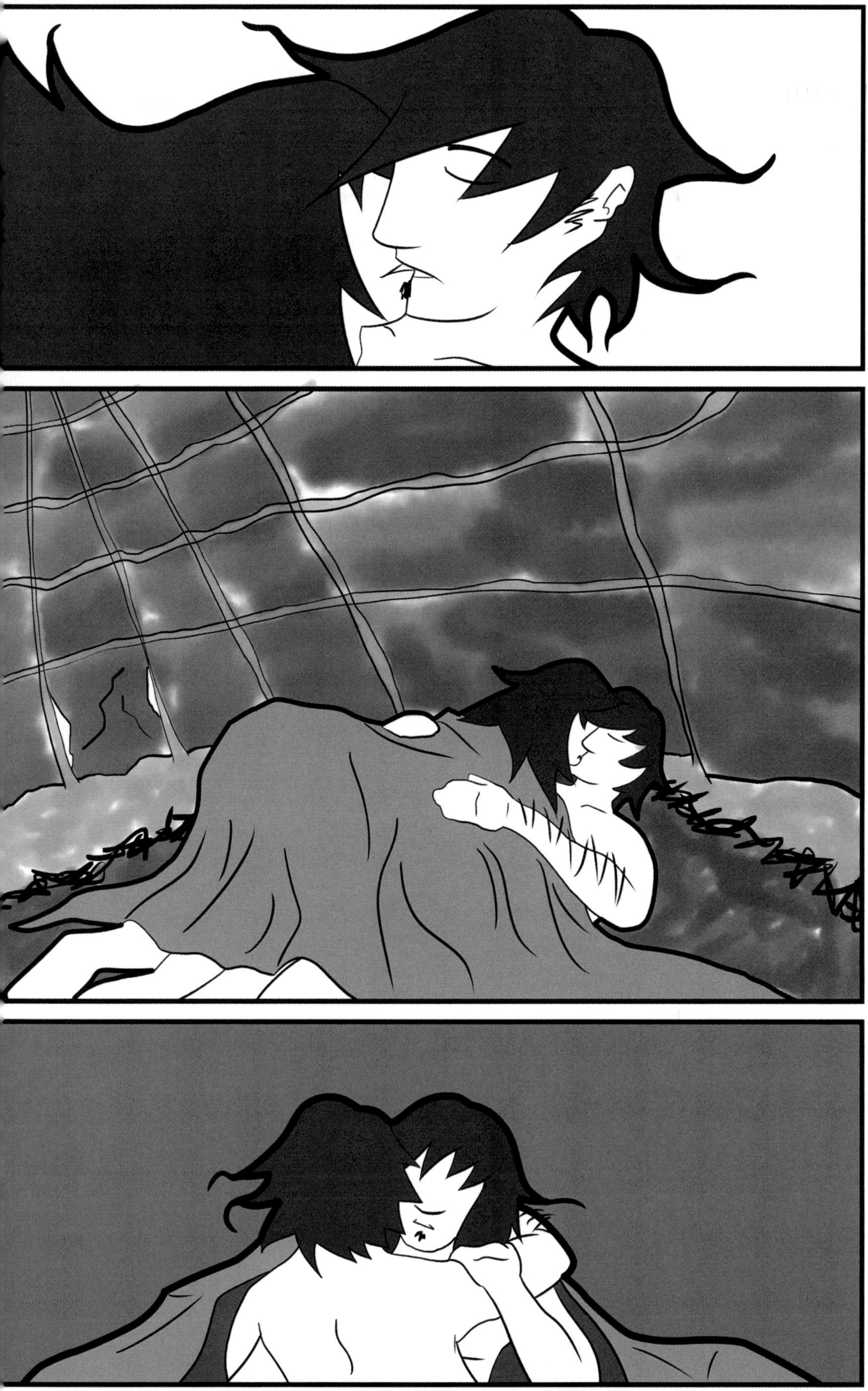

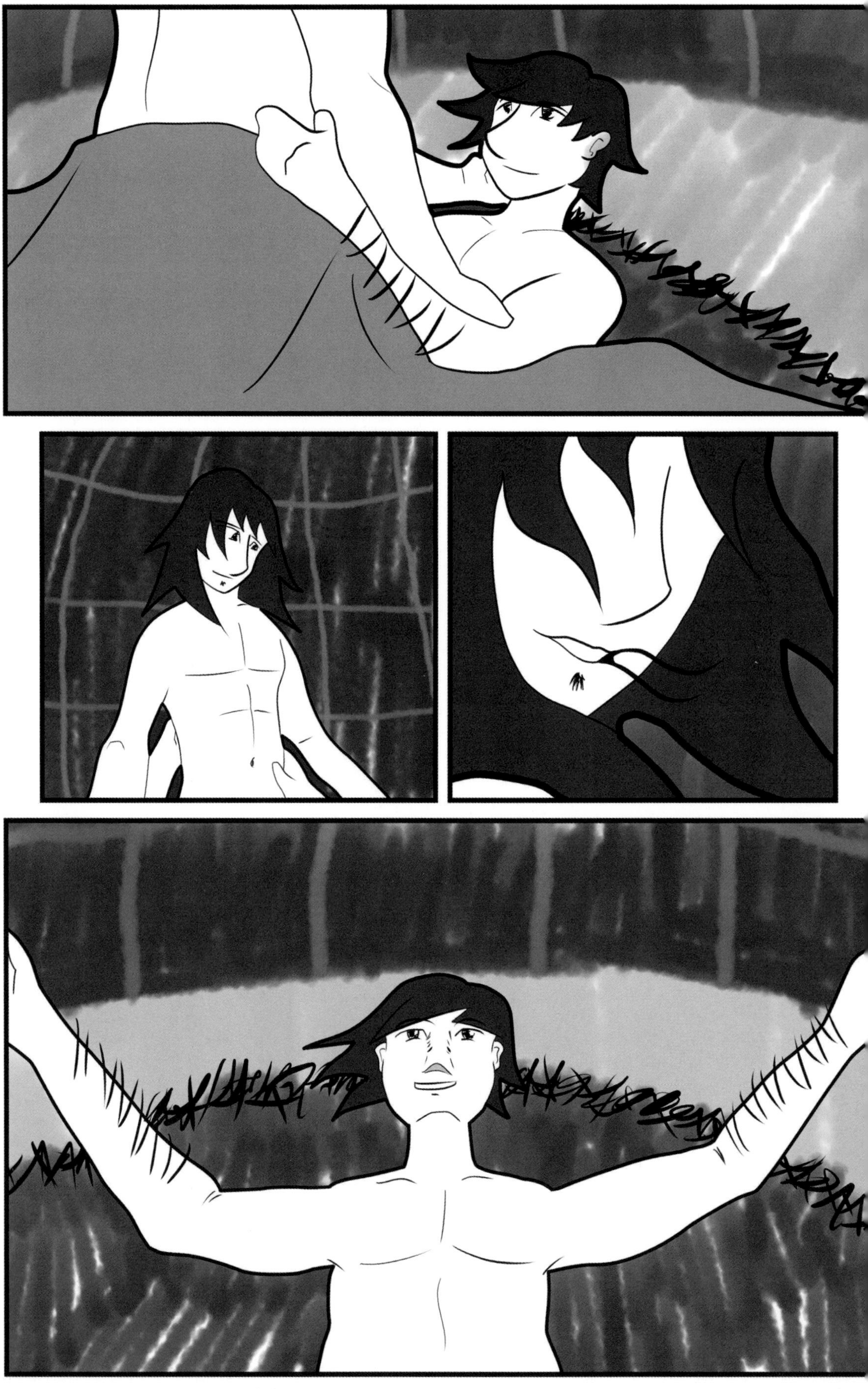

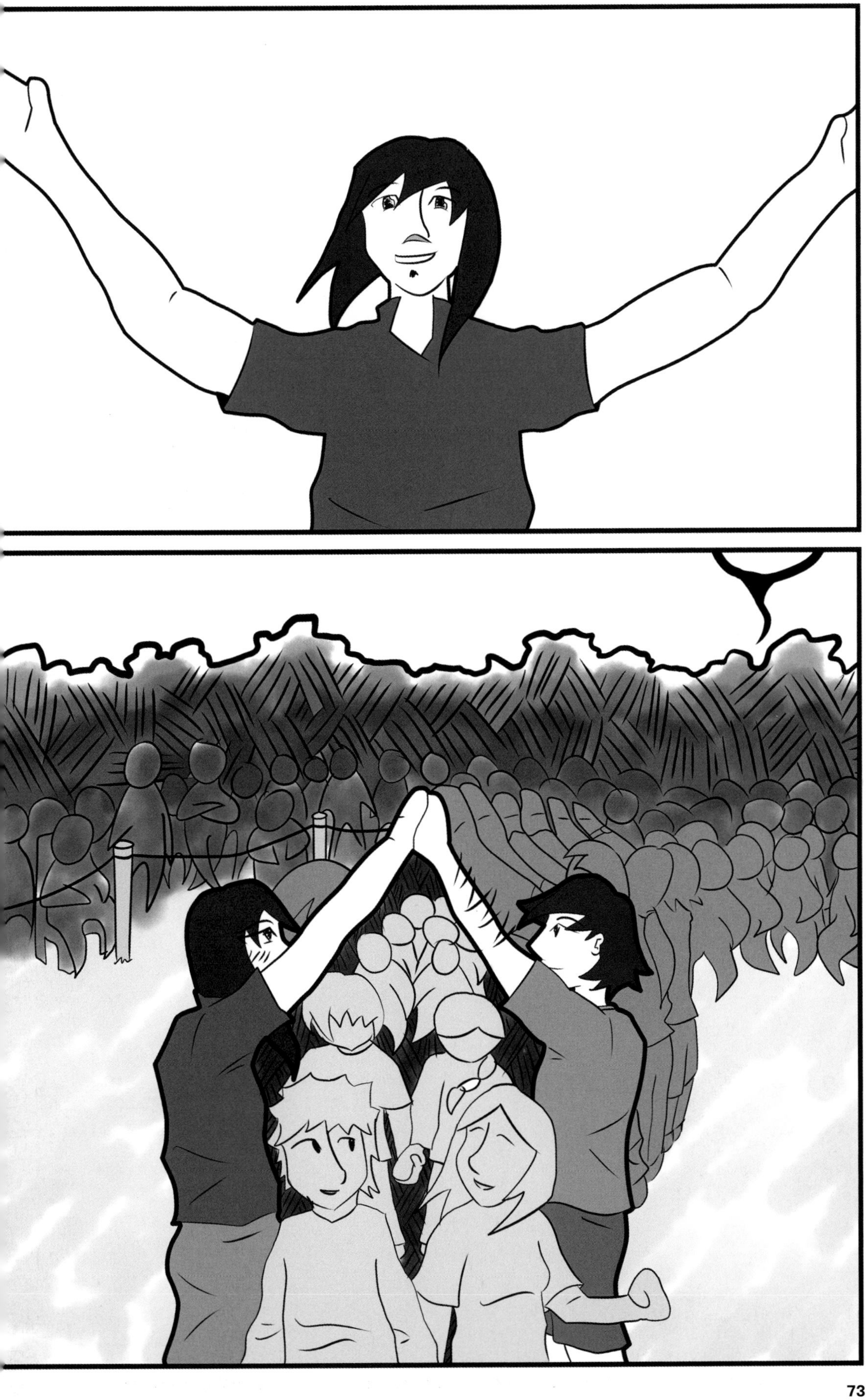

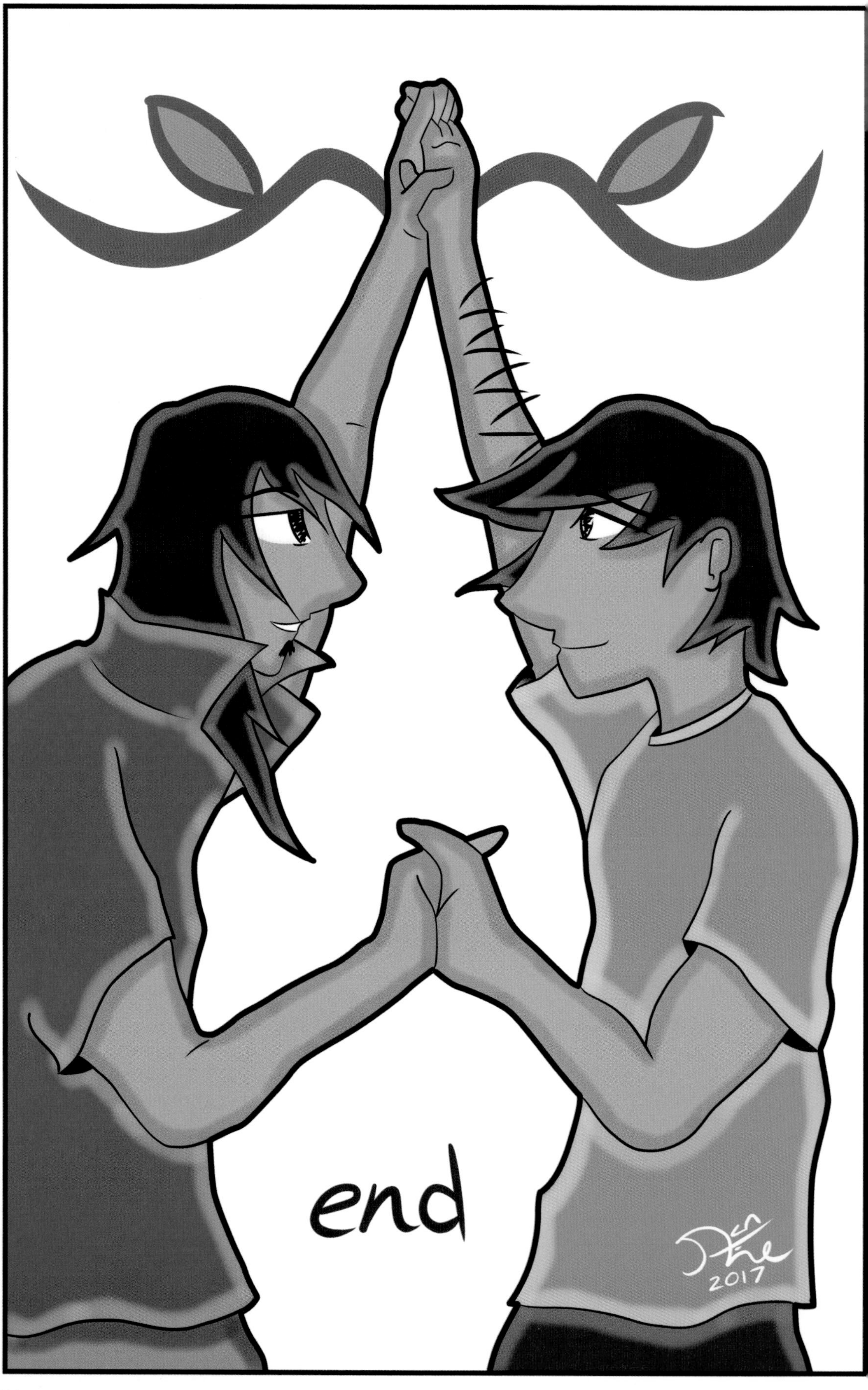
end
2017

Taste/Speak
Salt Lick
Electric Muscadine

Written by Rain Prud'homme-Cranford

These three poems are as much about the body of our homelands as the bodies of ourselves, our lovers, and Gulf South Indigenous/Post-Contact Indigenous Peoples. These lands are Atakapa-Ishak, Louisiana Creole, Choctaw, Tunica-Biloxi, Houma, Chitimacha, Creek, Latinidad Mestiz@s, and many other tribes and communities—folks whose culture and memory are intimately tied to the humid waters of our birth. Like the southern Gulf spaces we call home, from Florida to Louisiana and even Oklahoma, we know the power in the wind and water: from the fury of hurricanes, where the center of peace lurks in the eye of the storm, to the swirling winds of Thunder Beings as they twirl counterclockwise across the Red, Calcasieu, Canadian, and Oklahoma Rivers to the low plains. Love is sensual, empowering, devastating, graceful, and as resistant as the lands and ancestors we call home.

Taste/Speak

Rain Prud'homme-Cranford

Outside—
wraps warm
wet shawl
around shoulders.
Dampness beads
on forehead, upper lip,
dampens hair
at nape, and by ears.

Breathe deep air
tastes green,
and brown, wet.
Olfactory memory
rushes, time warp.

I am young again
taste of muscadines,
green onions, and clover
honey. My body fully
ripe as round plump
persimmons. Your hair
long waves and
dances water down
in rhythm to movement.

You are young and
taste of sugar skulls
barley hops, tobacco,
lemon, and sweat.

My roundness bleeds
into you, meshes in a
language of rock to water.

Now I move into outer
realm of age and distance
staving stale taste of
copper and moss.
My body beginning to
drip lazily in heat.
My curves speak a
weeping willow language.

Salt Lick

Rain Prud'homme-Cranford

They say some of our people fell from sky,
others crept from inside earth,
and still others came crawling up
from beneath the waves of the Gulf.
Into shores they rose like alligator people—
this was our emergence narrative.

How naturally you coax the waters from inside
    me.
Easy falling rain from ducts of my eyes,
slithering tongue proboscis spreading nectar on
    lips.
Fluids slipping greedily from the crease of my
    thighs.
In pleasure and pain you pull waters from me—
heavy and thick with salt, licked and dried.

I wonder if there was any pun intended
when you told me your people were fishermen,
oyster men, cuz you shuck me so very well,

with hard worn fingers practiced in the art.
Sucking briny fluids from mother–of–pearl
    shells—
locate my pearl every time.

You are the salt and bone of home.
Your touch, taste, a thrall, draws me into old wire
crab traps, locks me down to wait for you.
The knuckles of your hand scraping my flesh
creates a call and response leaping from your
blood into mine it shuffle steps a Gulf breeze
rhythm older than this myth called time.

This wind carries voices singing mimetic cries of
fishing streams and humid thick rains.
We move with the fury of a hurricane—
until limbs weep like Spanish moss, spent
fluttering ripples. Till again you coax the tides
in me to rise, as you swirl away—
leave me in the devastation.

Electric Muscadine

Rain Prud'homme-Cranford

Tips of fingers write electric language over
skin from peach powder soft to firm fine brown.
Tips whorls of memory imprint swirling like
dancers round fire. Fingers leave their
marks—like stomp dancers on grass.

Examining fingers, know they are sturdy like
vines of muscadine plants—persistent, growing
in ravines, up trees, over fences, and through
years of changing climate and the push of tar
pavement through southern sun, they return.

And so, in returning, these fingers on hands,
pick muscadines. Fill baskets, buckets, holding
up hem of skirt to catch falling fruit. In these
plucking hands, memory of cotton, river cane,
sugarcane, tobacco, and peanuts.

When the skin is peeled away from the meat
of the grape I slip it into your mouth—
Tingle of electric story slithers from fingertip
across your tongue mingling with eruption
of musk grape nectar . . .

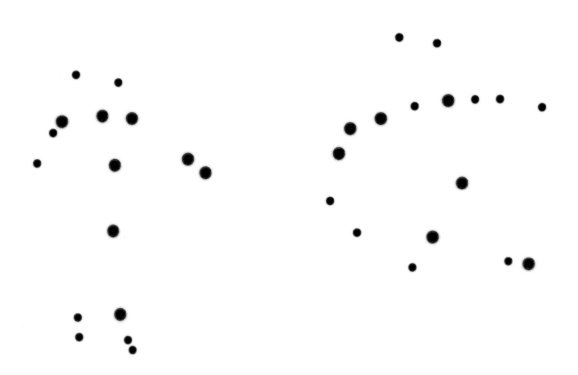

Arasy

**Written and Illustrated
by Gabriela Aveiro-Ojeda**

EVER SINCE I LAY EYES ON

ARASY

TIME HAS NEVER FELT THE SAME

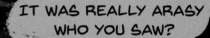

IT WAS RIGHT AROUND HERE THAT I SAW HER!

IT WAS REALLY ARASY WHO YOU SAW?

YES, IT REALLY WAS THE GODDESS ARASY! SHE STOOD RIGHT HERE AND LOOKED AT ME.

AND I AM CERTAIN SHE'LL APPEAR AGAIN IF I KEEP COMING BACK!

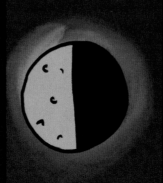

IT'S BEEN A YEAR... BUT I STILL CAN'T SHAKE OFF THAT FEELING.
I HAVEN'T BEEN ABLE TO DREAM SINCE THAT DAY.
ALL I THINK OF NOW IS GODDESS ARASY STANDING IN THE FOREST.
I KNOW SHE'LL COME HERE AGAIN. MAYBE IF MY SPIRIT IS STRONG ENOUGH...SHE WILL APPEAR ONCE MORE.

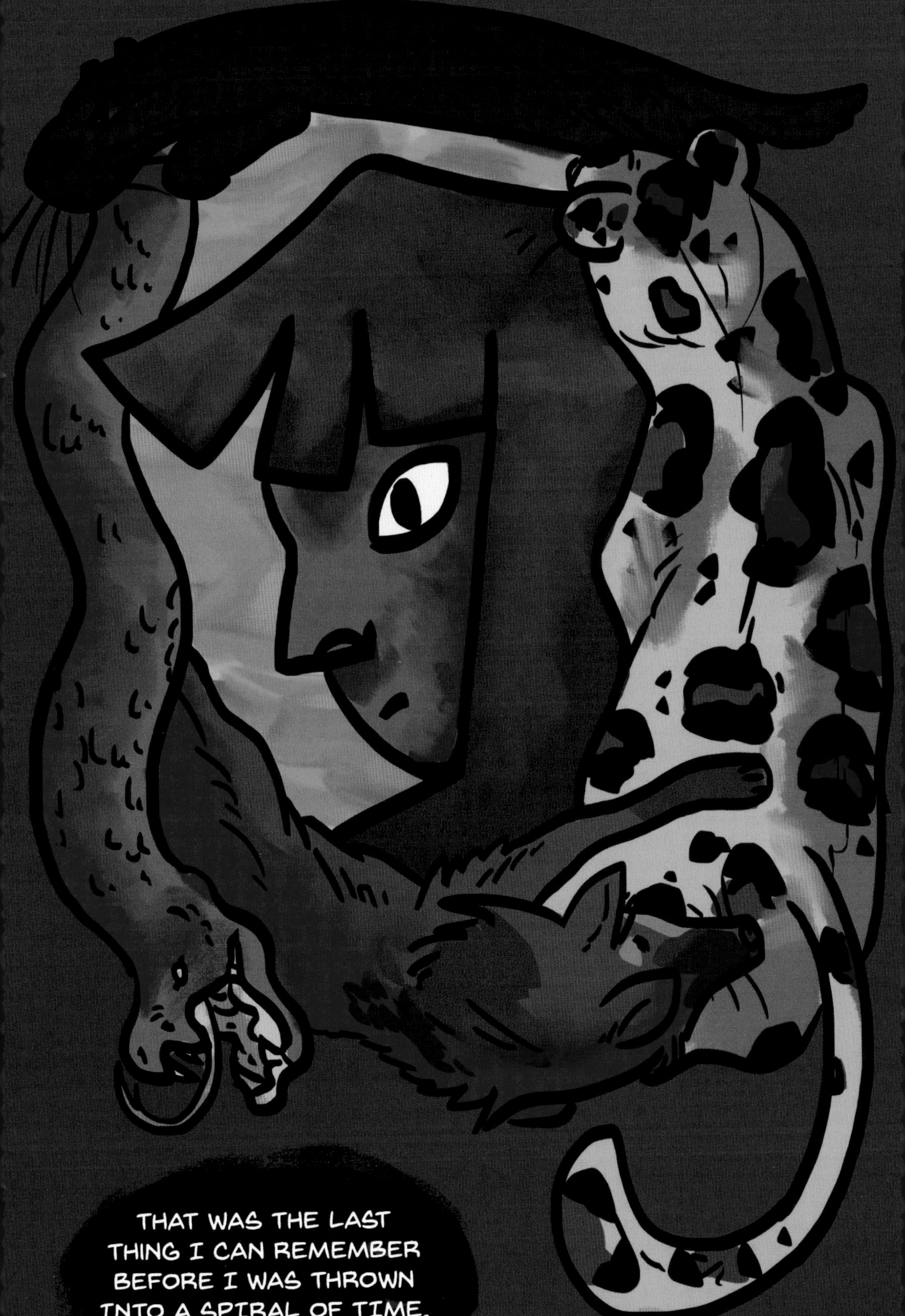
THAT WAS THE LAST THING I CAN REMEMBER BEFORE I WAS THROWN INTO A SPIRAL OF TIME.

I WAS A PARROT, AN OTTER, A YAGUARETE, AN AGUARA GUASU, AND MANY OTHER ANIMALS...
...BEFORE I REALIZED I WAS TRAVELING FORWARD IN TIME.
WHAT WAS I DOING BEFORE THIS HAPPENED?
OH...WAITING FOR ARASY TO SHOW UP.
THAT'S NOT ME.
I JUST FEEL...LIKE I MISS ARASY SO MUC
HEY!
ARE YOU GONNA PASS ME THAT PITCHER OR NOT?
UH...RIGHT.

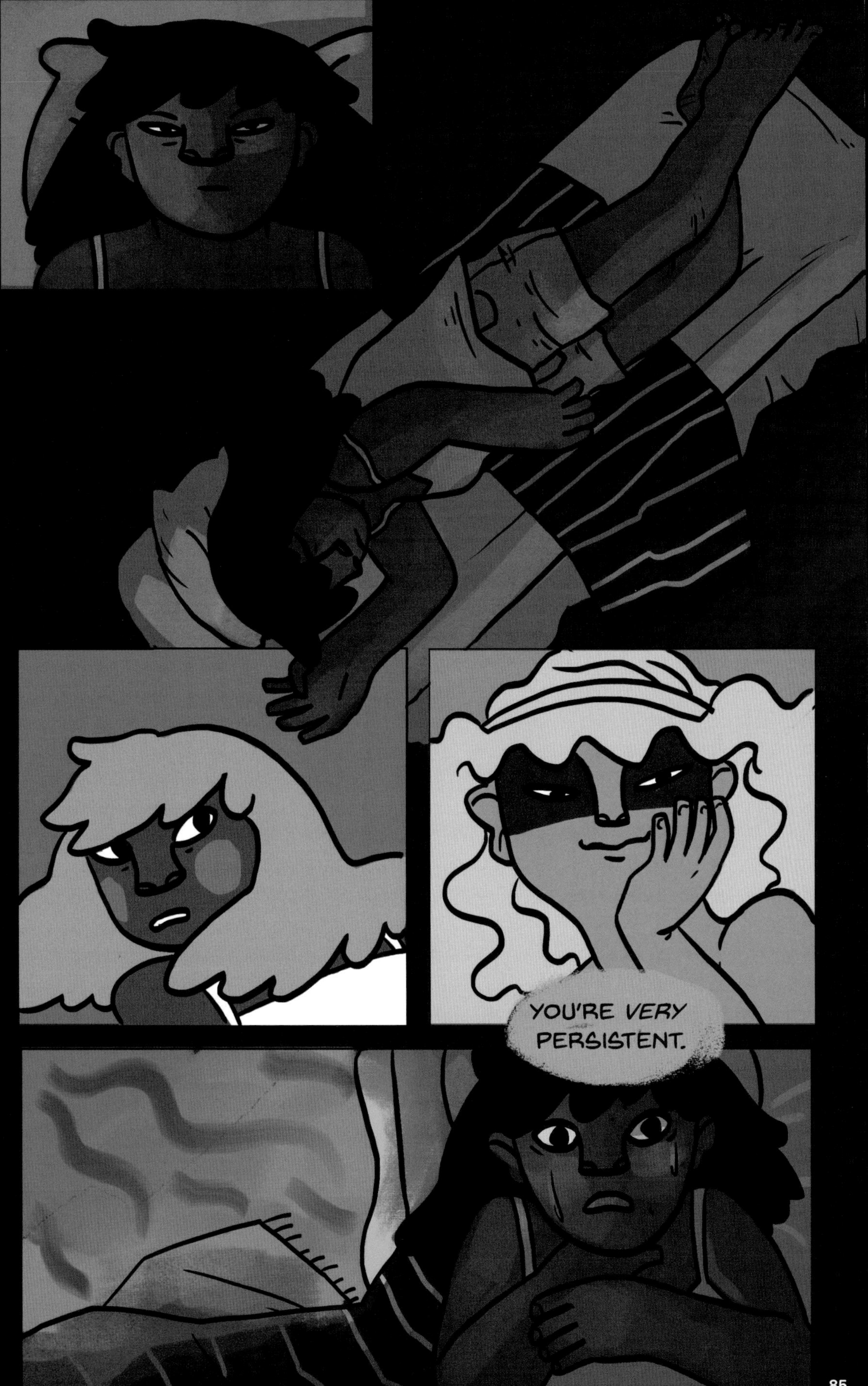
YOU'RE VERY PERSISTENT.

HUH?
WHO'S DOING THIS TO ME?
THERE YOU ARE, MARCELA.
I'VE BEEN TRYING TO SHAKE YOU OFF MY PATH, BUT YOU KEEP FOLLOWING ME AROUND.
YOU KNOW MY NAME!
AH, UM, I...I JUST REALLY WANTED TO SEE YOU AGAIN... JUST...
YES...I'M SORRY YOU GOT CAUGHT IN MY STREAM OF TIME. I CAN SEND YOU BACK.

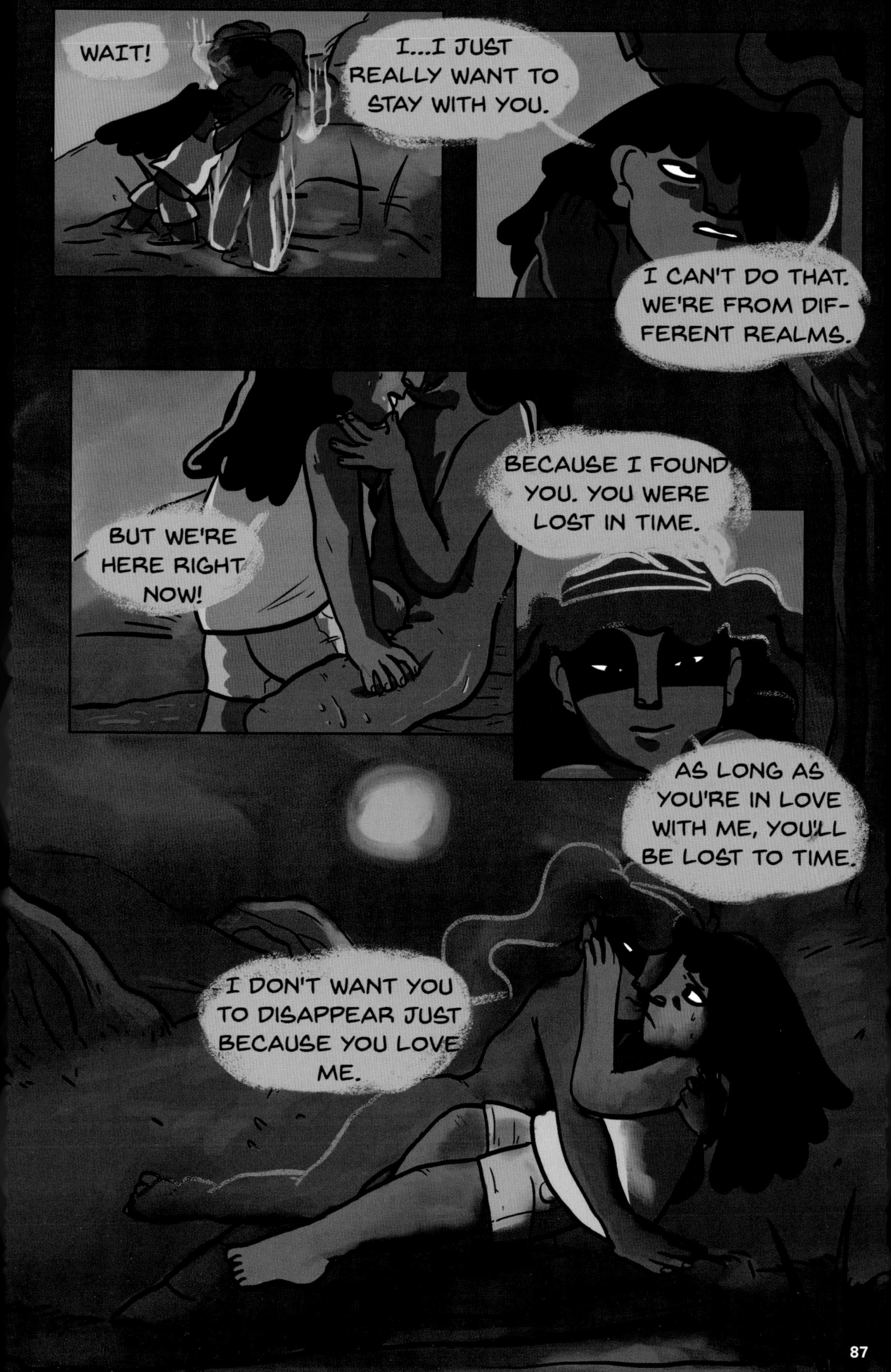
WAIT!
I...I JUST REALLY WANT TO STAY WITH YOU.
I CAN'T DO THAT. WE'RE FROM DIF-FERENT REALMS.
BUT WE'RE HERE RIGHT NOW!
BECAUSE I FOUND YOU. YOU WERE LOST IN TIME.
AS LONG AS YOU'RE IN LOVE WITH ME, YOU'LL BE LOST TO TIME.
I DON'T WANT YOU TO DISAPPEAR JUST BECAUSE YOU LOVE ME.

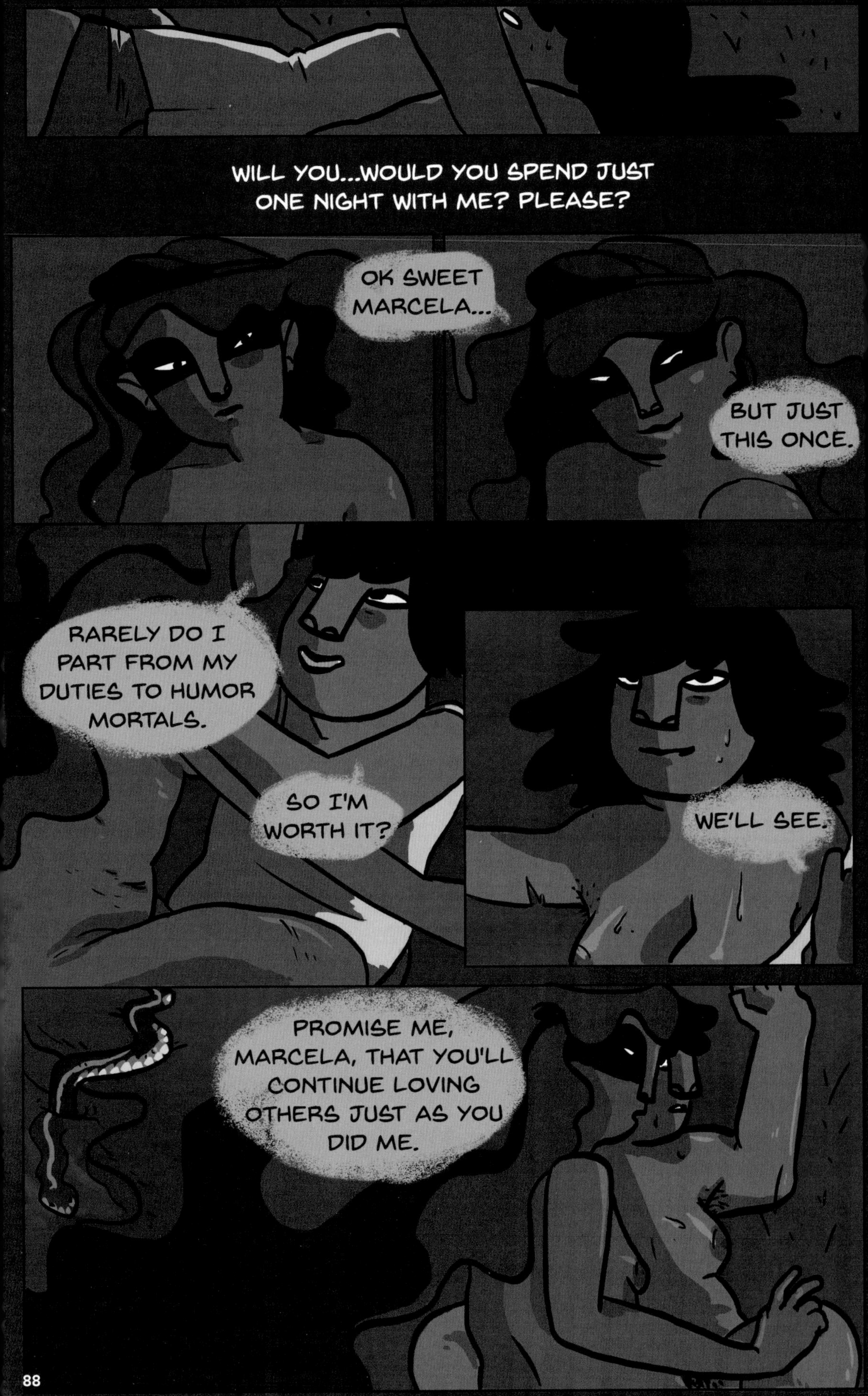
WILL YOU...WOULD YOU SPEND JUST ONE NIGHT WITH ME? PLEASE?
OK SWEET MARCELA...
BUT JUST THIS ONCE.
RARELY DO I PART FROM MY DUTIES TO HUMOR MORTALS.
SO I'M WORTH IT?
WE'LL SEE.
PROMISE ME, MARCELA, THAT YOU'LL CONTINUE LOVING OTHERS JUST AS YOU DID ME.

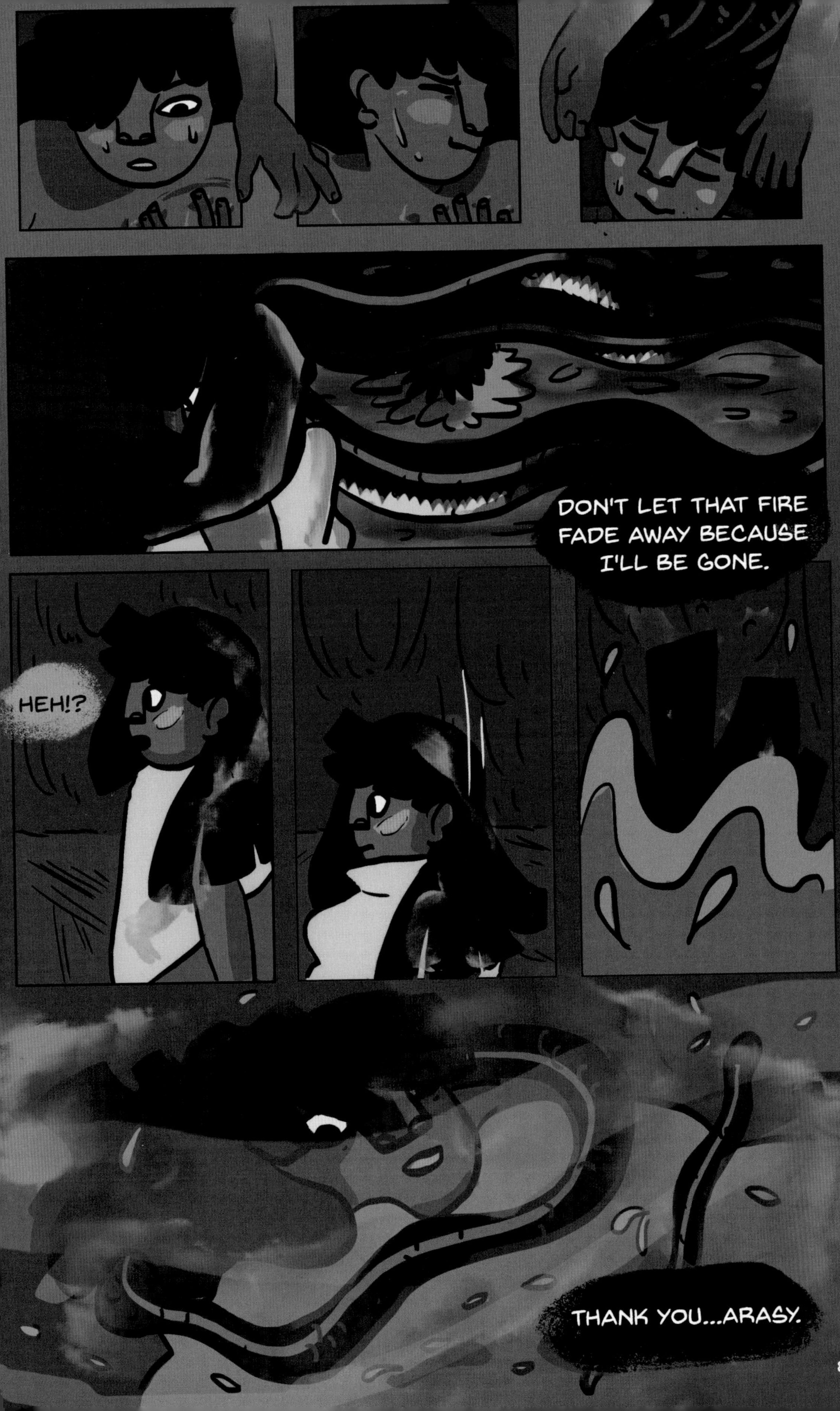
DON'T LET THAT FIRE FADE AWAY BECAUSE I'LL BE GONE.
HEH!?
THANK YOU...ARASY.

Kwe Loves Herself Despite All Odds

Illustrated by Quill Violet Christie-Peters

My work centers on an Anishinaabekwe conception of art-making that focuses on the processual building, strengthening, and reclamation of all my relations through artistic practice. When I paint, I enter into a conversation with my ancestors and those relations that exist beyond the material plane, making my practice an explicitly spiritual one that allows me to communicate knowledge I cannot otherwise express. Inherently, my work is about Anishinaabe futurisms and how our relationships to our ancestors must inform and shape our trajectories to the decolonial future, particularly in the context of displacement and urban Indigenous realities. As well as exploring my own spiritual landscape, my practice involves curating and facilitating collaborative Indigenous youth-based projects embodied through radical relationality. In this work we enact accountability to one another through our collective artistic practice while also exploring and strengthening the relationships settler colonialism seeks to destroy. Although I have explored various media and materials, I am by and large an acrylic painter. I stand on the shoulders of Anishinaabe artists who have always practiced art-making as an enactment of governance both over the self and extending outward to the nation. I stand lovingly on the shoulders of my own family of Anishinaabe artists who, within the violence of colonialism, have always used art as a tool for storytelling, resistance, survival, and, most importantly, creatively envisioning Anishinaabe futurities.

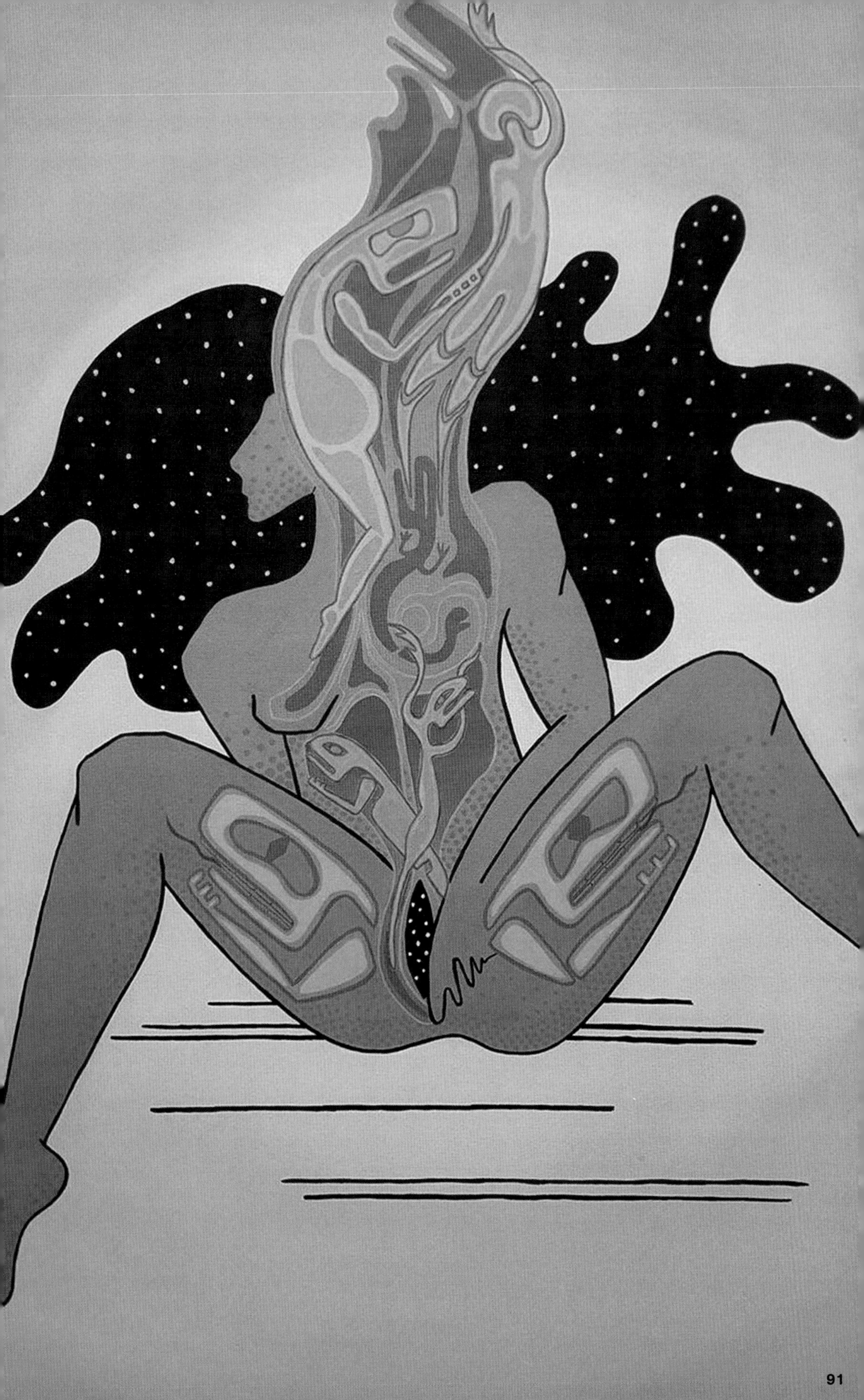

to love your name

**Written and Illustrated
by Weshoyot Alvitre**

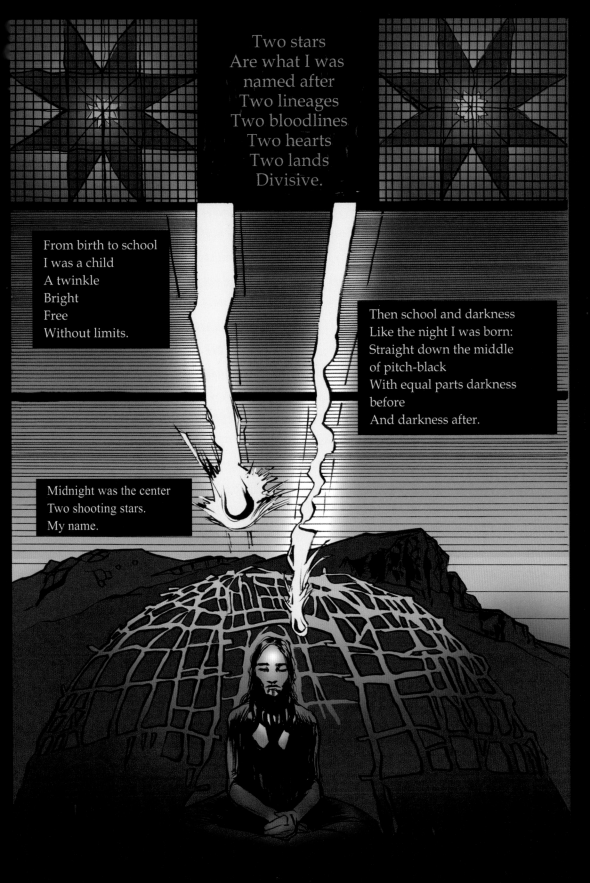

Two stars
Are what I was
named after
Two lineages
Two bloodlines
Two hearts
Two lands
Divisive.

From birth to school
I was a child
A twinkle
Bright
Free
Without limits.

Then school and darkness
Like the night I was born:
Straight down the middle
of pitch-black
With equal parts darkness
before
And darkness after.

Midnight was the center
Two shooting stars.
My name.

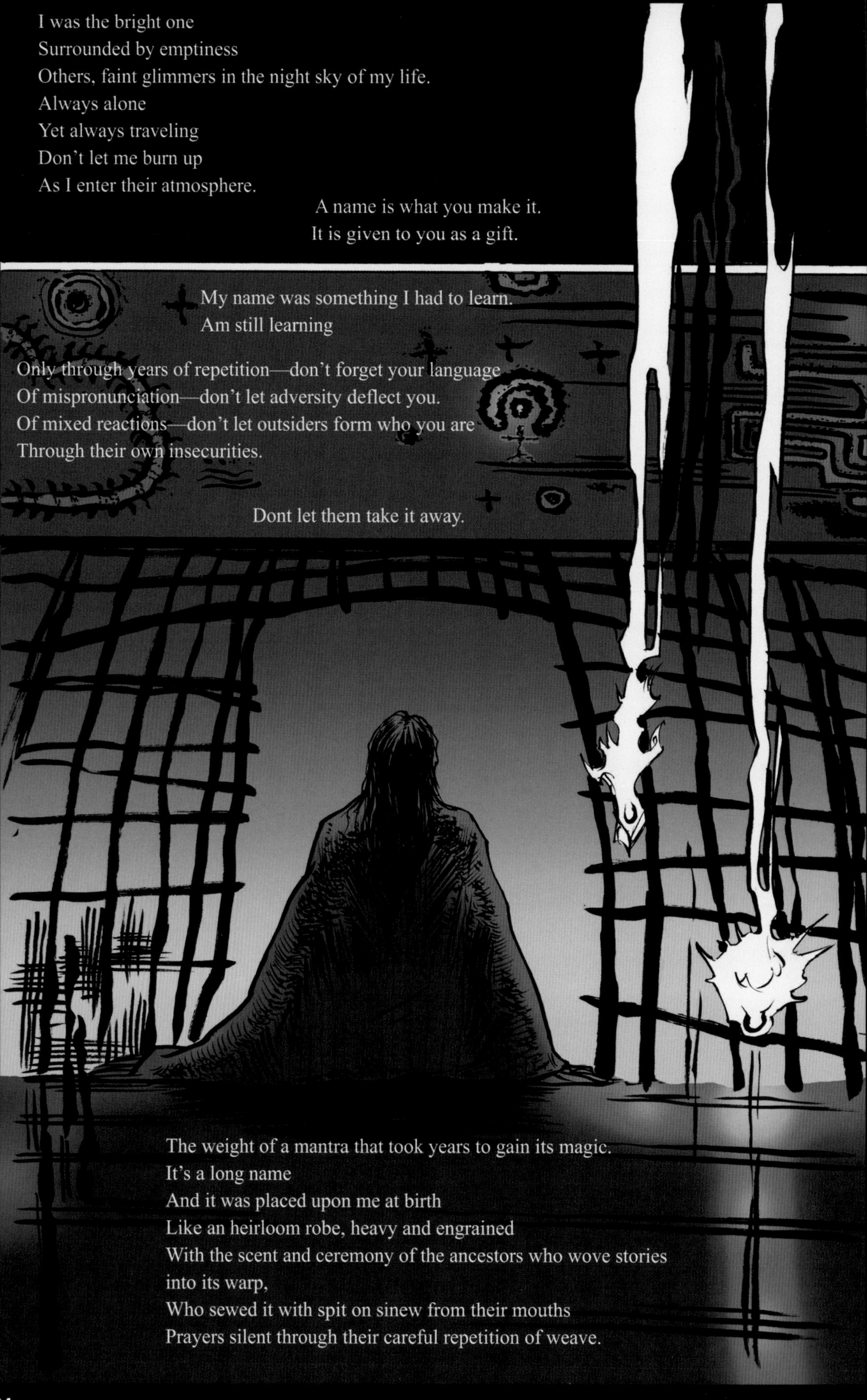
I was the bright one
Surrounded by emptiness
Others, faint glimmers in the night sky of my life.
Always alone
Yet always traveling
Don't let me burn up
As I enter their atmosphere.
A name is what you make it.
It is given to you as a gift.
My name was something I had to learn.
Am still learning
Only through years of repetition—don't forget your language
Of mispronunciation—don't let adversity deflect you.
Of mixed reactions—don't let outsiders form who you are
Through their own insecurities.
Dont let them take it away.
The weight of a mantra that took years to gain its magic.
It's a long name
And it was placed upon me at birth
Like an heirloom robe, heavy and engrained
With the scent and ceremony of the ancestors who wove stories
into its warp,
Who sewed it with spit on sinew from their mouths
Prayers silent through their careful repetition of weave.

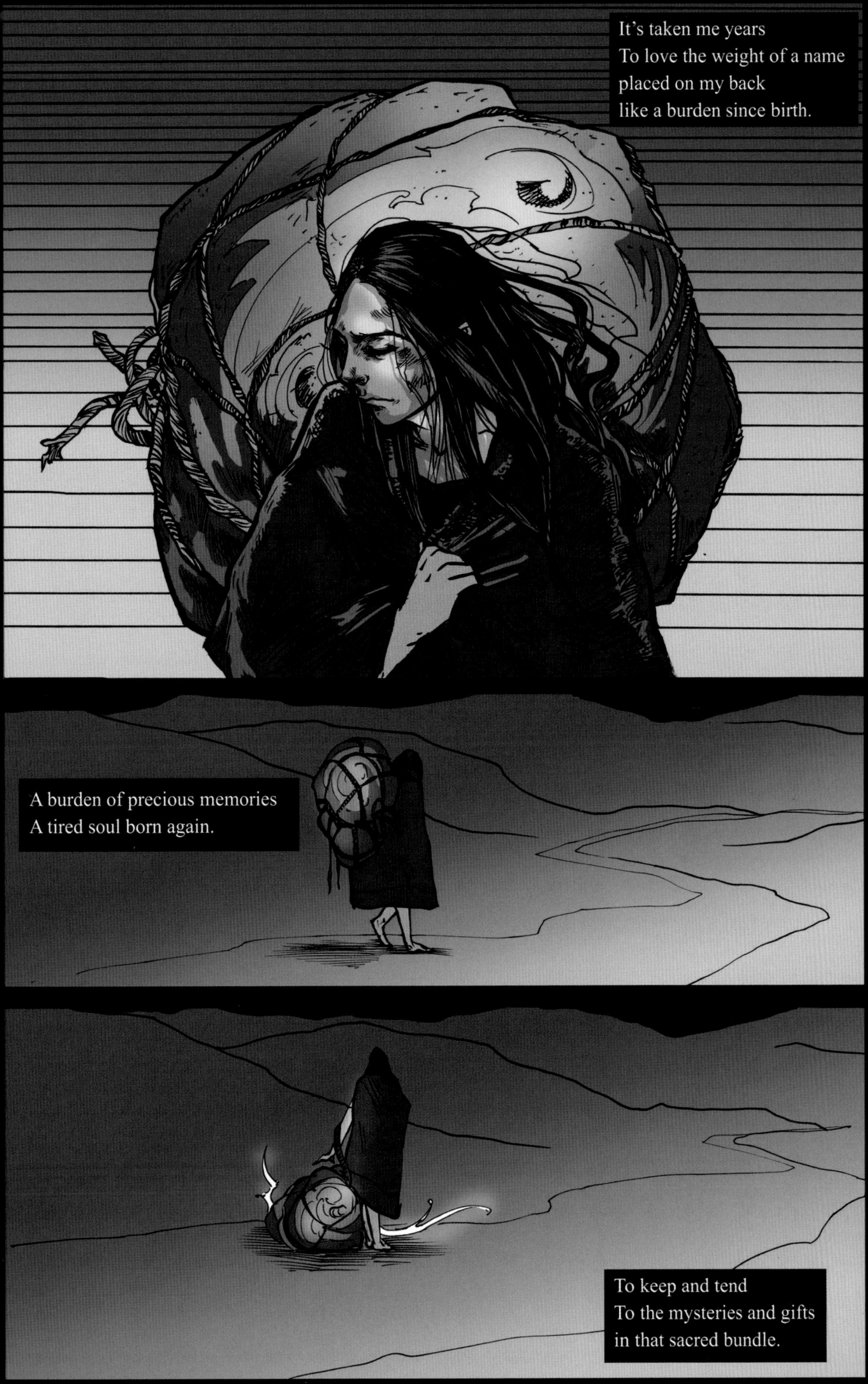
It's taken me years
To love the weight of a name
placed on my back
like a burden since birth.
A burden of precious memories
A tired soul born again.
To keep and tend
To the mysteries and gifts
in that sacred bundle.

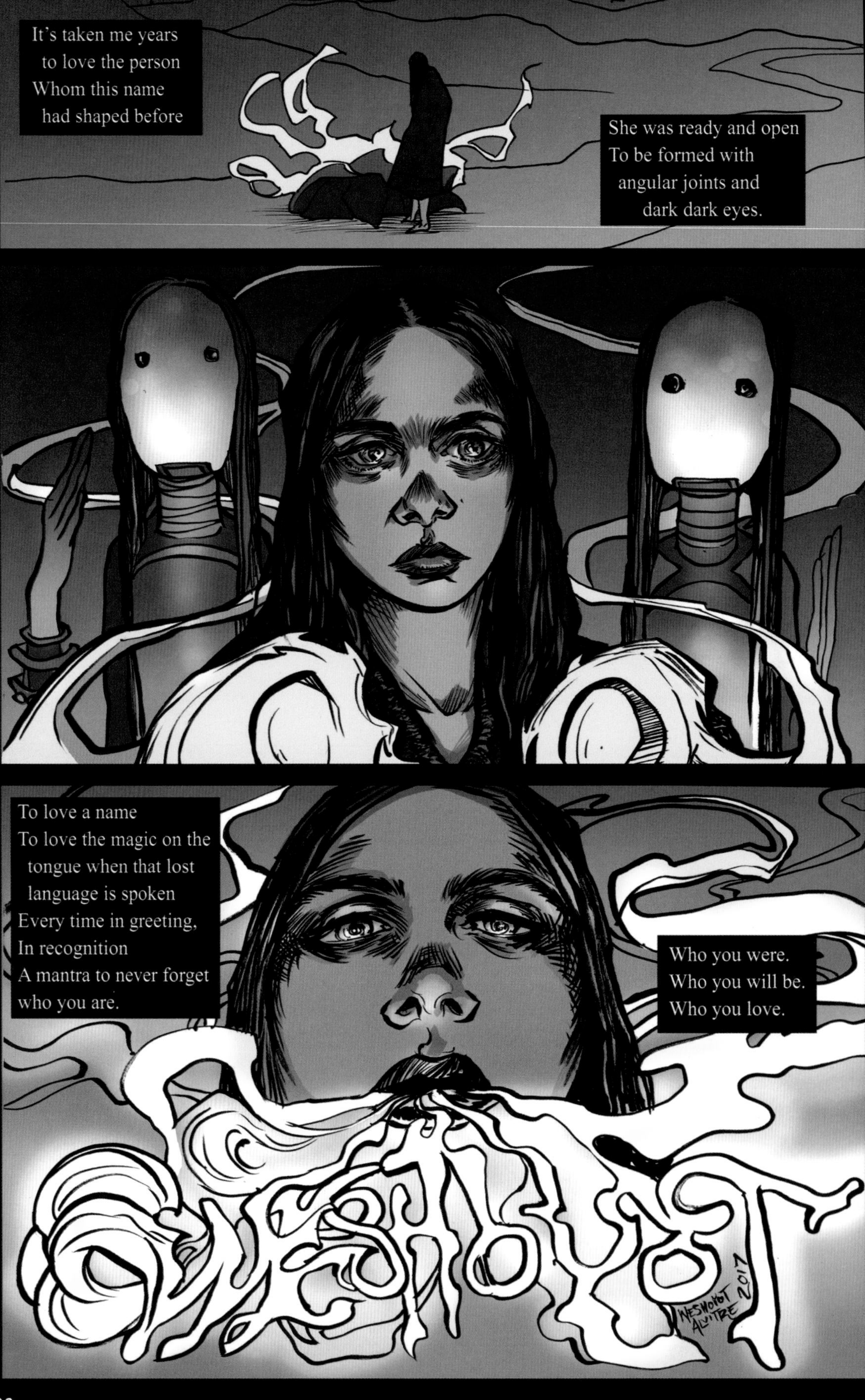
It's taken me years to love the person Whom this name had shaped before
She was ready and open To be formed with angular joints and dark dark eyes.
To love a name To love the magic on the tongue when that lost language is spoken Every time in greeting, In recognition A mantra to never forget who you are.
Who you were. Who you will be. Who you love.
WESHOYOT ALVITRE 2017

Nuliajunga

Marion Lewis

What else to say.
She went down there.
As a girl, up here; now woman, down there.
She was up here, but his fear and panic sank her.

No. Not her. No reflection of her is her circumstance.
She is who she is. She isn't what happened to her.
She always will be, because she was.
Go down to her. See her and help; it's just hair; she is no fear.

Patronize was fear manifest.
Cut from her, she gave to you. Skilled hand cut to the marrow
to give you yours.
Exceptional is scary to some, but fearless returns with life.
Acquainted with grief but posing no threat. Intensity means
ingenious.

No. Not stuck, not captured.
Her reason, she knows.
Her fingers swim and grow into food and light.
Understand. You will do what she can't: resurface.

It's just hair; she asks one thing, only one help, two braids.
It's just nice; she demands, only be nice, her digits your food.

What else to say.
Her platform is perspective. Respect can meet her eye to eye.
Courage meets no fear down there.
Take the plunge where she was forced.
I am Sedna.

Holy Wild

Gwen Benaway

my gookum said only
the wild ones are holy.

bush in northern Michigan
is the ancestral field of my body,

a girl who tastes of summer ragweed
in the high heat of noon.

my body grows by night in secret,
wet with yearling dew.

breasts and hips spread
like bushfires in a dry season,

skin pale as moonlight at dawn,
soft as a muskrat's pelt skinned in March.

my mouth is a damselfly's wings,
iridescent breath on your sex.

my hips hold a cock the color
of crushed blueberries, bittersweet purple.

my breasts dart from your hands
like minnows, chase deeper water.

my gookum said a woman moves
like the sway of cattails in a June wind.

I lean to you like an otter dives, slick
and glistening against your chest.

underneath the cedar of my thighs,
past the birch tree of my spine

is an opening, a rattlesnake den,
when you press your body in me,

the sound I make is a blackbird's cry.
here is the wild heart of me,

rush of heat on your fullness,
this is the holy wild she made me.

a woman's sex is as sacred as her land,
my ancestors learned from creation,

a woman is as holy wild as
her body's made to be.

This poem was published in the Summer 2017 issue of Canadian Art.

Of Ash and Snow

**Written by Elizabeth LaPensée,
Illustrated by Mitchell Bercier,
Colors by Elizabeth LaPensée**

This is an act of reclamation, a response to the limitations of being pinned into "educational" comics for the settler gaze, and for every Native man who has ever been told they look like a werewolf thanks to *Twilight*.

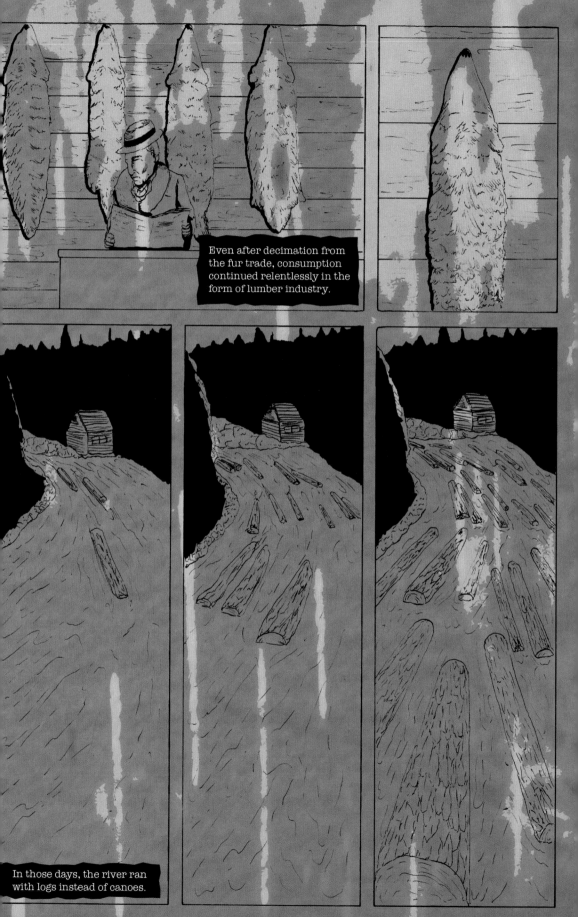

Even after decimation from the fur trade, consumption continued relentlessly in the form of lumber industry.

In those days, the river ran with logs instead of canoes.

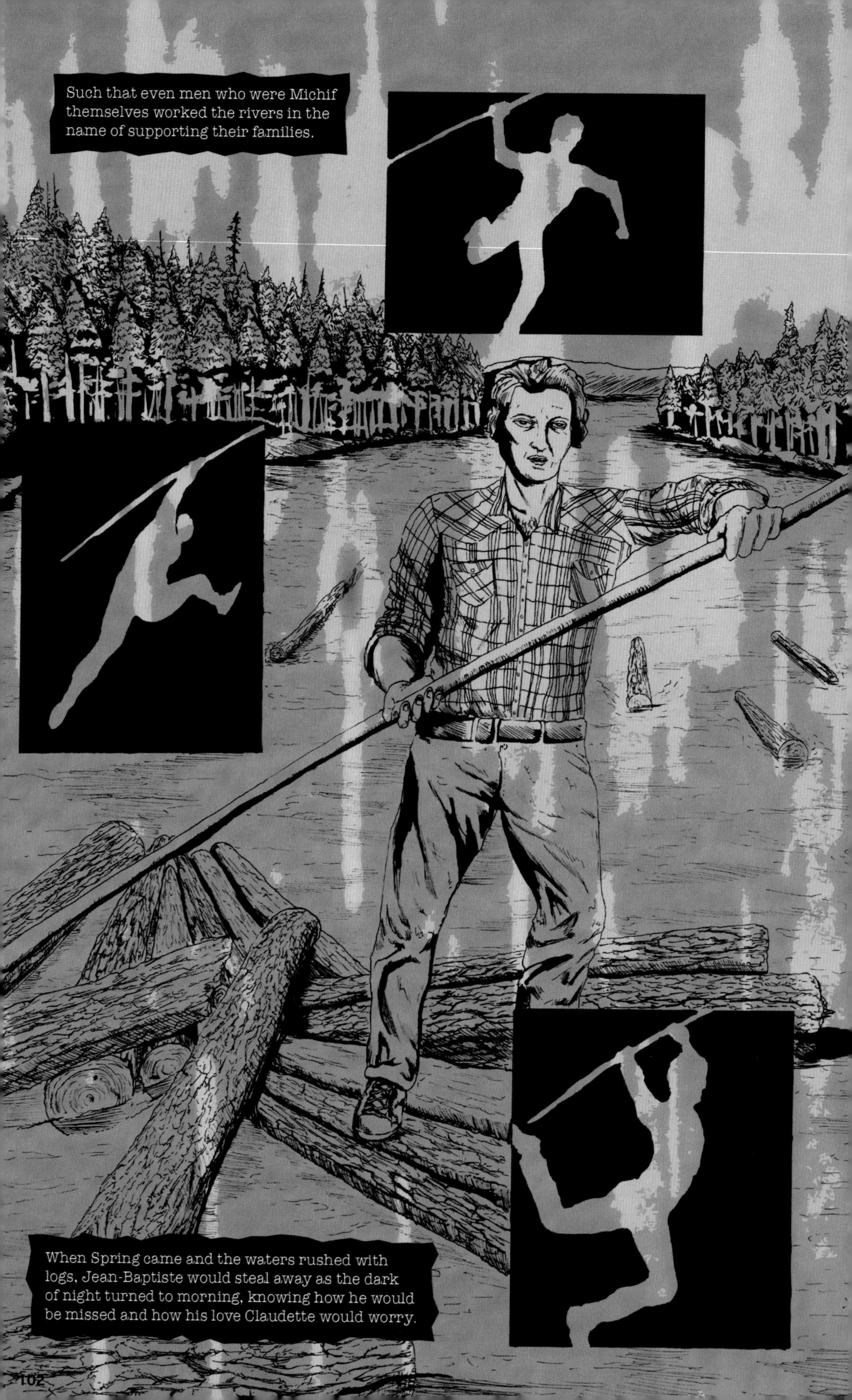
Such that even men who were Michif themselves worked the rivers in the name of supporting their families.
When Spring came and the waters rushed with logs, Jean-Baptiste would steal away as the dark of night turned to morning, knowing how he would be missed and how his love Claudette would worry.

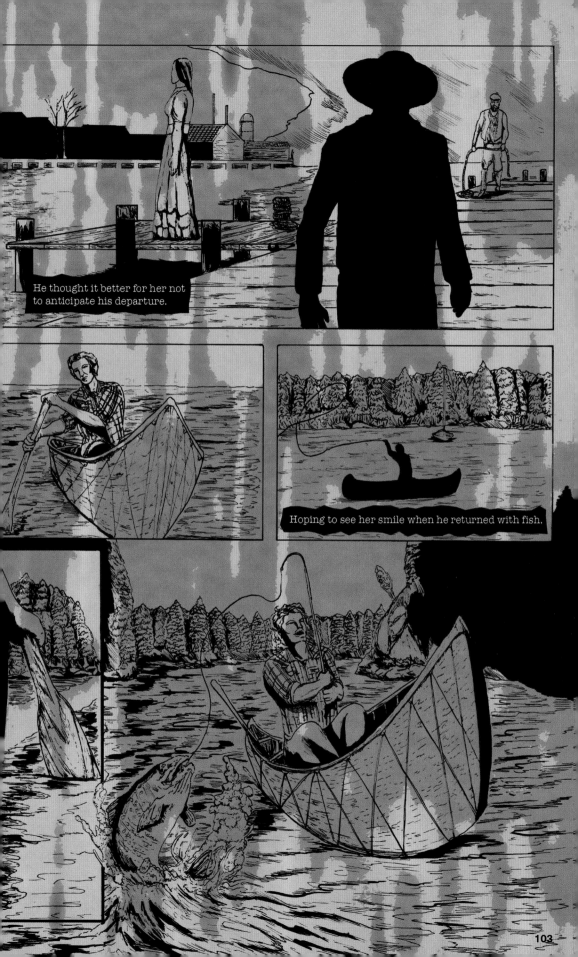

He thought it better for her not to anticipate his departure.

Hoping to see her smile when he returned with fish.

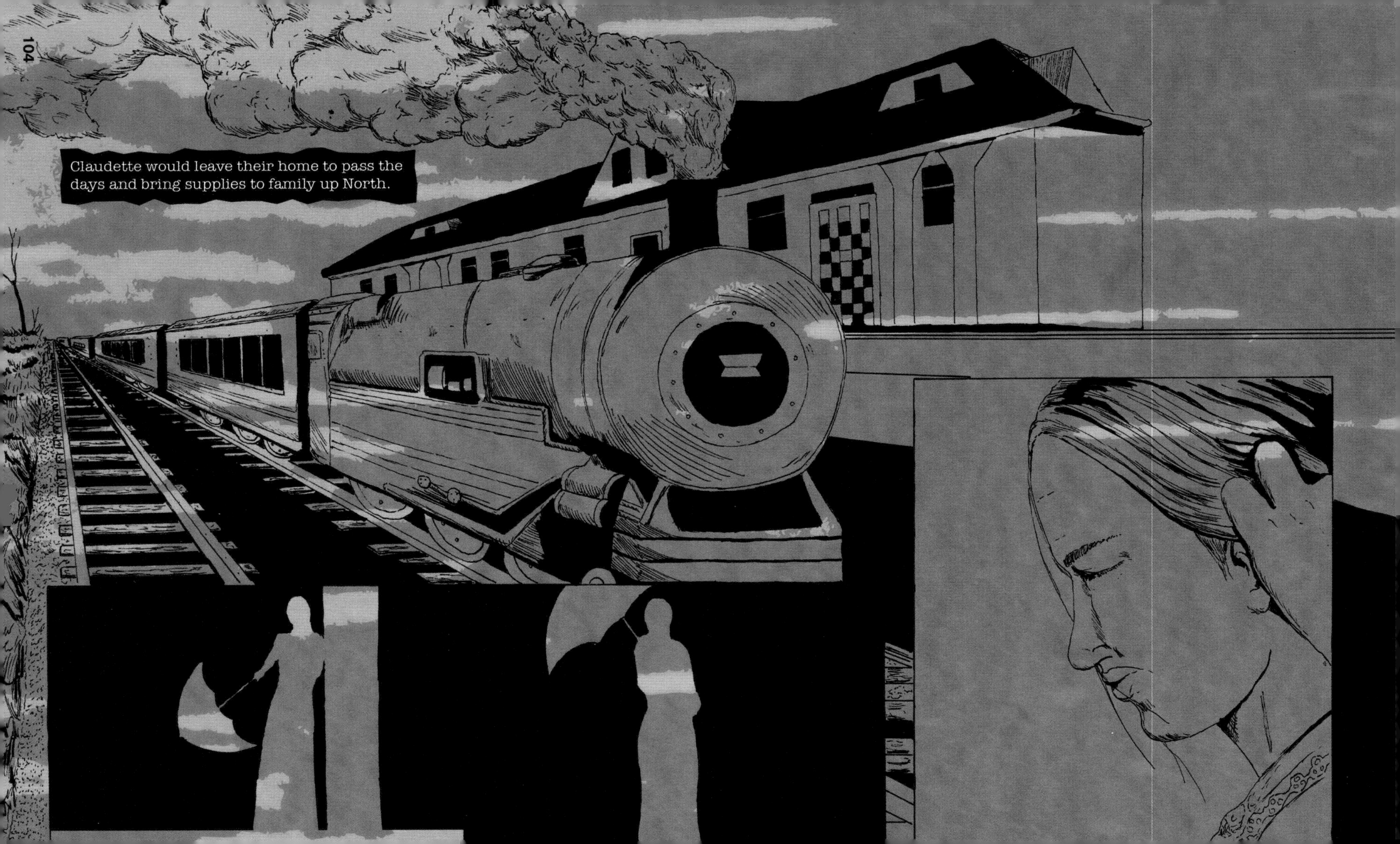
Claudette would leave their home to pass the days and bring supplies to family up North.

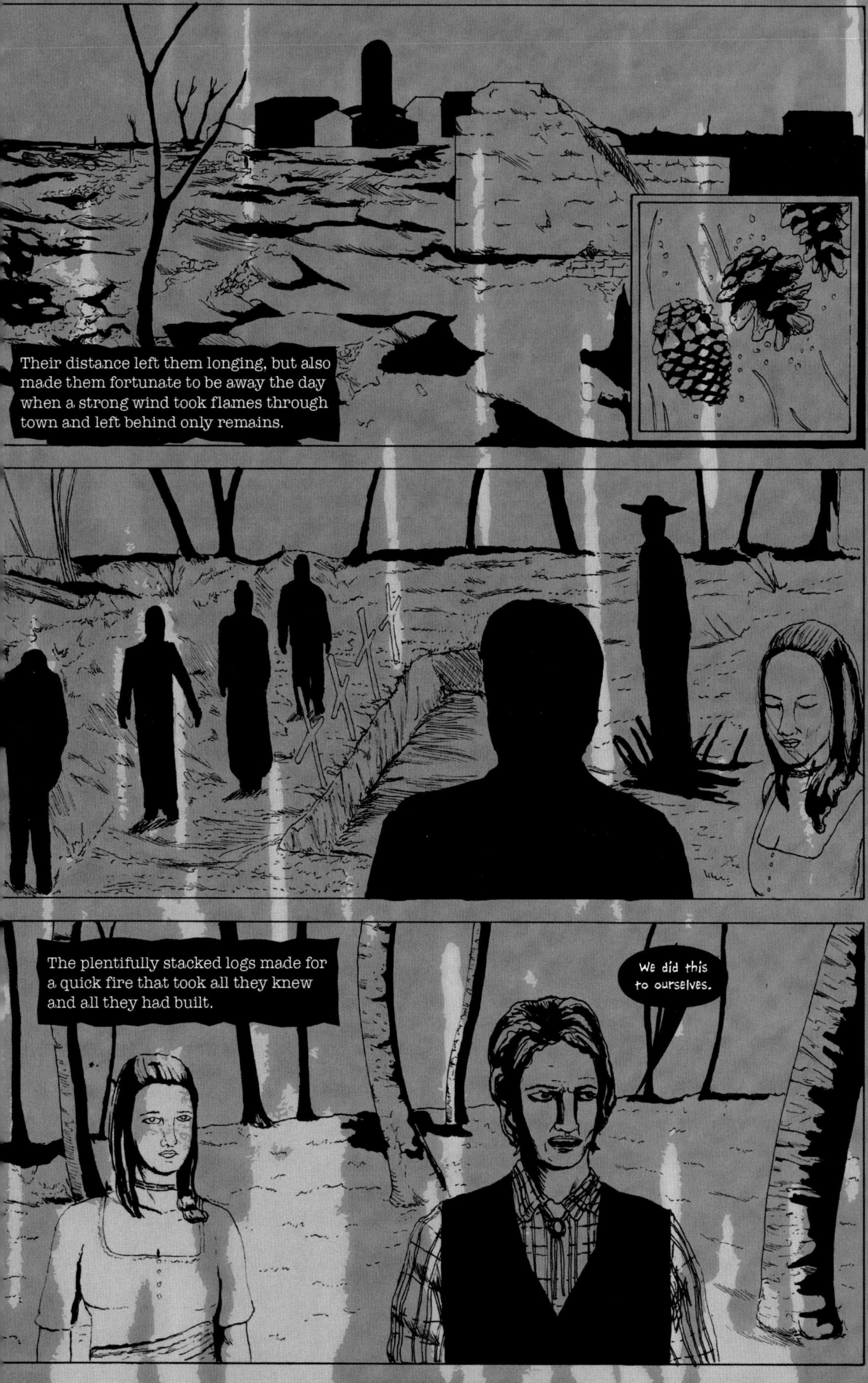
Their distance left them longing, but also made them fortunate to be away the day when a strong wind took flames through town and left behind only remains.
The plentifully stacked logs made for a quick fire that took all they knew and all they had built.
We did this to ourselves.

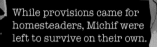
While provisions came for homesteaders, Michif were left to survive on their own.

And so it was with his acclaimed strength that Jean-Baptiste set about making a new home with Claudette.

They worked side by side, with their hands and hearts close to the land.

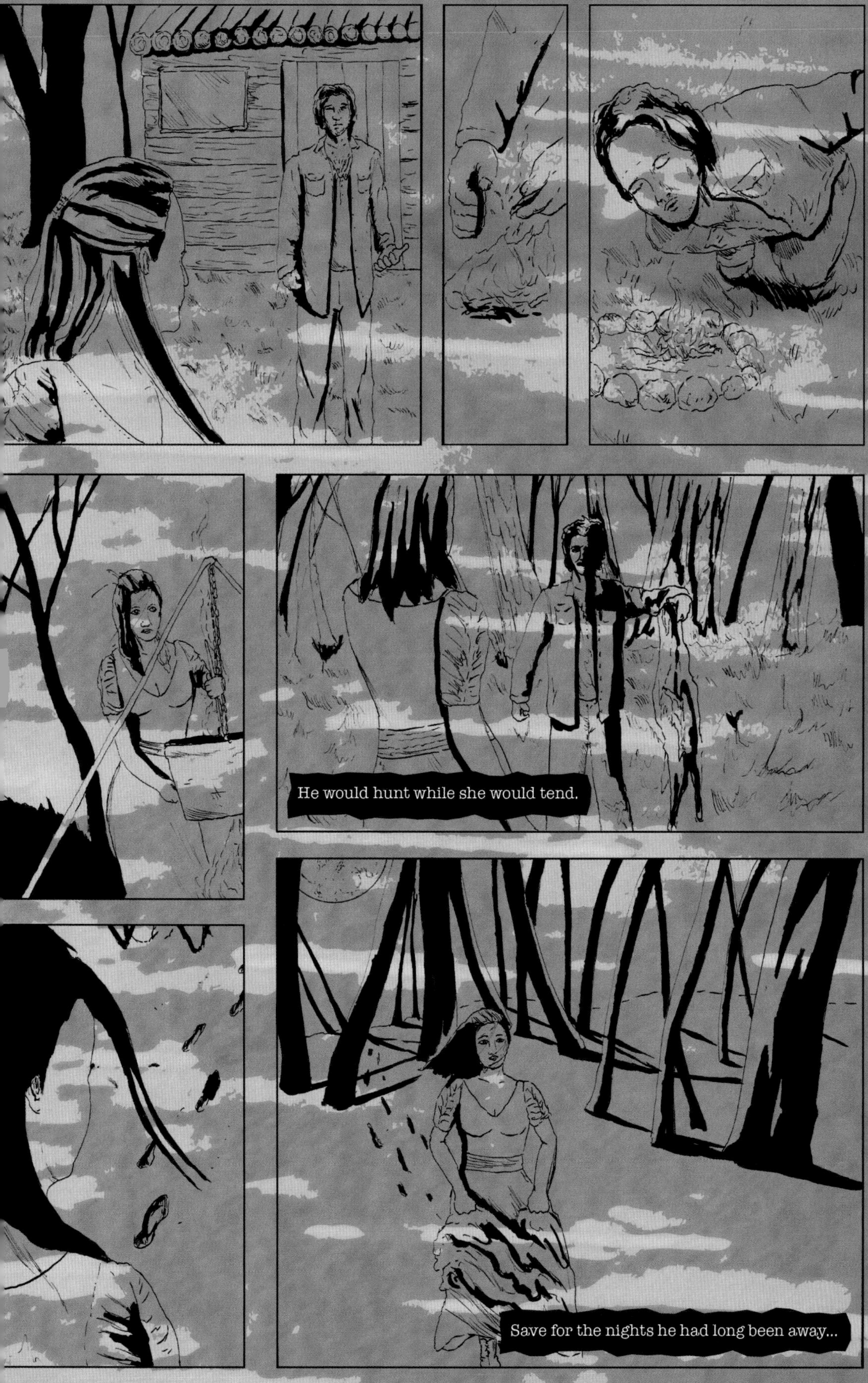
He would hunt while she would tend.
Save for the nights he had long been away...

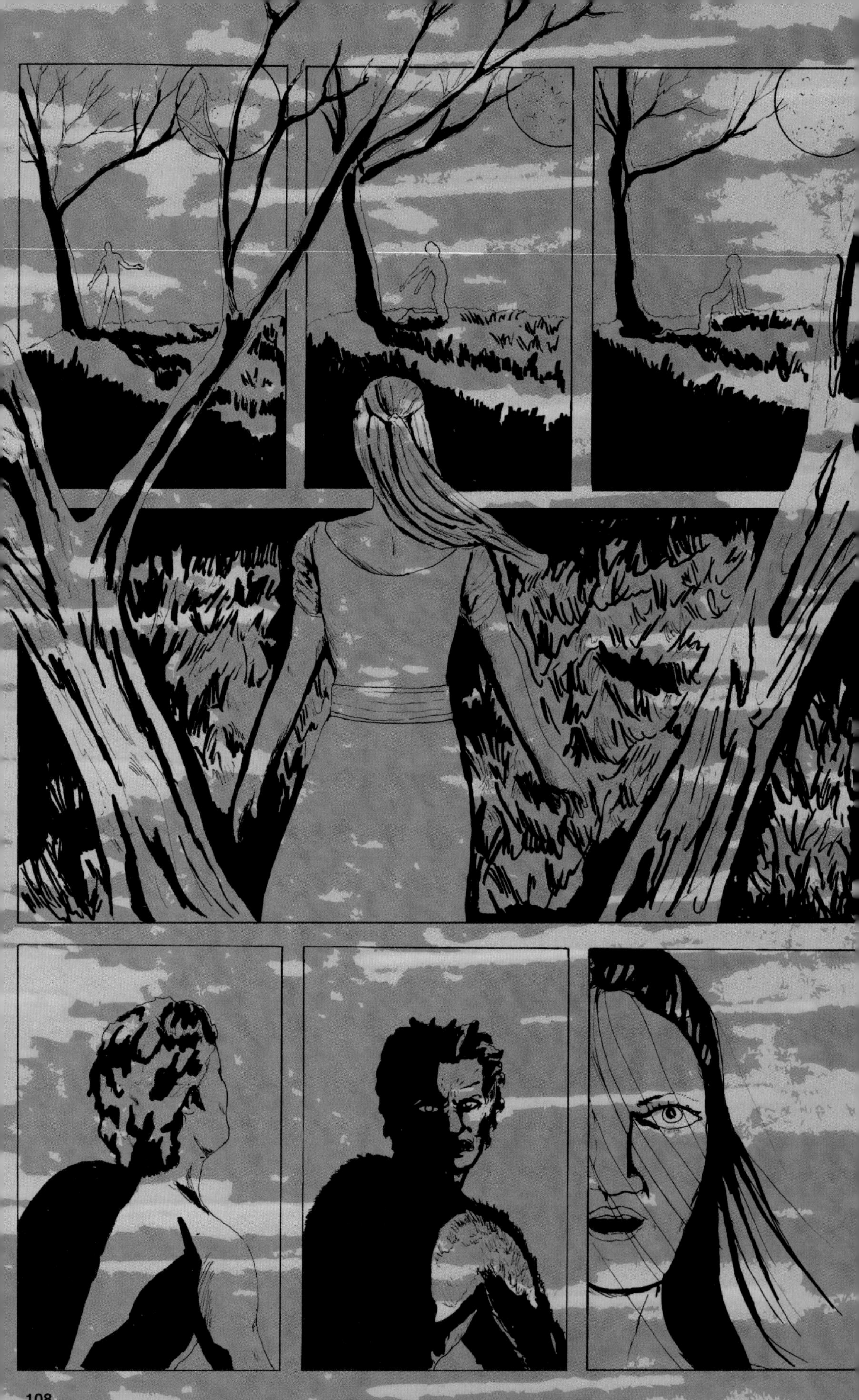

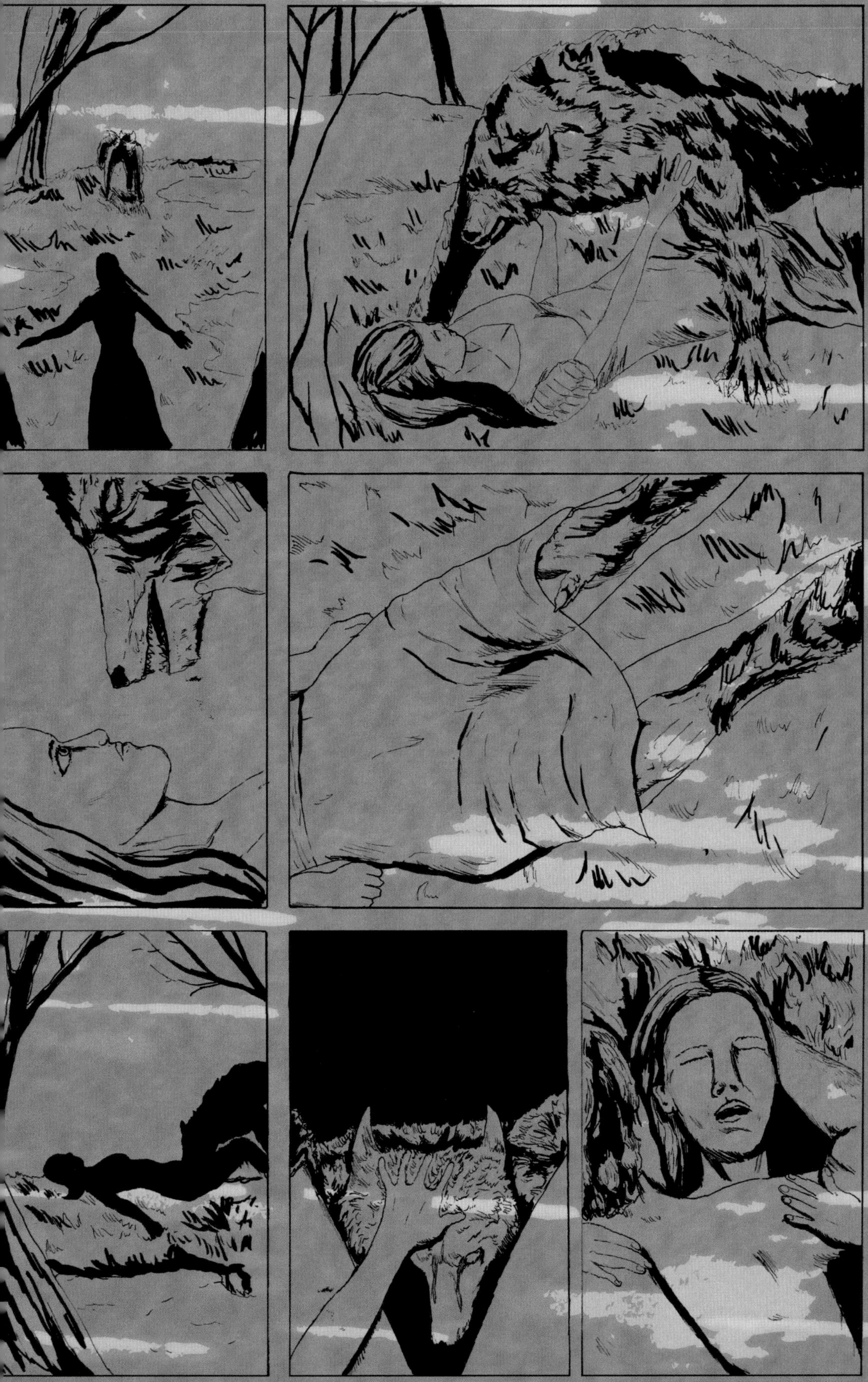

Teeming (with Self Love and Tattoos)

Illustrated by Chief Lady Bird

"Teeming (with Self Love and Tattoos)" was created in response to an InkTober prompt. While conceptualizing "Teeming," I began to see images of the women in my community who are so full and bursting with power. Power in relation to the land, the rock faces with petroglyphs painted on them, the sacredness of our stories being told and retold since time immemorial. Power in relation to self-pleasure, self love, and reconnecting to ourselves—a beautiful rejection of the unbodiment and disconnection forced on us through colonization.

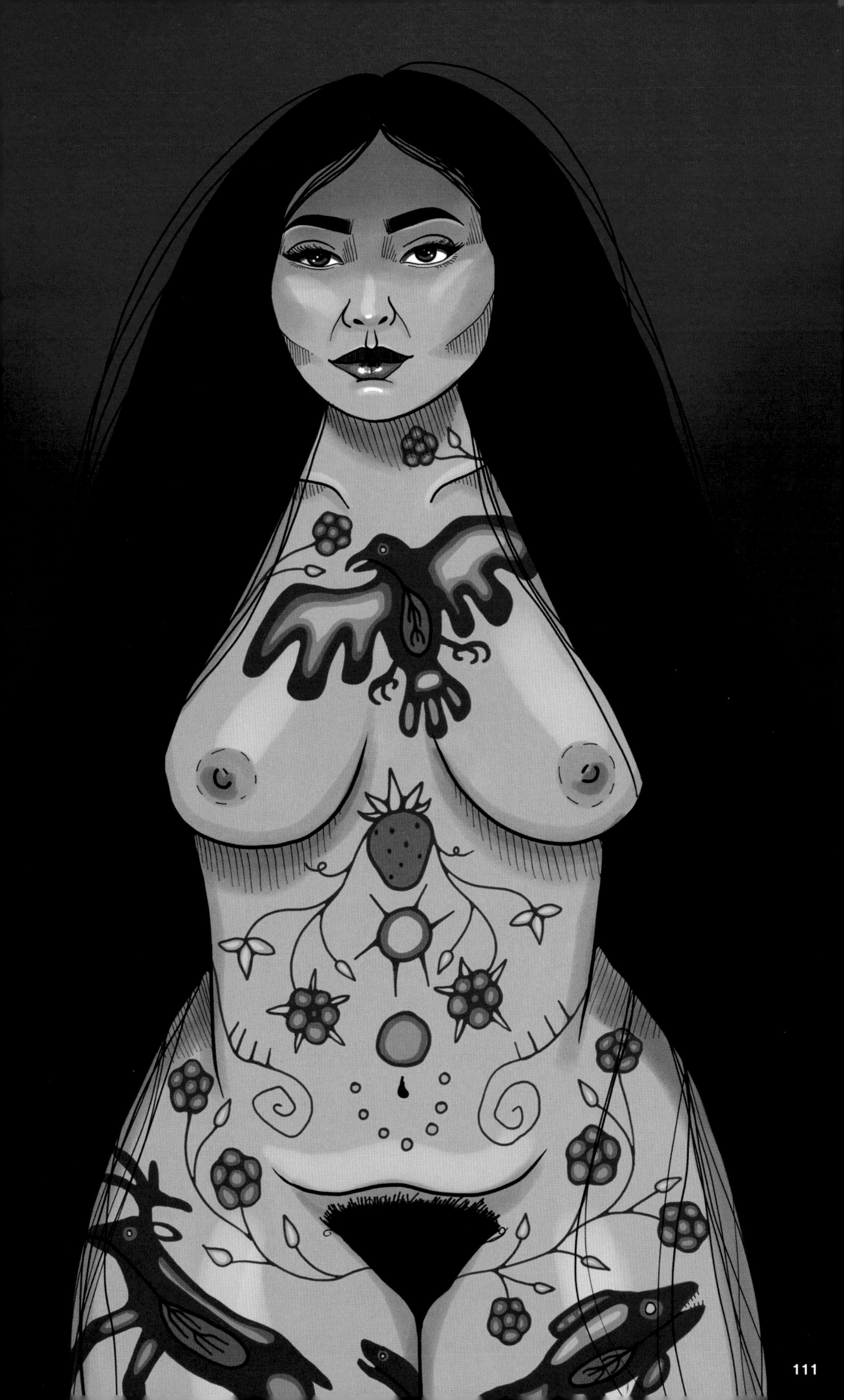

Linger

**Written and Illustrated
by Nshannacappo**

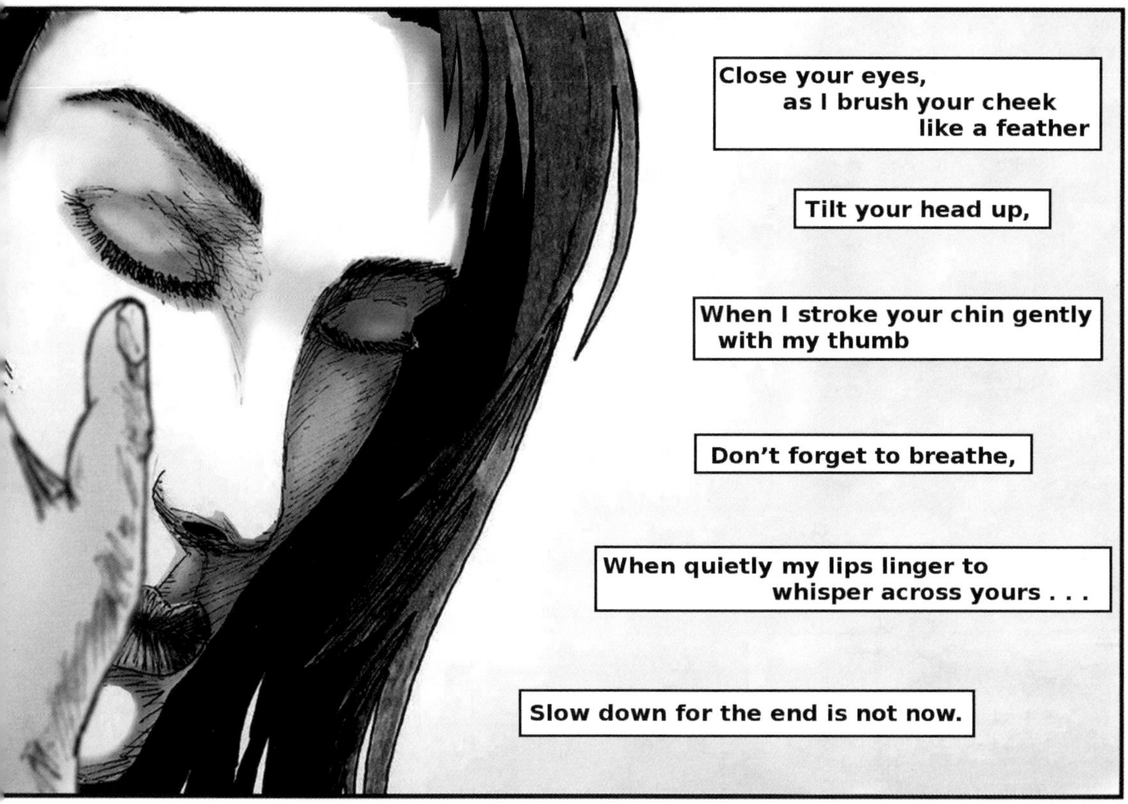
Close your eyes,
as I brush your cheek
like a feather
Tilt your head up,
When I stroke your chin gently
with my thumb
Don't forget to breathe,
When quietly my lips linger to
whisper across yours . . .
Slow down for the end is not now.

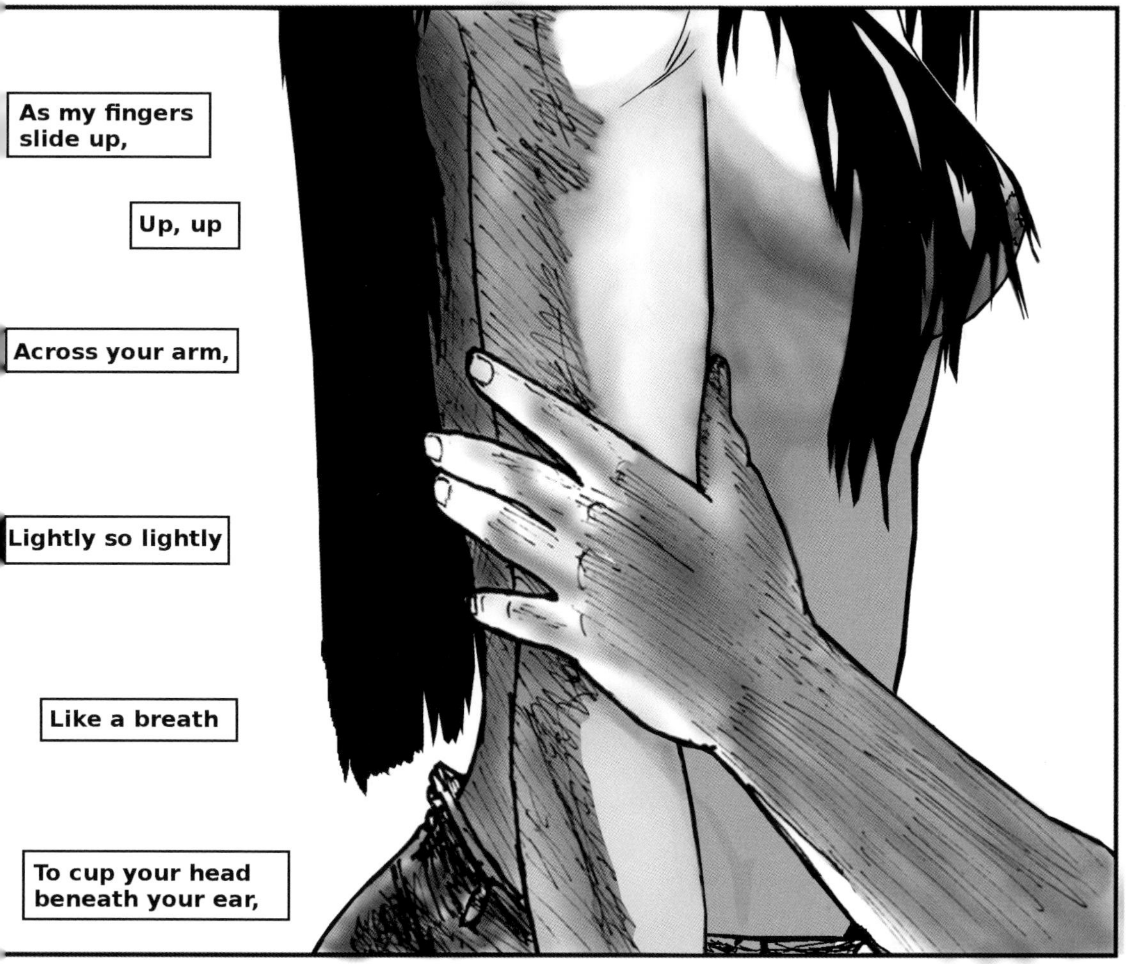
As my fingers
slide up,
Up, up
Across your arm,
Lightly so lightly
Like a breath
To cup your head
beneath your ear,

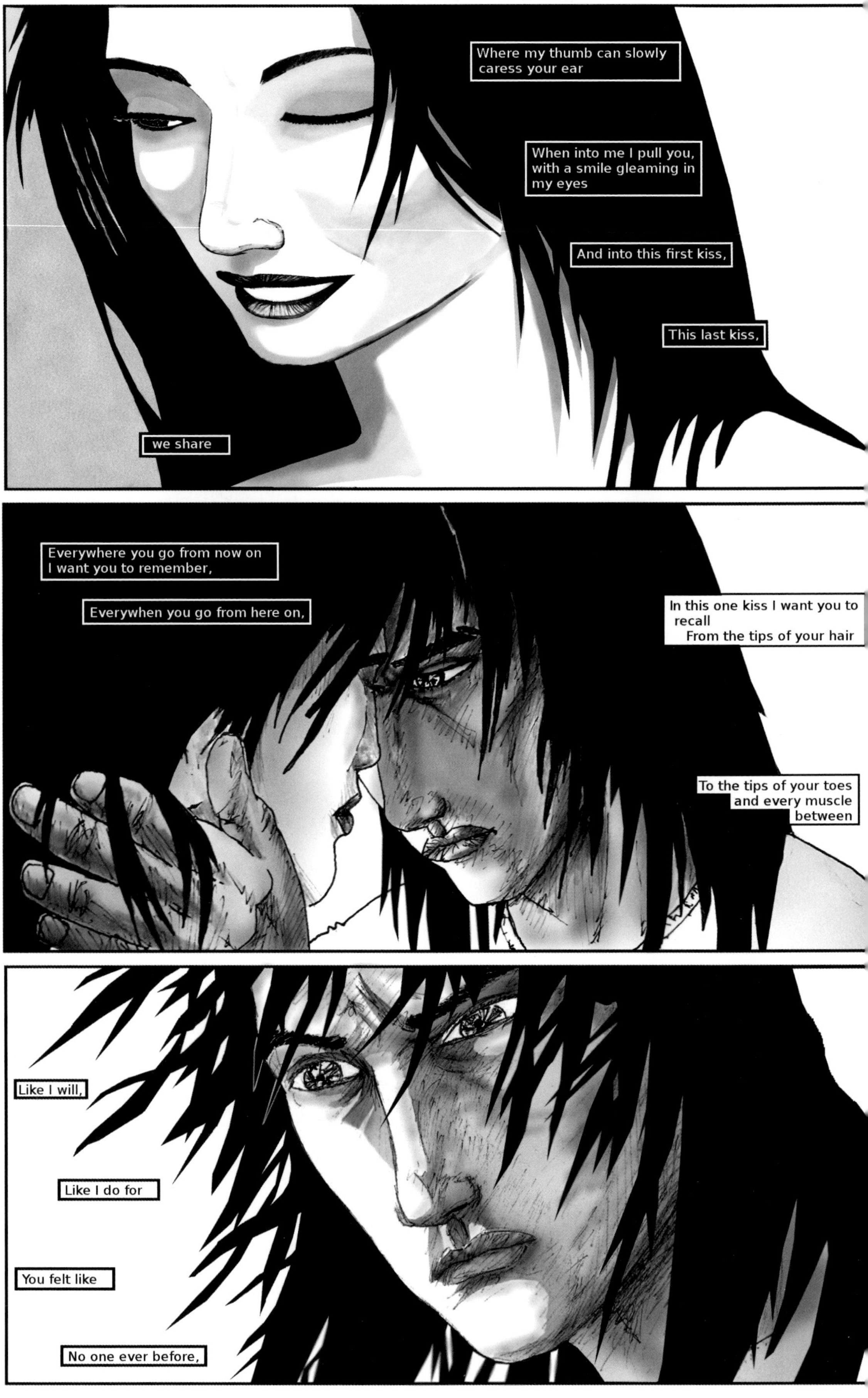
Where my thumb can slowly caress your ear
When into me I pull you, with a smile gleaming in my eyes
And into this first kiss,
This last kiss,
we share
Everywhere you go from now on I want you to remember,
Everywhen you go from here on,
In this one kiss I want you to recall
From the tips of your hair
To the tips of your toes and every muscle between
Like I will,
Like I do for
You felt like
No one ever before,

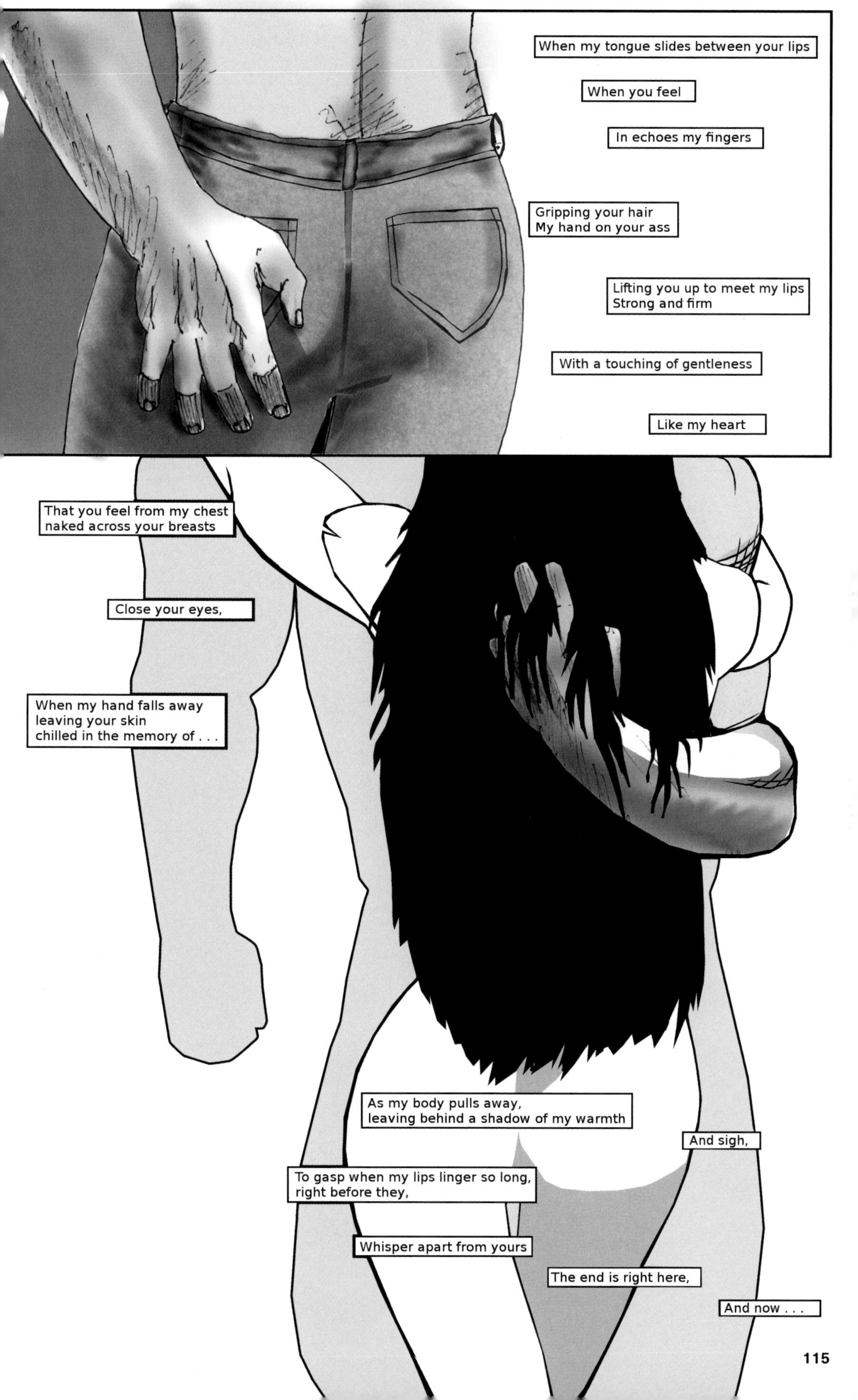
When my tongue slides between your lips
When you feel
In echoes my fingers
Gripping your hair
My hand on your ass
Lifting you up to meet my lips
Strong and firm
With a touching of gentleness
Like my heart
That you feel from my chest
naked across your breasts
Close your eyes,
When my hand falls away
leaving your skin
chilled in the memory of . . .
As my body pulls away,
leaving behind a shadow of my warmth
And sigh,
To gasp when my lips linger so long,
right before they,
Whisper apart from yours
The end is right here,
And now . . .

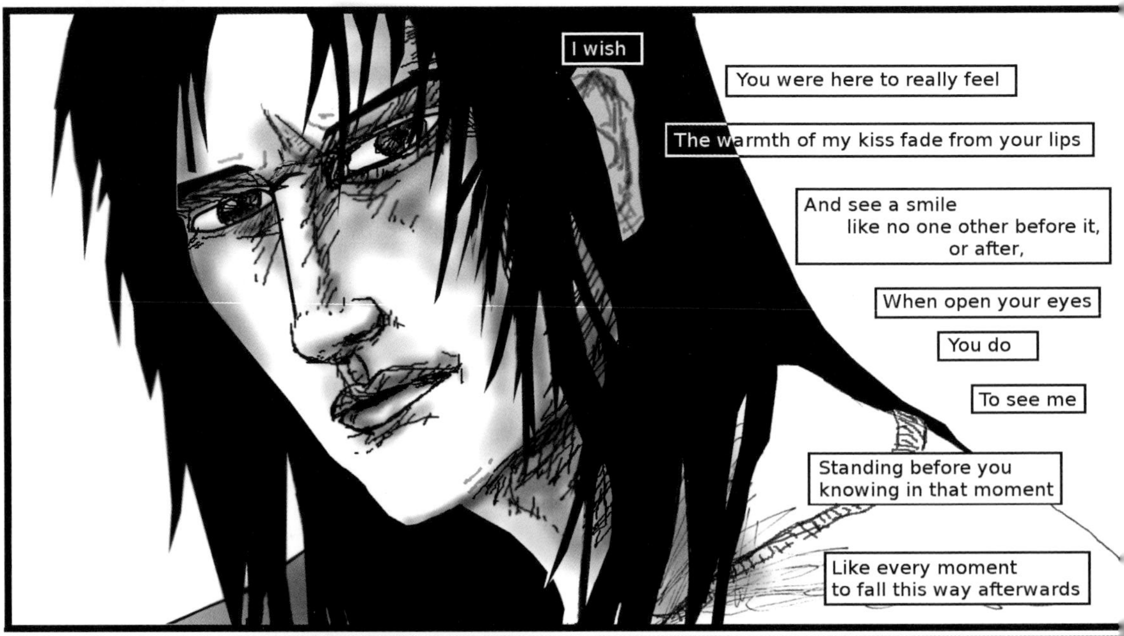
I wish
You were here to really feel
The warmth of my kiss fade from your lips
And see a smile
like no one other before it,
or after,
When open your eyes
You do
To see me
Standing before you
knowing in that moment
Like every moment
to fall this way afterwards

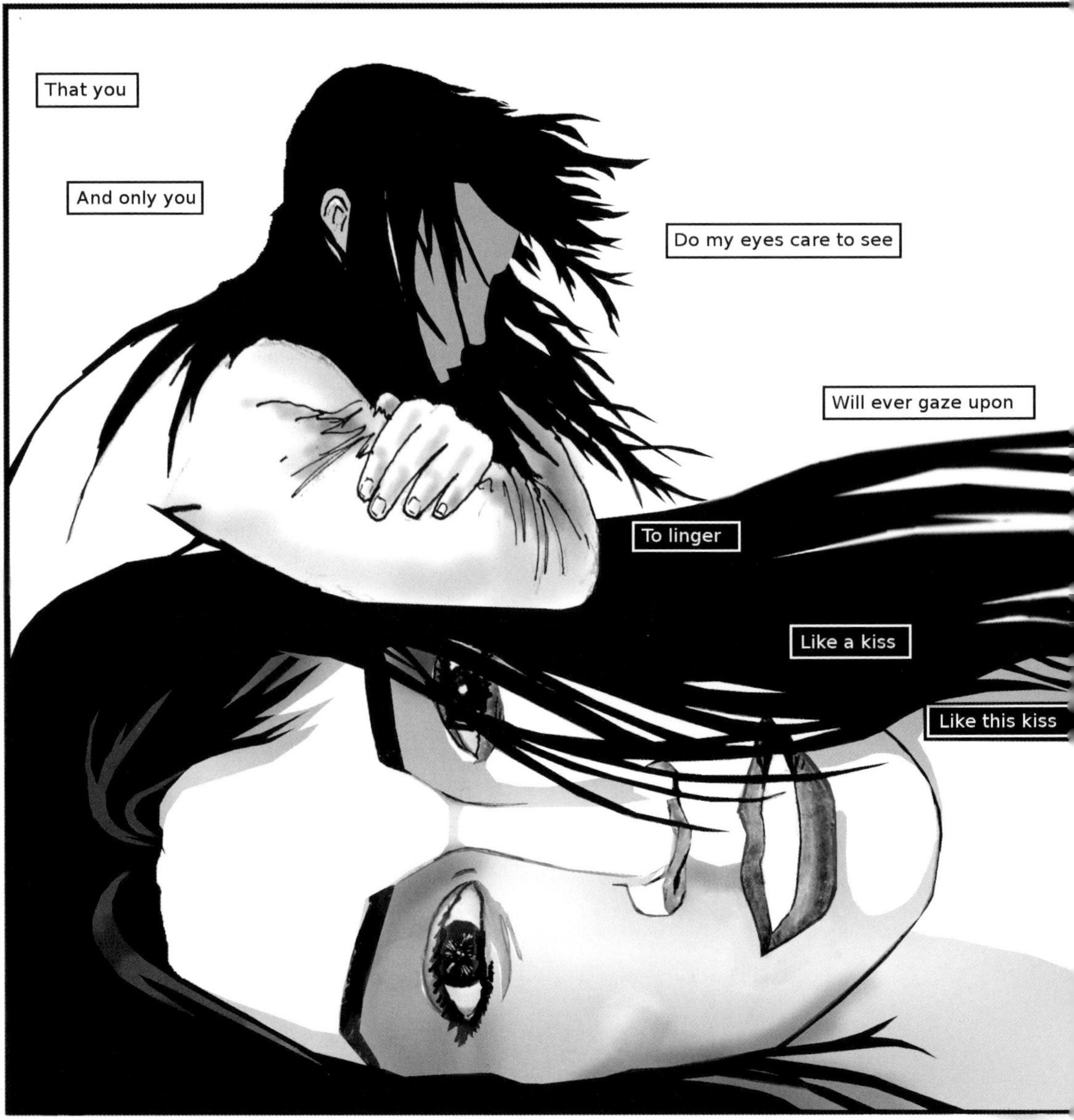
That you
And only you
Do my eyes care to see
Will ever gaze upon
To linger
Like a kiss
Like this kiss

Hot and Bothered

Written by Lee Francis IV,
Illustrated by Shaun Beyale

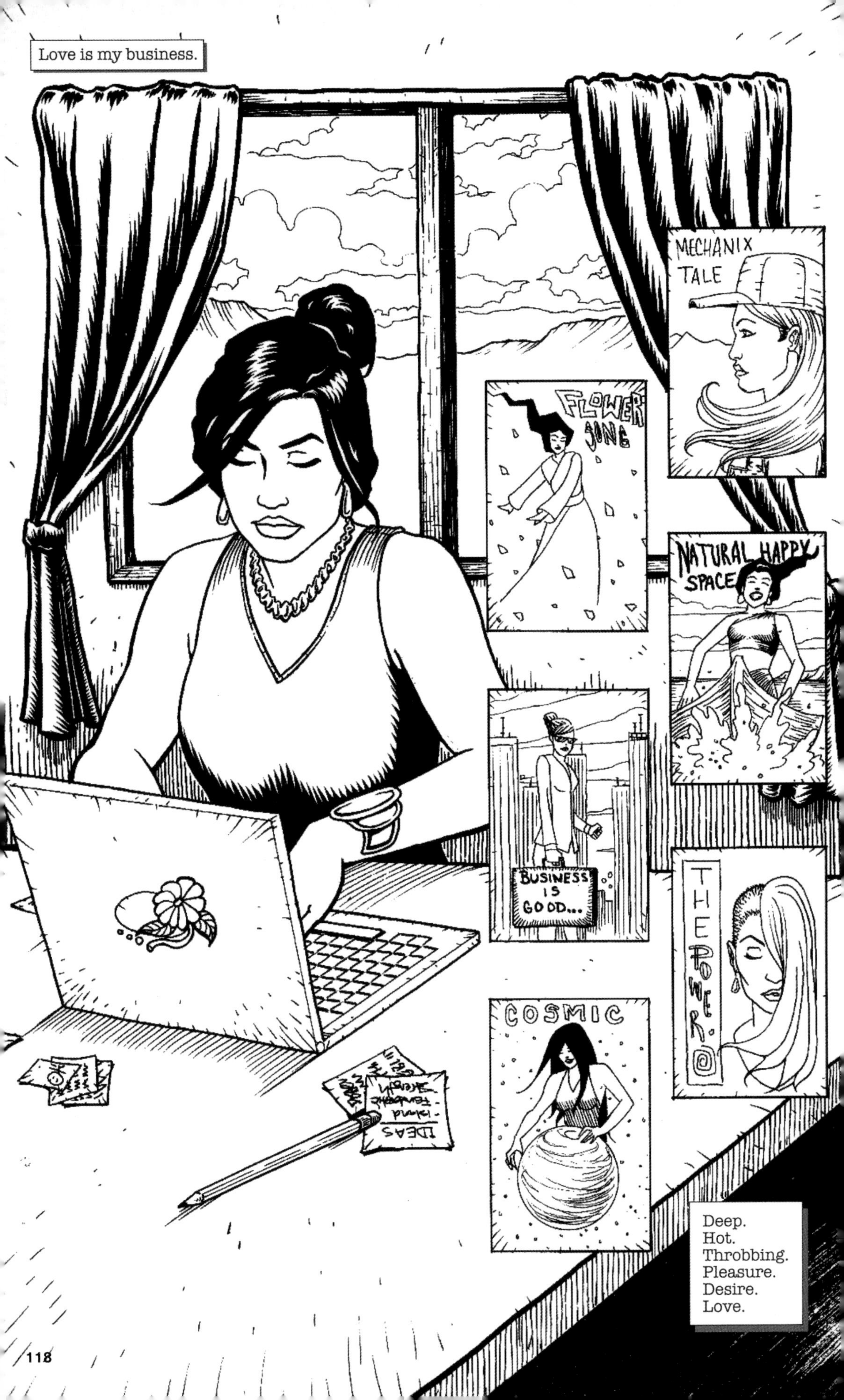
Love is my business.
MECHANIX TALE
FLOWER SONG
NATURAL HAPPY SPACE
BUSINESS IS GOOD...
THE POWER
COSMIC
Deep.
Hot.
Throbbing.
Pleasure.
Desire.
Love.

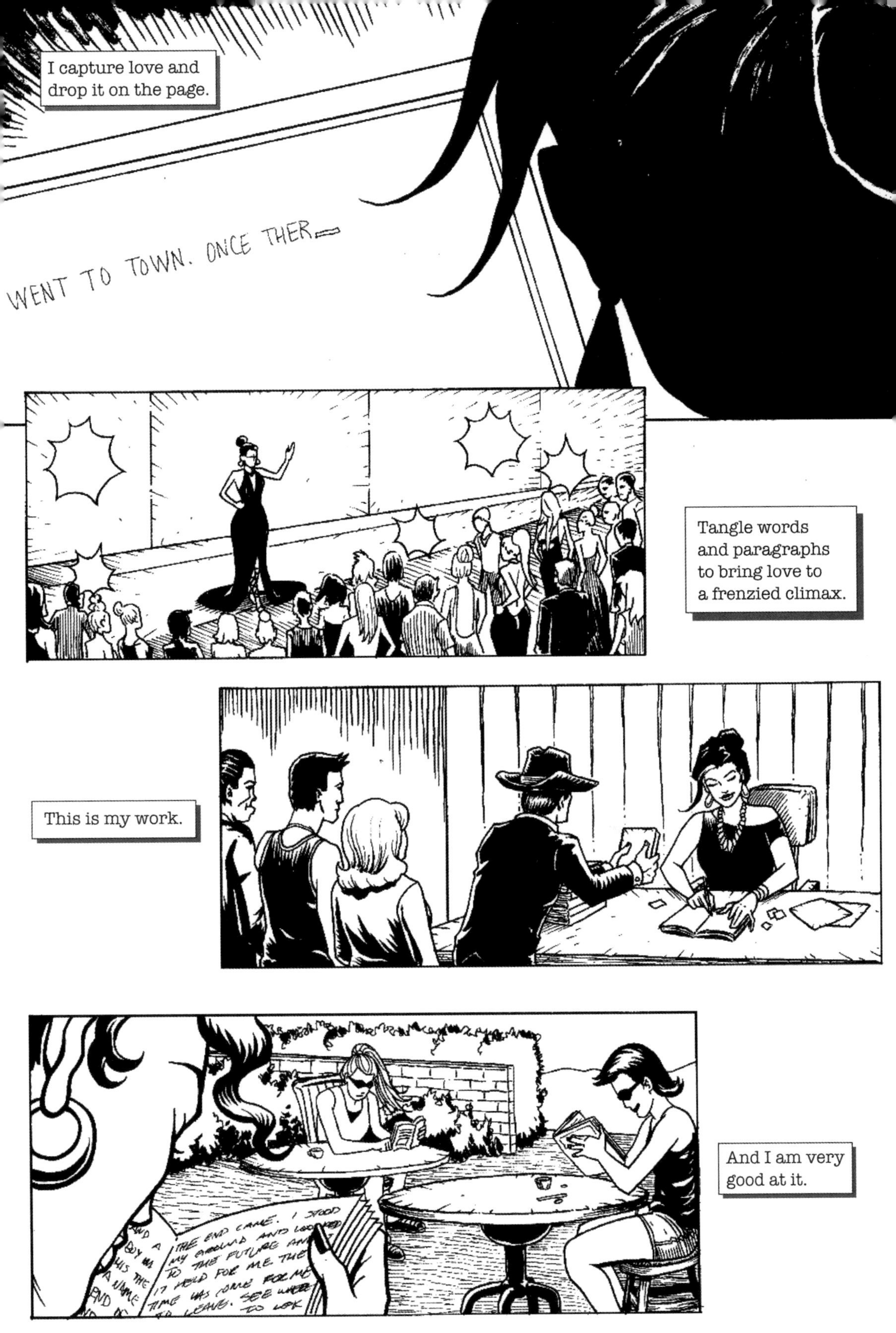
I capture love and drop it on the page.
WENT TO TOWN. ONCE THER—
Tangle words and paragraphs to bring love to a frenzied climax.
This is my work.
And I am very good at it.

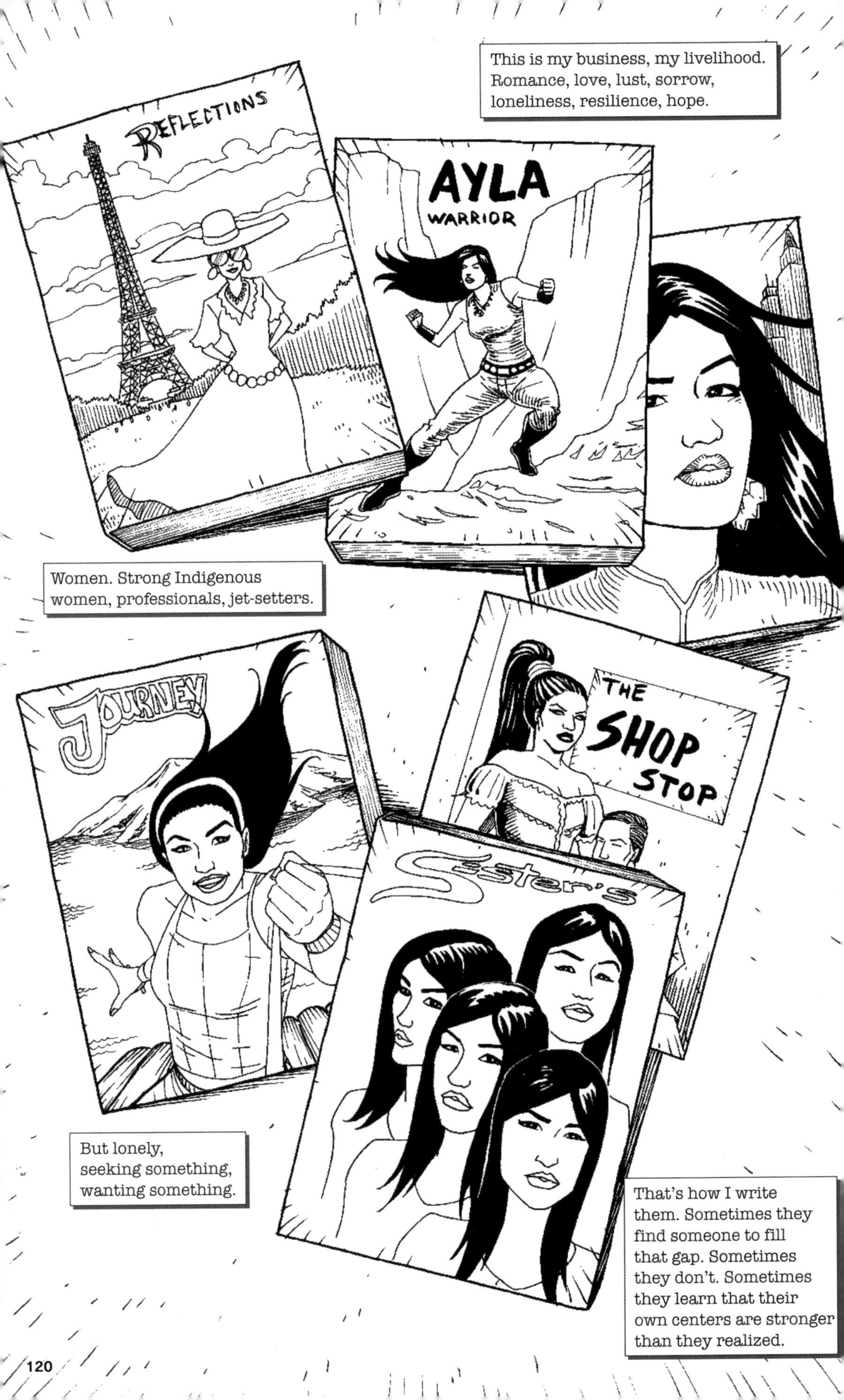
This is my business, my livelihood. Romance, love, lust, sorrow, loneliness, resilience, hope.
REFLECTIONS
AYLA
WARRIOR
Women. Strong Indigenous women, professionals, jet-setters.
JOURNEY
THE SHOP STOP
Sister's
But lonely, seeking something, wanting something.
That's how I write them. Sometimes they find someone to fill that gap. Sometimes they don't. Sometimes they learn that their own centers are stronger than they realized.

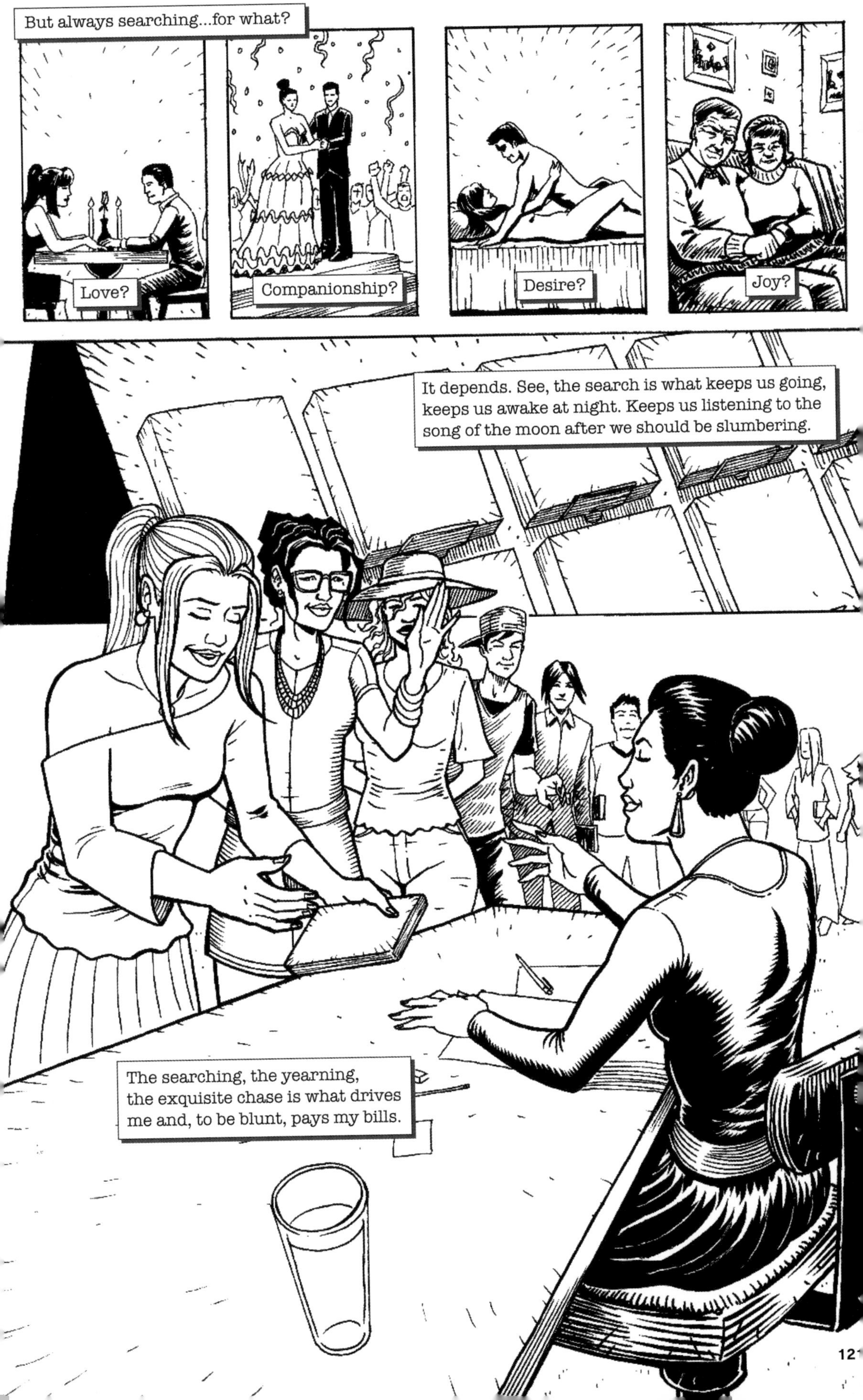

But always searching...for what?
Love?
Companionship?
Desire?
Joy?
It depends. See, the search is what keeps us going, keeps us awake at night. Keeps us listening to the song of the moon after we should be slumbering.
The searching, the yearning, the exquisite chase is what drives me and, to be blunt, pays my bills.

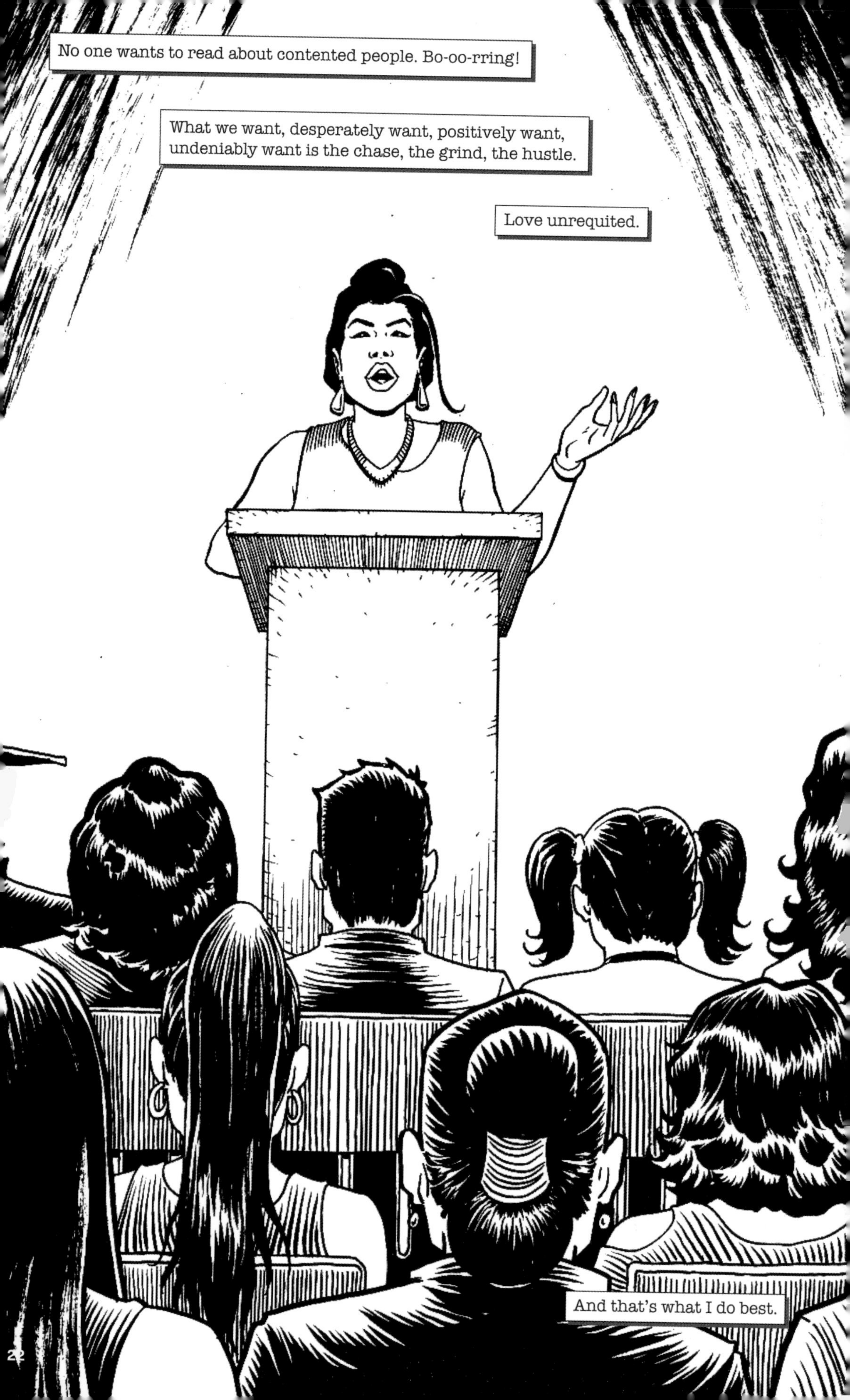
No one wants to read about contented people. Bo-oo-rring!
What we want, desperately want, positively want, undeniably want is the chase, the grind, the hustle.
Love unrequited.
And that's what I do best.

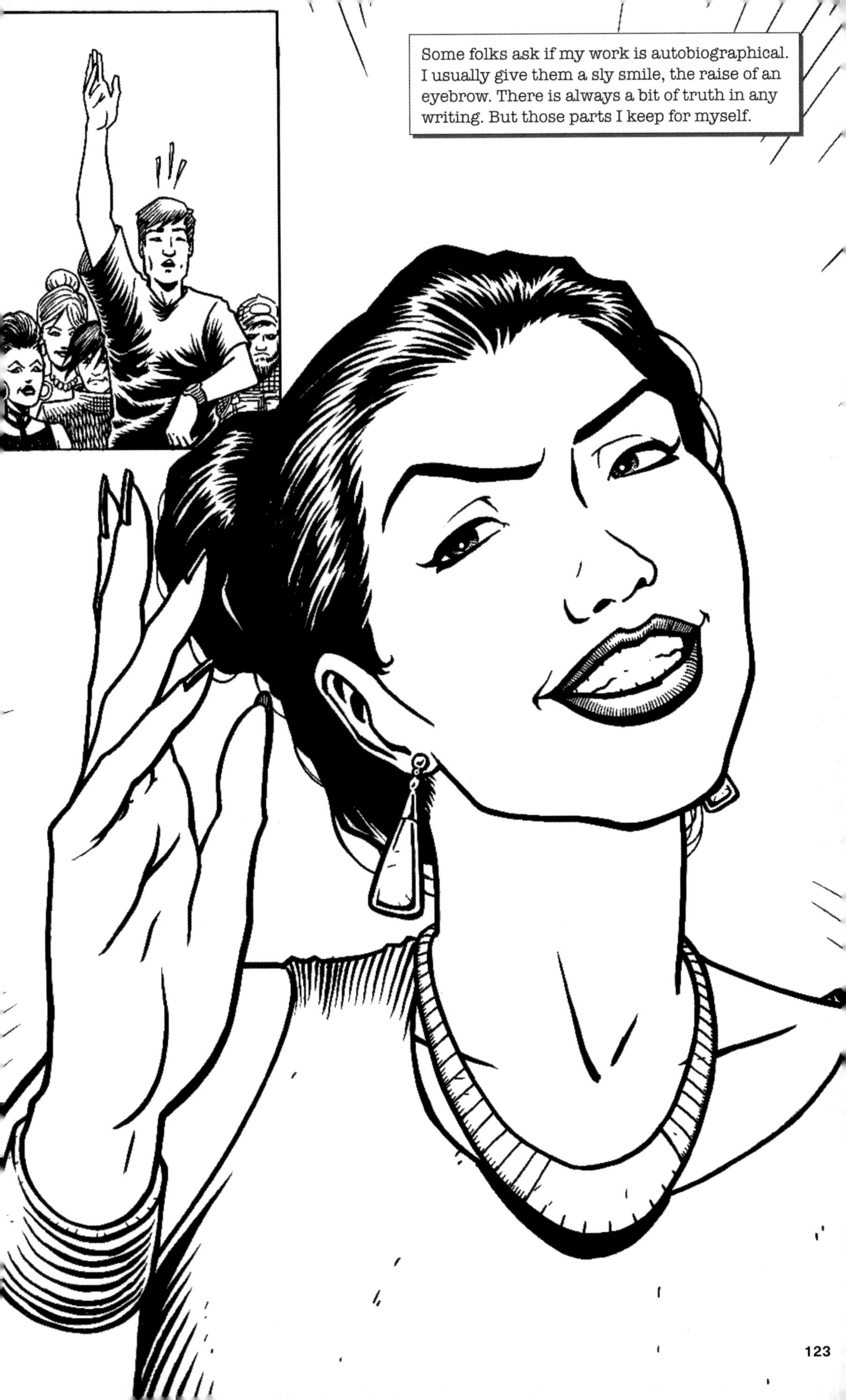
Some folks ask if my work is autobiographical. I usually give them a sly smile, the raise of an eyebrow. There is always a bit of truth in any writing. But those parts I keep for myself.

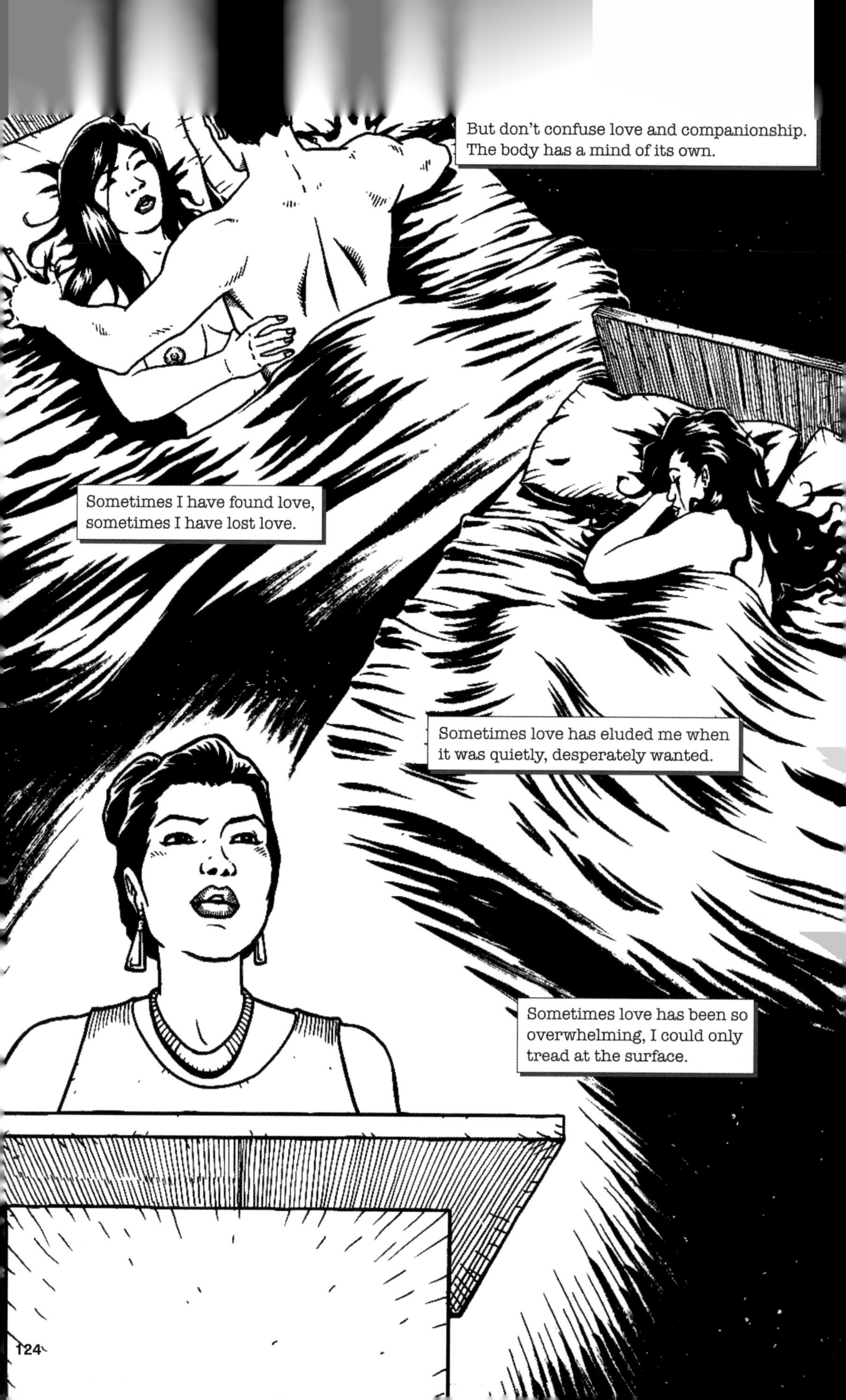
But don't confuse love and companionship. The body has a mind of its own.
Sometimes I have found love, sometimes I have lost love.
Sometimes love has eluded me when it was quietly, desperately wanted.
Sometimes love has been so overwhelming, I could only tread at the surface.

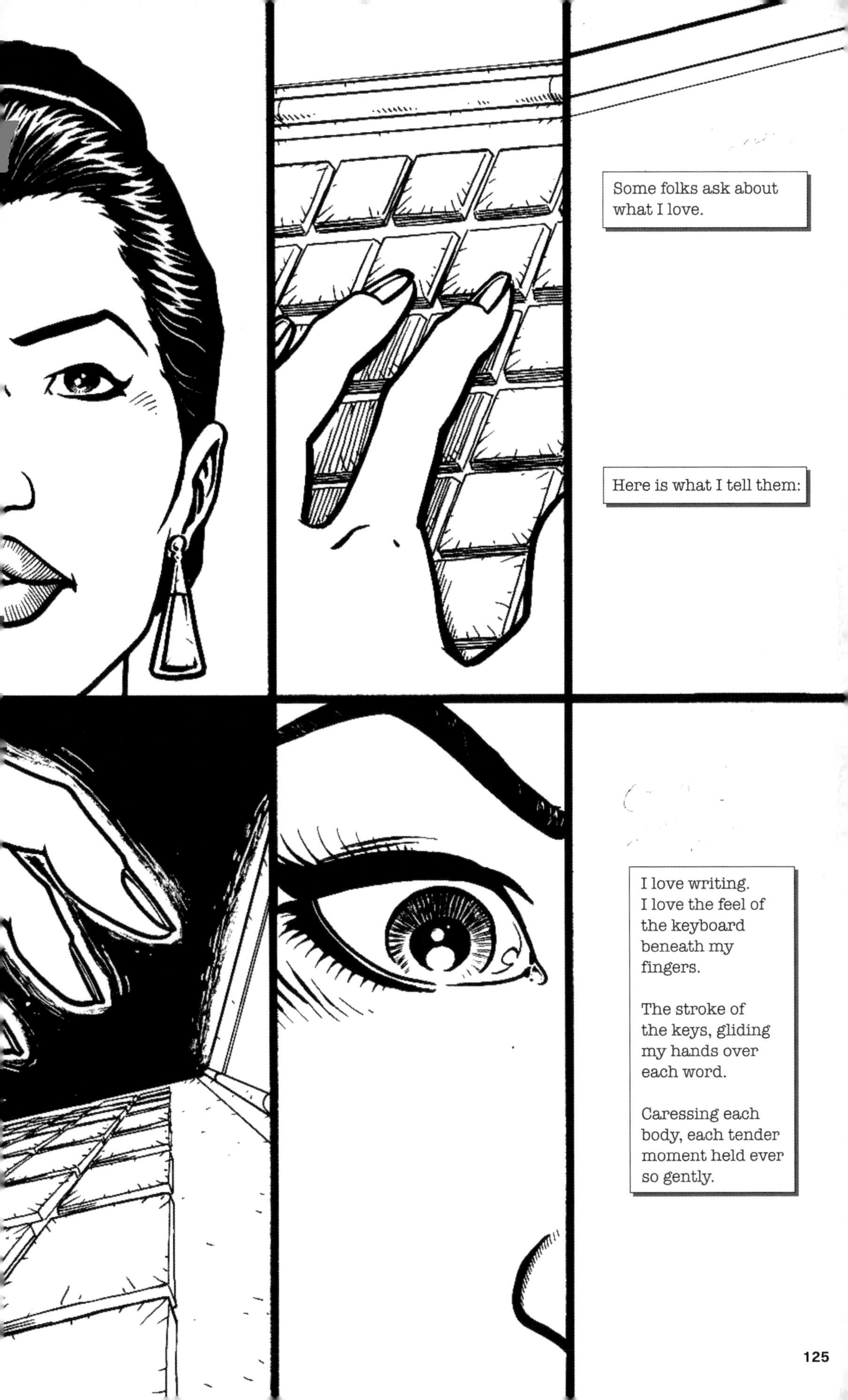
Some folks ask about what I love.
Here is what I tell them:
I love writing. I love the feel of the keyboard beneath my fingers.
The stroke of the keys, gliding my hands over each word.
Caressing each body, each tender moment held ever so gently.

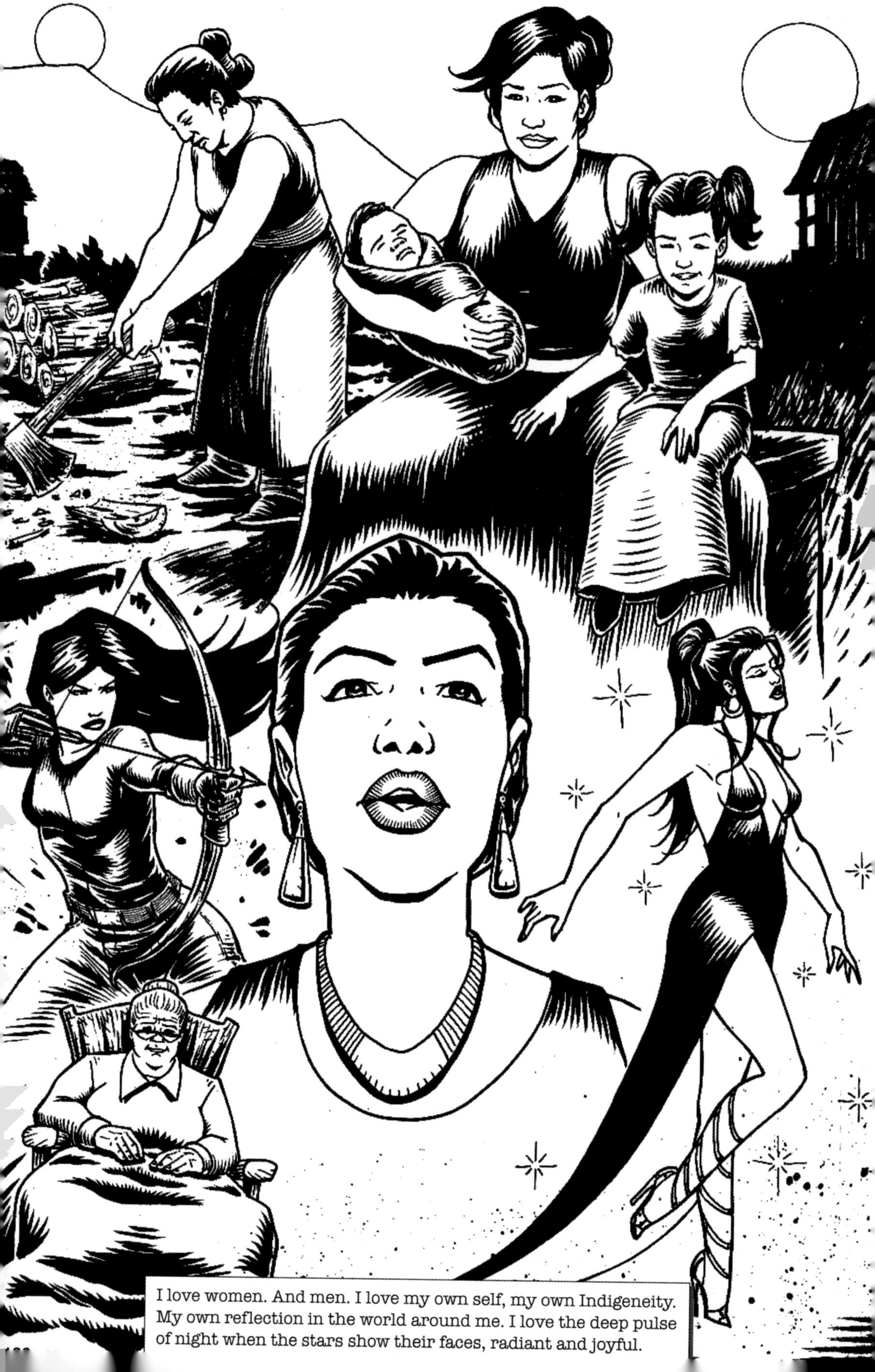
I love women. And men. I love my own self, my own Indigeneity. My own reflection in the world around me. I love the deep pulse of night when the stars show their faces, radiant and joyful.

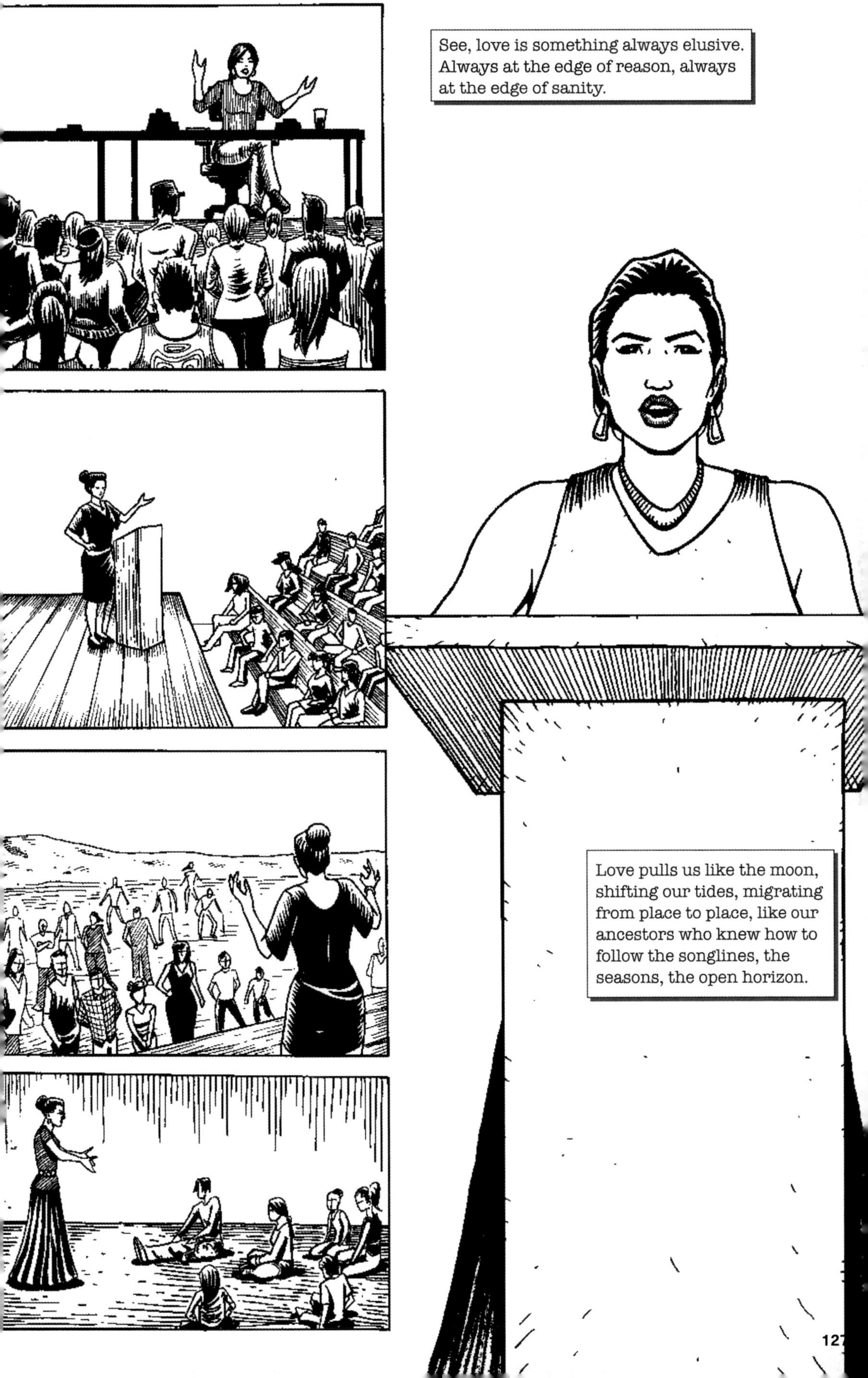
See, love is something always elusive. Always at the edge of reason, always at the edge of sanity.
Love pulls us like the moon, shifting our tides, migrating from place to place, like our ancestors who knew how to follow the songlines, the seasons, the open horizon.

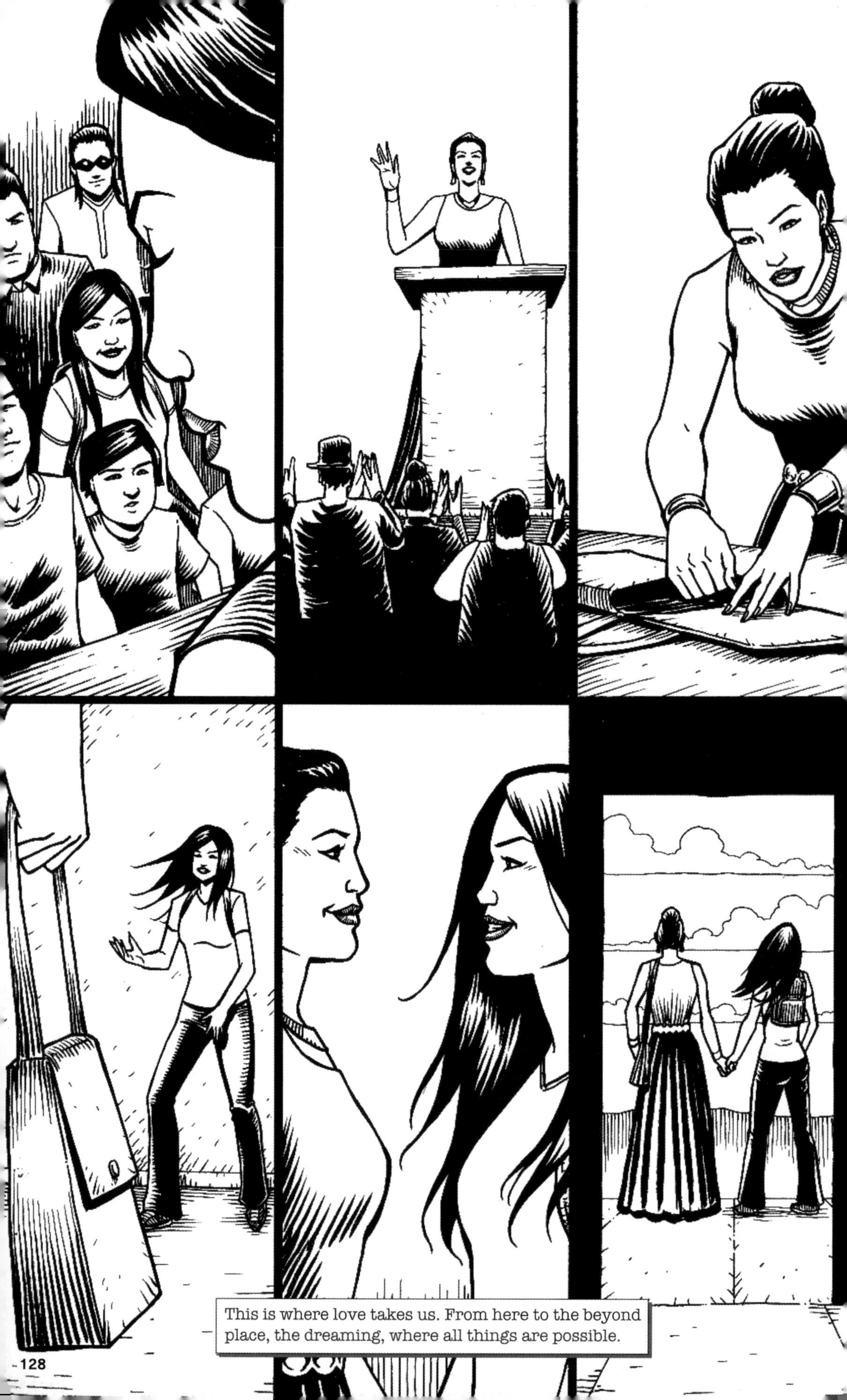
This is where love takes us. From here to the beyond place, the dreaming, where all things are possible.

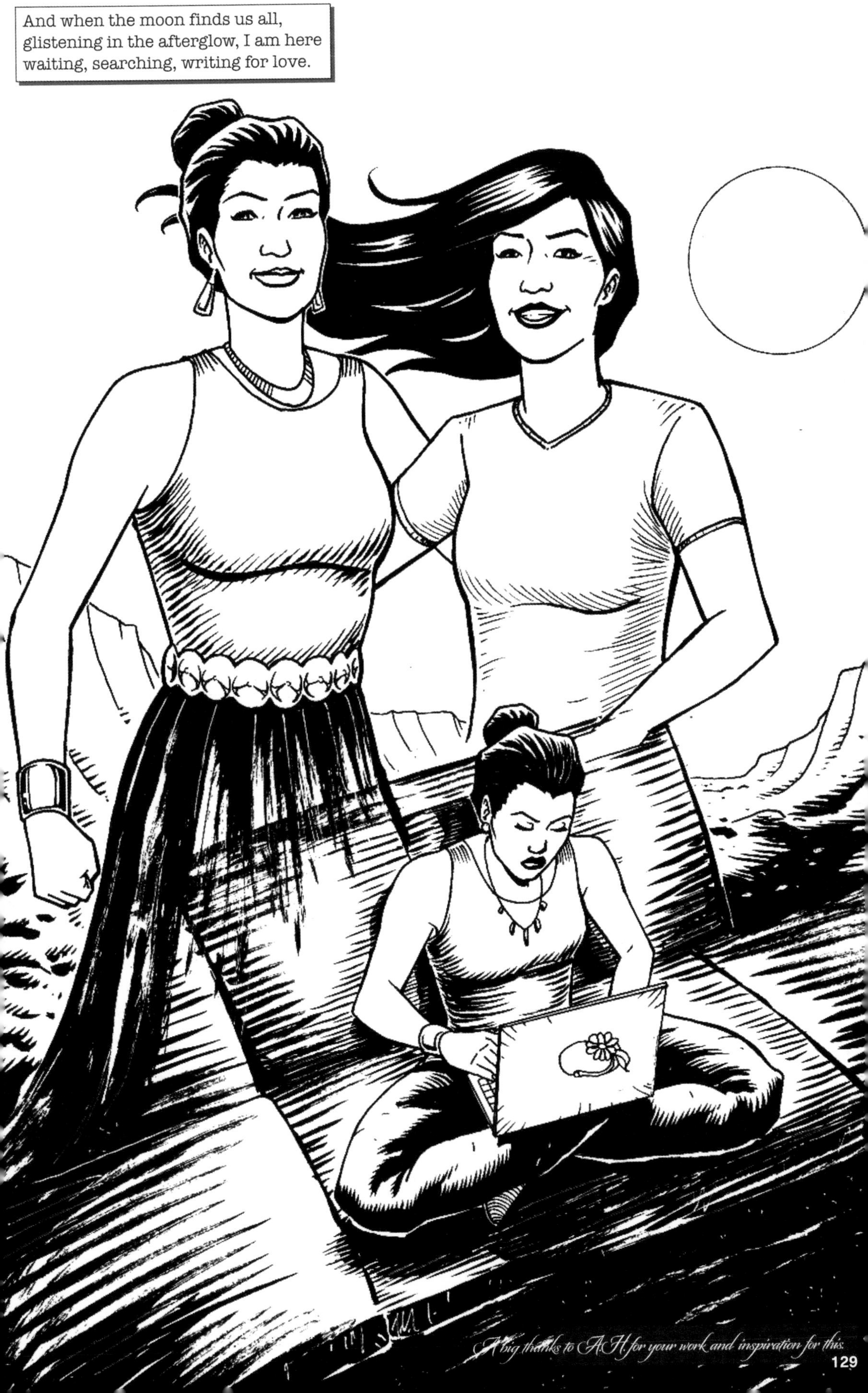
And when the moon finds us all, glistening in the afterglow, I am here waiting, searching, writing for love.
A big thanks to AH for your work and inspiration for this.

Nagamtadizowag

Elizabeth LaPensée

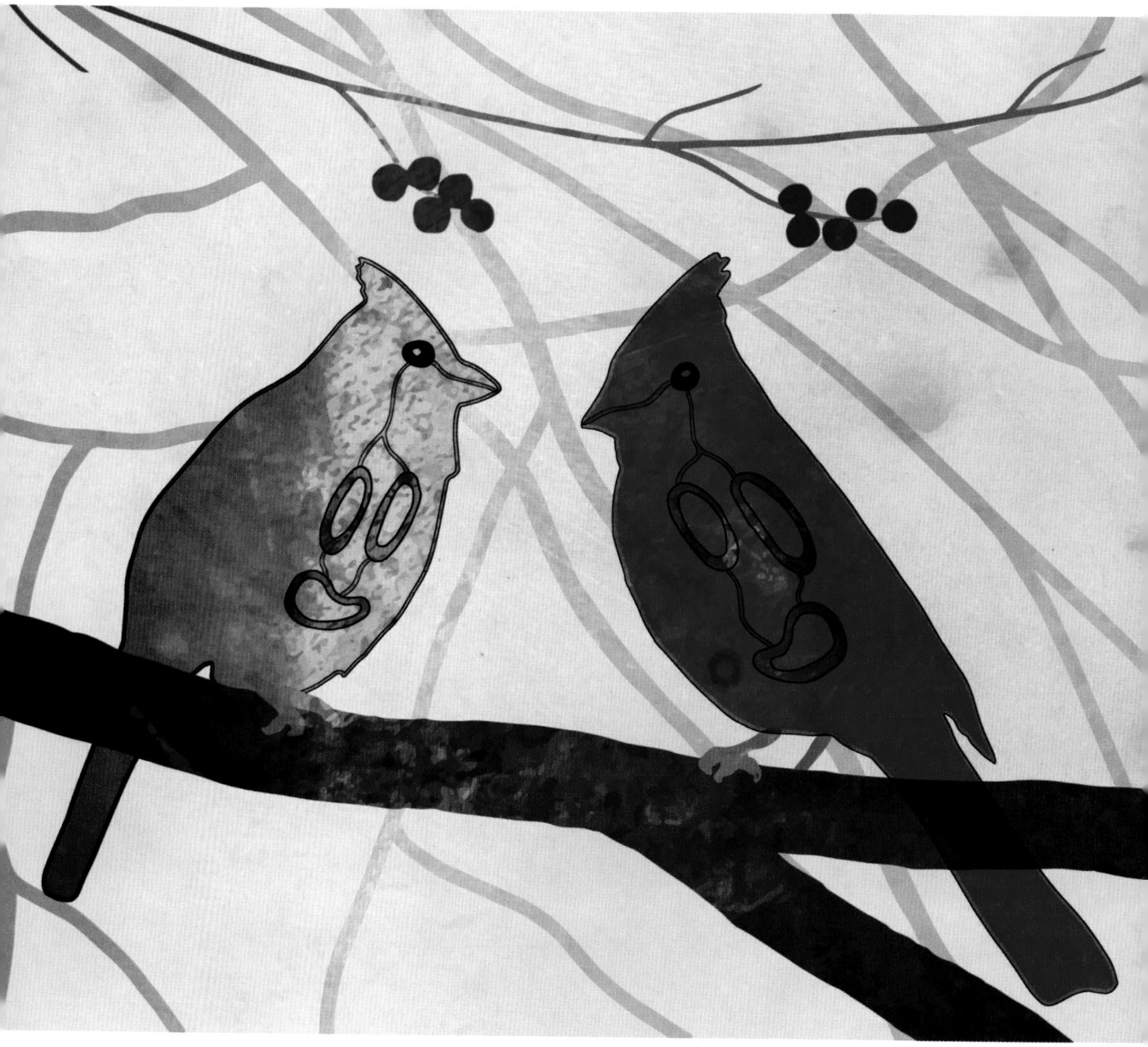

about the authors

Weshoyot Alvitre is an illustrator and comic book artist. She has a BA in fine art and studied illustration and animation. She is Tongva and Scottish. She has contributed to many award-winning books including the Eisner award–winning *Umbrella Academy* and *Little Nemo: Dream Another Dream*. Her most recent projects include art for *Tales of the Mighty Code Talkers*, volume 1, *MOONSHOT: The Indigenous Comics Collection*, volume 2, and *Rosebud* magazine #61, as well as work in several gallery shows across the country to bring awareness to the fight against the Dakota Access Pipeline and missing and murdered Indigenous women.

Gabriela Aveiro-Ojeda is an artist, speaker, and gamemaker. She currently resides in Toronto, Canada, where she creates art based around expressions of Latinidad, witchcraft, and ancestral traditions. Her latest project, *Don't Wake the Night*, is a 2-D point-and-click game funded by the Ontario Art Council's Emerging Media Artist grant.

Liv Barney is a Diné (Navajo) artist who is passionate about what she does because she sees art as a power that can bring communities together, express cultures, and tell people's stories. She practices and has a love for many of the arts from painting to technical theatre to animation and film. Additionally, she received a Bachelor of Fine Arts degree from the Savannah College of Art and Design in 2017. Her work often relates back to her Indigenous identity, as well as diversity and embracing people's differences.

Her work is viewable on Instagram @ artistlivbarney, at www.livbarney.com, and on Vimeo.

Gwen Benaway is of Anishinaabe and Métis descent. She has published three collections of poetry, *Ceremonies for the Dead*, *Passage*, and *Holy Wild*. A Two-Spirited Trans poet, she has been described as the spiritual love child of Tomson Highway and Anne Sexton. She has received many distinctions and awards, including the Dayne Ogilvie Honour of Distinction for Emerging Queer Authors from the Writer's Trust of Canada. Her poetry and essays have been published in national publications and anthologies, including *The Globe and Mail*, *Maclean's Magazine*, and *CBC Arts*. She was born in Wingham, Ontario, and resides in Toronto, Ontario.

Mitchell Bercier is a Turtle Mountain Chippewa comic artist and writer whose work has appeared at the AltCom international comic festival. His independently published comics, including *Fables of Other*, have received support from Minnesota State Arts Board as well as the Arrowhead Regional Arts Council.

Shaun Beyale was born in Shiprock, New Mexico, on the Navajo Nation reservation. He is an enrolled member of the Navajo Nation and grew up in Farmington, New Mexico. He is known for his comic book–style illustrations and paintings. He discovered comic books and heavy metal music growing up, and both have been huge influences on him and his art. He grew up with no electricity and running water, conveniences that many take for granted, so comic books were his main source of entertainment and escape for his imagination. Shaun graduated from the Institute of American Indian Arts in Santa Fe in 2014 with a BFA. He is based out of Winslow, Arizona, with his wife and daughter.

Molly Billows is swift waters, secrets, and salal berries. Northern Coast Salish from the Homalco Nation, they were adopted-out and grew up in and around Victoria. They have been living as a visitor in Vancouver, on the unceded territory of the Musqueam, Squamish, and Tsleil-Waututh Nations since 2011. They are a two-spirit, queer, trans non-binary, mixed, urban Indigenous feminist, spoken word poet, facilitator, and youth worker. Molly hopes to weave together stories in ways that lift up their communities, and contribute to collective healing, rage, resurgence, and love.

Henrietta Black is a respected elder from Tobique First Nation, New Brunswick, who is recognized for her contributions as a Maliseet language teacher, translator, and consultant. She is actively sharing traditional knowledge with community members through many language and culture programs sponsored by members of Tobique First Nation.

Michelle Lee Brown is a doctoral candidate in the subfields of Indigenous Politics and Futures Studies within the Political Science Department at the University of Hawaiʻi at Mānoa. Her areas of focus are Indigenous video games and oceanic relations. Euskaldun, her ancestral land and waters are Lapurdi, the Bidart/Plage D'Erretegia area.

Quill Violet Christie-Peters is an Anishinaabe arts programmer and self-taught visual artist residing in Thunder Bay. She is the creator of the Indigenous youth residency program, an artist residency that relies on a radically relational praxis that allows youth to reclaim relationships to self, homeland, ancestors, and community while exploring land-based arts practices. Quill holds a master's degree in Indigenous governance on Anishinaabe art-making as a practice of falling in love and sits on the board to directors for Native Women in the Arts. In her free time, she paints and writes about self-love and self-pleasure as resistance to the settler colonial project, and is very interested in exploring the body as a site of ancestors/homelands/creation.

Dale Ray Deforest grew up in the Four Corners area of the Navajo Nation, around Shiprock and Farmington, New Mexico. He graduated high school from the Navajo Preparatory School in 1995, then studied 2-D arts and photography at the Institute of American Indian Arts (IAIA) in Santa Fe. He later graduated IAIA in the summer of 2000. Much of his artistic endeavors stem from his love of the craft itself. In terms of photography, he fell in love with grainy film and rough edges while maintaining crisp and cleverly captured moments in a solid frame. His other primary practice is sequential and 2-D art. He employs high-contrast and thick lines to convey bold imagery matched with bright and vivid colors. Artwork that can be used to not only express but also captivate and manipulate thought and action has always been his goal as an artist.

Lee Francis IV (Pueblo of Laguna) is the head Indigenerd and CEO of Native Realities, the only Native and Indigenous pop culture company in the United States. Native Realities hope to change the perceptions of Native and Indigenous people through dynamic and imaginative pop culture representations. He has been published in multiple publications ranging from poetry to short stories. His first comic book is *Sixkiller*. He lives in Albuquerque with his family.

Dawn Karima is the winner of two Global Music Awards and a Native American Music Award Winner. This Indigenous Artist Activist Award

Winner hosts an award-winning syndicated radio show, *A Conversation with Dawn Karima*, which was nominated for an Indigenous Music Award. She is the author of two award-winning novels, *The Marriage of Saints* and *The Way We Make Sense*, in addition to many other published books and a volume of poetry.

Chief Lady Bird is a Chippewa and Potawatomi artist from Rama First Nation and Moosedeer Point First Nation, who is currently based in Toronto. She graduated from OCAD University in 2015 with a BFA in drawing and painting and a minor in Indigenous visual culture. In her thesis year she received the Donna McLean award for Portraiture and Life Study. Through her art practice, Chief Lady Bird uses street art, community-based workshops, digital illustration, and mixed media work to challenge the lens that Indigenous people are often viewed through. Her work subverts the dominant culture's frequent fetishization of Indigenous culture by highlighting the diverse experiences that we all come from. In 2017 Chief Lady Bird received the Leading Women, Leading Girls, Building Communities Recognition Award alongside her sister Aura for their active roles in educating youth through collaborative mural projects. The sister duo are widely recognized for their murals and empowering imagery; their work can be seen throughout Ontario and Quebec and will be spreading throughout the rest of Canada and the United States in the coming years.

Elizabeth LaPensée is an award-winning designer, writer, artist, and researcher of Indigenous-led media such as comics and games. She is Anishinaabe from Baawaating, Metis, and Irish, and Assistant Professor of Media & Information and Writing, Rhetoric, & American Cultures at Michigan State University. She has contributed to comics as an illustrator, writer, and editor, including *MOONSHOT: The Indigenous Comics Collection*, volumes 1 and 2, *Deer Woman: An Anthology*, and *Sovereign Traces, Volume 1: Not (Just) (An)Other*.

Marion Lewis was born in Iqaluit, Nunavut. She has lived in communities throughout the Arctic including Qikiqtarjuaq, Nunavut; Watson Lake, Yukon; and Inuvik, Northwest Territories. Marion was introduced to the imaginative and beautiful world of Inuit traditional stories while studying at the Nunavut Teacher Education Program in Iqaluit. That introduction sparked her love for Inuit literature and inspired her to write the poem, "Nujiajunga."

Darcie Little Badger is a Lipan Apache scientist and writer. Her short fiction and nonfiction have appeared in places like *Strange Horizons*, *The Dark*, *Mythic Delirium*, *Take the Mic: Fictional Stories of Everyday Resistance*, *Cicada Magazine*, *Love Beyond Body, Space, and Time: An Indigenous LGBT Sci-Fi Anthology*, and *Deer Woman: An Anthology*. Darcie's debut comic, "Worst Bargain in Town," was published in *MOONSHOT: The Indigenous Comics Collection*, volume 2.

beyon wren moor condenses the power of movement into capturing images whose invitations are specifically elusive to oral or written mediums. She is Pimicikamāk Nīhithawī Cree, a two spirit printmaker, painter and tattoo artist. Her art practice is woven into land defense movements; she travels to stand with bodies to defend landscapes and illustrates landscapes that become bodies. She tells stories of intergenerational trauma and stitches the edges back together with images of queer resilience. Her paintings are filled with painstaking detail, repeating stories of resistance that have been told for the five hundred years of colonial occupation of Turtle Island. Interested in many mediums, beyon creates art that always invokes a spectrum of feeling, from full chaos to an emptiness that will grip you by the belly and hold you firmly where you stand.

Renee Nejo is a freelance artist and professor of game design in Bellevue, Washington. She is a proud Diegueno Native and a literal card-carrying tribal member of the Mesa Grande Band of Mission Indians. Renee is an unapologetic advocate for education and self-determination of Native people. She has recently contributed to the art of *Ever, Jane* and *Gravity Ghost*. She was volunteer mentor for at risk youth at Thomas Jefferson High School in Denver, Colorado. Renee is the creator and designer of the video game *Blood Quantum*, her "experiment in educational games."

Margaret Noodin is currently director of the Electa Quinney Institute for American Indian Education and associate professor of English at the University of Wisconsin–Milwaukee. She is the author of *Bawaajimo: A Dialect of Dreams in Anishinaabe Language and Literature* and *Weweni: Poems in Anishinaabemowin and English*. She also serves as editor of www.ojibwe.net.

Nshannacappo is a Nakawe (Saulteaux) from Ditibineya-ziibiing (Rolling River First Nations). He's Eagle Clan and living, working, and playing in Ottawa. He's been an artist working on his craft since he was eight years old, and over the years, he has written and illustrated many of his own comic books and graphic novels. Artistically he is influenced by his Indigenous culture. Some reflection of his First Nations heritage can be seen in all his artwork; however, he rejects the traditional stereotypes of feathers and beads. He hopes to inspire Indigenous children and youth to see their own creative dreams through to fruition.

Bernard Perley is a member of Tobique First Nation, New Brunswick, and an association professor of anthropology at the University of Wisconsin–Milwaukee. He is the author of *Defying Maliseet Language Death: Emergent Vitalities of Language, Culture, and Identity in Eastern Canada* and uses his creative skills and scholarship to promote Indigenous language and cultural vitality.

Rain Prud'homme-Cranford (Rain C. Goméz) PhD is a "FAT-tastically Queer IndigeNerd" whose *Smoked Mullet Cornbread Crawdad Memory* (2012) won the First Book Award in Poetry from Native Writers' Circle of the Americas. She is an assistant professor of Indigenous literatures in the Department of English and affiliated faculty in the International Indigenous Studies Program at the University of Calgary. She is coeditor and chief (along with Carolyn Dunn) of That Painted Horse Press: A Borderless Indigenous Press of the Americas. Rain is a Louisiana Creole, whose paternal ancestry includes Choctaw-Biloxi, Ishak, Muskogean Freedmen, African, French, and Gulf Spanish Latinidad and whose maternal ancestry includes Alberta Métis and Celtic American.

Ishki Ricard is a Chahta, two-spirit, freelance writer and artist, interested in all things nerdy, artistic, and aesthetically chill. They write for games, short stories, fiction, sci-fi, reviews, and poetry.

Kimberly Robertson (Mvskoke) is an artivist, scholar, teacher, and mother who works diligently to employ Native feminist theories, practices, and methodologies in her hustle to fulfill the dreams of her ancestors and to build a world in which her daughters can thrive. She was born in Bakersfield, California, and lives on unceded Tongva lands. She earned an MA in American Indian studies and a PhD in women's studies from the University of California, Los Angeles in 2012. She is an assistant professor of women's, gender, and sexuality studies at California State University, Los Angeles.

Lucas Rowley was born and raised in Homer, Alaska, and is of Inupiaq, Scottish, and Italian descent. He is an award-winning playwright and science fiction author, and has had readings in Anchorage, New York City, Los Angeles, and Albuquerque. Lucas is developing his full-length play, *William, Inc.*, for production and contributed a short story to the Dirigibles of Denali project. He has been drawing and writing Alaska Native comic books, and is working on his first novel. Lucas struggles to find the time to hunt caribou, deer, bears, and ducks, but does so to fill his freezer with meat every year. He attends local comic book and anime conventions with his children, and enjoys putting together costumes for these events.

Nunatsiavut Inuit artist **Jason Sikoak** was born and raised in the Big Land, Labrador, in the province of Newfoundland and Labrador. Jason's love of art began watching his uncle Jack Mugford as a child. Wishing he could command the materials as his uncle did, Jason vowed to learn as much as he could. Evolving an artistic style that is all his own, he started with using materials at hand: wood first, like his uncle; paper and pencil as it became available; and stone, bone, and antler later in life. Pen and ink are now his main mediums. His subject matter varies, depending on the day, maybe mood-based or inspired by world events. He tries to render his interpretation of Inuit life, Inuit hardship, and spirituality on paper. At times his work is very controversial, but he would have it no other way. He believes that if his controversial work challenges those who view his work to think, ask questions, and maybe learn a little he has succeeded.

Dan Stinehart is a fine arts freelancer pursuing careers in the comics industry, graphic design, writing, and freelance art. Having earned a Bachelor of Fine Arts at Lake Superior State University in 2012, Stinehart plans to further his fine arts studies under the university's graduate program in the near future. He was born in Sault Ste. Marie, Michigan, and is a member of the Sault Ste. Marie of Chippewa Indians. His portfolio, comics, and other contributions are available on his website at jiibaydan.wordpress.com.

Not (Just) (An)Other

Edited by Gordon Henry Jr. and Elizabeth LaPensée
ISBN: 978-1-938065-06-4

SOVEREIGN TRACES VOL. 1

STORIES BY:

Warren Cariou

Louise Erdrich

Joy Harjo

Gordon Henry Jr.

Stephen Graham Jones

Niigaanwewidam James Sinclair

Richard Van Camp

Gerald Vizenor

Gwen Nell Westerman

ILLUSTRATIONS BY:

Weshoyot Alvitre

Evan Buchanan

Nicholas Burns

GMB Chomichuk

Scott B. Henderson

Elizabeth LaPensée

Tara Ogaick

Neal Shannacappo

Delicia Williams

Donovan Yaciuk

SOVEREIGN TRACES

Sovereign Traces merges works of contemporary North American Indian literature with imaginative illustrations by U.S. and Canadian artists to provide a unique collection of reimagined fiction and poetry.

Gordon Henry Jr. and Elizabeth LaPensée *Series Editors*